Viva Studymates

Better German

Achieving fluency with everyday speech

Viva Studymates

Better German

Achieving fluency with everyday speech

Christian Otto

Viva Books

New Delhi | Mumbai | Chennai | Kolkata | Bengaluru | Hyderabad | Kochi | Guwahati

First Indian Edition 2007
Reprinted 2011

VIVA BOOKS PRIVATE LIMITED

- 4737/23 Ansari Road, Daryaganj, New Delhi 110 002
  E-mail: vivadelhi@vivagroupindia.net, Tel. 42242200
- 76, Service Industries, Shirvane, Sector 1, Nerul, Navi Mumbai 400 706
  E-mail: vivamumbai@vivagroupindia.net, Tel. 27721273, 27721274
- Jamals Fazal Chambers, 26 Greams Road, Chennai 600 006
  E-mail: vivachennai@vivagroupindia.net, Tel. 28290304, 28294241
- B-103, Jindal Towers, 21/1A/3 Darga Road, Kolkata 700 017
  E-mail: vivakolkata@vivagroupindia.net, Tel. 22836381, 22816713
- 7, Sovereign Park Apartments, 56-58, K. R. Road, Basavanagudi, Bengaluru 560 004
  E-mail: vivabangalore@vivagroupindia.net, Tel. 26607409, 26607410
- 101-102 Mughal Marc Aptt., 3-4-637 to 641, Narayanguda, Hyderabad 500 029
  E-mail: vivahyderabad@vivagroupindia.net, Tel. 27564481, 27564482
- First Floor, Beevi Towers, SRM Road, Kaloor, Kochi 682 018, Kerala
  E-mail: vivakochi@vivagroupindia.net, Tel: 0484-2403055, 2403056
- 232, GNB Road, Beside UCO Bank, Silpukhuri, Guwahati 781 003
  E-mail: vivaguwahati@vivagroupindia.net, Tel: 0361-2666386

Published by arrangement with

Studymates Limited
PO Box 2
Bishops Lydeard,
Somerset TA4 3YE
United Kingdom

ISBN 978-81-309-0721-5

Published by Vinod Vasishtha for Viva Books Private Limited, 4737/23, Ansari Road, New Delhi - 110 002. Printed and bound by Anand Sons, Delhi - 110 092.

Contents

Preface

Why German?

The world has become a village. Around the globe countries are moving closer together. Especially in Europe with its thriving common market and the advance of the internet we are witnessing a vigorous interchange between countries at all levels (trade, economy, politics, media, etc.). To participate actively and wholeheartedly in this development it has become more important than ever to be able to speak at least one major foreign language. Spoken in Germany, Austria, Switzerland and in small parts of Belgium and Italy, German is the language used by most people in Western and Central Europe and is arguably second only to English **as** the most important lingua franca on the European continent. Thus learning German will take you to modern Europe.

Who this book is for?

This book is designed for students of German at an elementary and intermediate level who want to revise their vocabulary and to practise difficult grammatical structures. Thus it is ideal for preparing oneself for a test or an exam. Additionally it is a useful handbook for those who intend to stay in Germany for some time, whether as tourists or for business reasons. Not only does this book help you to master the little problems and difficulties of everyday life – like finding your way about – this book is also a great help to a first-hand experience of the German way of life. In fact, communicating in German whether as a holidaymaker or a businessman helps you to grasp the German culture and lifestyle more deeply and enables you to participate in it actively.

What this book is about?

This book helps you to improve and to extend your command of German by focusing on everyday situations, especially those situations a traveller might come across when staying in Germany. Not only can it be used as a reference book for those who need some quick information about what to say in everyday situations, it is also designed as a self-study book for the revision of problem words and phrases as well as grammatical structures that cause difficulties for the English-speaking learner of German. This book draws attention to the pitfalls of German and points to ways of mastering difficult sentence structures. Thus a greater fluency is achieved.

Christian Otto
Christian.Otto@studymates.co.uk

How to use this book

Speaking complete sentences – the first step to fluency

Fluency always involves the ability to speak complete sentences. We are not talking about single words or phrases; fluency is about speaking elaborate sentences for which words and phrases are used. So if you want to learn to speak a foreign language fluently and to write it properly, you must be able to build complete sentences.

Sentences are made up of words, consequently we have to find out how all these various types of words (nouns, verbs, adjectives, etc.) are put together to form a complete sentence. The first chapter of this book introduces the most important types of words and how they are used in a sentence as subject, verb or object. This chapter is therefore useful for those who are not familiar with the most common grammatical terms used in language learning. Since some of these grammatical terms will turn up again and again in this book, the first chapter provides a solid basis for the grammar dealt with in the chapters to come.

In the subsequent chapters we take a closer look at the usage of the various types of words and pick out specific problems that native speakers of English might come across when learning German; e.g. sometimes one word in English can be translated by two or more words in German, which are not interchangeable.

So for those who need some revision of the basic grammatical terms in language learning it is advisable to start with chapter 1. But if you only want to revise or practise one or two specific grammatical problems, you can of course simply concentrate on the revelant chapters.

In each chapter you will find useful exercises which help you to check your progress in understanding the given language problem. These exercises are also ideal for practising and revising your grammar and certain problem words. At the end of the book you will find the answers to the exercises.

man for travellers

ldition to being a useful grammar book, this is an ideal *vade mecum* hose who plan to visit and to stay in a German-speaking country. ı chapter provides you with a set of examples to illustrate the use of ain words or certain grammatical structures. But not only do these nples help you to grasp the grammar, they also provide you with ›ful phrases and expressions needed for everyday communication.

ng abroad in a German-speaking country, whether as a tourist or a inessman, you often encounter a number of situations in which a ›d command of German is almost indispensable. For these situations ı have to master a specific vocabulary and specific expressions in ler to communicate properly.

Chapter 1:
The Basics of Sentence Building

One-minute overview

This first chapter will give you a basic understanding of how the standard German sentence is made up. It is very useful and beneficial for the language learning process to take a closer look at how the words in German are put together to create complete sentences. If you have a basic understanding of the inner structure of a foreign language, you will find it easier to relate to its vocabulary and grammar. This basic knowledge about German grammar will surely speed up your language learning process and you will achieve a greater fluency in a shorter time. This chapter will show you:

- the most important types of words (nouns, verbs, adjectives, etc.) and how they are put together to create complete sentences;
- how nouns are used as subject and object;
- where subject and object are placed in a sentence;
- how to use adjectives;
- the position of adverbs;
- how to use pronouns, prepositions and conjunctions.

Nouns and verbs – the core of a sentence

Nouns and verbs are the most important words in every language and form the core of a sentence. Imagine what language would be like, if we did not have any nouns and verbs.

Nouns refer to persons and things in our world. Grammatically speaking the world surrounding you is a world of nouns. Just take a look at it for a second and test it, you will find plenty of nouns in your immediate environment, whether it be people (*Mann* – husband, *Frau* – wife, *Kinder* – children, *Chef* – boss, *Kollege* – colleague, *Verkäufer* – *shop-assistant,*

Postbote – postman, etc.,) or man-made objects (*Haus* – house, *Wolkenkratzer* – skycraper, *Wohnung* – flat, *Tisch* – table, *Auto* – car, *Hose* – trousers, etc.), whether it be things that exist in nature (*Wald* – forest, *Bäume* – trees, *Berge* – mountains, *Flüsse* – rivers, *Regen* – rain, *Sonne* – sun, etc.) or things that exist in the invisible world, such as feelings or abstract ideas (*Liebe* – love, *Angst* – fear, *Einsamkeit* – loneliness, *Beziehung* – relationship, *Idealismus* – idealism, etc.).

The world around you does not stand still. There is movement, action and change. The words that refer to these movements and actions are called **verbs**. They are concerned with what people or things do or what happens to them, they refer to someone's actions or behaviour or to the things that happen in your environment, at work, in nature, politics, etc. By connecting a noun to a verb you create a sentence. Consider the following German sentences and their English translations:

Touristen reisen. – Tourists travel.	*Polizisten helfen.* – Policemen help.
Bäume wachsen. – Trees grow.	*Wälder sterben.* – Forests are dying.
Ärzte heilen. – Doctors cure.	*Holz schwimmt.* – Wood floats.
Fische schlafen. – Fish sleep.	*Benzin stinkt.* – Petrol stinks.
Kinder spielen. – Children play.	*Hass tötet.* – Hate kills.

This combination of one noun and one verb is considered the shortest possible way of creating a grammatically correct and complete sentence. This simple way of putting nouns and verbs together can be regarded as the first stage in ordering words. At this stage the German and the English word order are identical.

The noun as subject

The simple sentences above consist of a **subject** (for which normally a noun is used) and a verb. The subject is the word in the sentence that represents the person or thing that is doing the action expressed by the verb, as in the following sentence:

subject	**verb**
Touristen	*reisen.*
Tourists	travel.

Here, subject and verb form a little unit which is absolutely essential if you want to form a complete and grammatically correct sentence. This little unit is the basis for longer and more intricate sentences.

In the following paragraphs we are going to make simple sentences more complex just by adding more words around the subject and the verb. As you will discover, you can create longer and more elaborate sentences by simply building words around this unit of noun and verb. As a matter of fact, more elaborate sentence structures are just complex variants of this simple noun-verb-combination.

The noun as direct object

The thing or person by which or by whom the action is performed is called subject. In English the subject has to be put in first position of the sentence. As far as the examples above are concerned this is also true for the German word order.

Certain verbs can be followed by another noun, which is commonly known as the **direct object**. The direct object refers to a thing or person to which or to whom the action is performed. The verbs that can take a direct object are called **transitive verbs** as opposed to **intransitive verbs,** which cannot take an object, such as *wachsen* (to grow), *stinken* (to stink) or *schlafen* (to sleep). Adding an object to the noun–verb combination of subject and verb is a very simple way of making a sentence more elaborate, as you can see in the following examples:

- *Männer spielen Karten.* – Men play cards.
- *Ärzte heilen Patienten.* – Doctors cure patients.
- *Hass tötet Beziehungen.* – Hate kills relationships.

Here the nouns *Karten*, *Patienten* and *Beziehungen* are direct objects. In German the objects have to be put into a **case**; the **direct object** is usually put in the **accusative case**. The word order of the examples above is subject + verb + object, **SVO** for short.

Exercise 1.1

Put the following plural nouns and verbs in the right order to form a sensible and complete sentence consisting of a subject, verb and a direct object.

nouns:	verbs:	subject + verb + object (accusative case)
1. *Mäuse, Katzen*	*transportieren*	1. *Katzen fressen Mäuse.*
2. *Unfriede, Eifersucht*	*besitzen*	2. *Eifersucht schafft ...*
3. *Fischer, Boote*	*jagen*	3. ...
4. *Schüler, Lehrer*	*fressen*	
5. *Häuser, Dächer*	*schenken*	
6. *Verbrecher, Polizisten*	*baut*	
7. *Computer, Menschen*	*liebt*	
8. *Güter, Schiffe*	*ersetzen*	
9. *Nächstenliebe, Frieden*	*haben*	
10. *Wolken, Regen*	*unterrichten*	
11. *Thomas, Kathrin*	*schafft*	
12. *Herr Müller, Brücken*	*verbreitet*	

Nouns and articles

So far we have done without any **articles**. Plurals and certain singular nouns – mostly generic terms that refer to a certain material like *Holz* (wood) or *Benzin* (petrol), or feelings such as *Eifersucht* (jealousy) or *Liebe* (love) – do not necessarily need an article **neither** in English **nor** in German.

When we talk about articles we have to keep in mind that German nouns and articles possess a **grammatical gender – masculine** (*der, ein*), **feminine** (*die, eine*) and **neuter** (*das, ein*). They therefore pose a special difficulty for English-speaking learners of German. With regard to nouns and articles the English language does without any grammatical gender.

In English as well as in German we must distinguish between a **definite article** (***der*** Baum, ***die*** Katze, ***das*** Kind) and an **indefinite article** (***ein*** Baum, ***eine*** Katze, ***ein*** Kind). The function of the definite article is to put a greater emphasis on the noun you are talking about or to specify something or someone so that it becomes clear who or what you mean. The indefinite article is used when you want to generalize something or if you do not want to put so much emphasis on this noun because this person, animal or thing is unimportant to you. We just add the article to the sentence by putting it in front of the noun it refers to:

The use of the **definite** and the **indefinite article** in the **subject case** (the **nominative** case):

masculine	***Der*** Baum wächst. – The tree is growing.	***Ein*** Baum wächst. – A tree grows.
feminine	***Die*** Katze frisst. – The cat is eating.	***Eine*** Katze frisst. – A cat is eating.
neuter	***Das*** Kind spielt. – The child is playing.	***Ein*** Kind spielt. – A child is playing.

Of course, articles are also used in the **object cases** (the **accusative** or the **dative** case). Used in other cases the articles often change their appearance to reflect the case they are used in. In the accusative case only the masculine articles change their appearance, as you can see in the following table:

The use of the **definite** and the **indefinite article** in the **object case** (the **accusative** case):

masculine	*Die Frau küsst* ***den*** Mann.	*Die Frau küsst* ***einen*** Mann.
feminine	*Der Hund jagt* ***die*** Katze.	*Der Hund jagt* ***eine*** Katze.
neuter	*Der Arzt untersucht* ***das*** Kind.	*Der Arzt untersucht* ***ein*** Kind.

There are certain verbs in German that do not take the accusative, but the dative case as direct object. The most common verbs are: *folgen* (to follow), *antworten* (to answer), *helfen* (to help), *danken* (to thank), *gefallen* (to please, to like), *glauben* (to believe). In the dative case all articles – masculine, feminine and neuter – change their appearance, which becomes obvious in the following table:

The use of the **definite** and the **indefinite article** in the **object case** (the **dative** case):

masculine	*Die Touristen folgen* ***dem*** *Reiseführer.*	*Die Touristen folgen* ***einem*** *Reiseführer.*
feminine	*Der Schüler antwortet* ***der*** *Lehrerin.*	*Der Schüler antwortet* ***einer*** *Lehrerin.*
neuter	*Die Lehrerin hilft* ***dem*** Kind.	*Die Lehrerin hilft* ***einem*** Kind.

Exercise 1.2

Put the following nouns, verbs and articles in the right order to form a sensible and complete sentence consisting of a subject (article + noun), a verb and a direct object (article + noun) in the accusative or dative case.

articles + nouns:	(transitive) **verbs**	**Subject** (noun + article) + verb + direct object (noun + article)
1. *den Patienten, der Arzt*	*dankt*	1. *Der Arzt untersucht den Patienten.*
2. *dem Professor, der Student*	*gefällt*	2. *Der Student dankt ...*
3. *der Junge, dem Mädchen*	*überholt*	3. ...
4. *die Schüler, dem Lehrer*	*untersucht*	
5. *das Haus, eine Garage*	*gehorcht*	
6. *einen Dieb, der Polizist*	*hat*	
7. *das Mädchen, eine Freundin*	*umarmt*	
8. *das Spiel, dem Kind*	*gefällt*	
9. *der Vogel, den Wurm*	*frisst*	
10. *den Radfahrer, das Auto*	*verfolgt*	
11. *einen Zoo, die Familie*	*besucht*	
12. *die Tochter, der Mutter*	*antworten*	

The direct object in front position

The word order in the examples above (*Der Arzt untersucht den Patienten.* – The doctor examines the patient.) is **SVO**: subject – verb – direct object (accusative), which is the standard word order in English as well as in German:

S **subject (article + noun)**	V **verb**	O **object (article + noun)**
Der Arzt The doctor	*untersucht* examines	*den Patienten.* the patient.

Unlike English, you can change the German standard word order from SVO to **OVS**. The object can be put in front position of the sentence:

O **object (article + noun)**	V **verb**	S **subject (article + noun)**
Den Patienten	*untersucht*	*der Arzt.*

If you changed the word order in English, you would change subject and object and alter the meaning of the sentence; its result would not make much sense either (The patient examines the doctor). In German, on the other hand, the change of words can be done without any misunderstandings: because the different articles and their nouns are marked by the respective cases they are used in, it becomes clear to the reader or the listener which word of the sentence serves as subject and which word serves as object. If you really wanted to translate that rather senseless sentence (The patient examines the doctor.) into German, you would have to change the article from the **nominative** to the **accusative** case: *Der Patient untersucht den Arzt.*

Exercise 1.3

Change the word order of the sentences completed in exercise 1.2 so that the direct object takes front position (OVS).

1. *Den Patienten untersucht der Arzt.*
2. *Dem Professor ...*

A sentence with two objects

A number of verbs in English and German can take two objects, a direct object and an indirect object, e.g. *geben* (to give), *mitbringen* (to bring), *senden* (to send), *versprechen* (to promise), *(an)bieten* (to offer), etc. These verbs are called **ditransitive verbs**. The indirect object refers to something which or someone who benefits from something or receives something as a result. In German the **indirect object** is always put in the **dative** case:

subject	verb (ditransitive)	**indirect object** (dative)	direct object (accusative)
The boss *Der Chef*	promises *verspricht*	**a woman** ***einer Frau***	a job. *einen Arbeitsplatz.*

As you can see in this example the English and the German word order are identical. It is regarded as the standard word order, in which the indirect object has to be put in front of the direct object.

Exercise 1.4

Put the following articles, nouns and verbs in the right order and form grammatically correct and complete sentences, which consist of a subject, verb, direct and indirect object.

nouns (with their articles in front of them)	**ditransitive verbs** (with the infinitive in brackets)
1. *das Kind, der Mutter, einen Blumenstrauß*	1. *schenkt (schenken)*
2. *der Lehrer, der Schülerin, einen Rat*	2. *gibt (geben)*

3.	*die Professorin, der Studentin, Mut*	3.	*macht (machen)*
4.	*der Vater, dem Kind, die Fahrkarte*	4.	*gibt (geben)*
5.	*Andrea, dem Arbeitskollegen, das Auto*	5.	*verkauft (verkaufen)*
6.	*der Verkäufer, dem Kunden, ein Angebot*	6.	*macht (machen)*
7.	*die Frau, der Tante, eine Postkarte*	7.	*sendet (senden)*
8.	*der Junge, der Freundin, ein Geschenk*	8.	*gibt (geben)*
9.	*der Lehrer, dem Schüler, ein Kompliment*	9.	*macht (machen)*
10.	*die Direktorin, dem Mitarbeiter, eine Urkunde*	10.	*überreicht (überreichen)*

Example:

1. *Das Kind schenkt der Mutter einen Blumenstrauß.*
2. *Der Lehrer gibt ...*

The indirect object in front position

As we said before, the German word order permits the change of subject and object; instead of the subject you can put the object in front position. Ditransitive verbs and their objects function in the same way as transitive verbs do. With ditransitive verbs you even have a choice: you can either put the direct or the indirect object in front position. But it must be pointed out that you cannot put both objects in front position, nor can you put an object together with the subject in front position. As you can see, the second position is always reserved for the verb; whatever word order you choose, ***the verb must be in second place.***

indirect object	verb	subject	direct object
Der Mutter	*schenkt*	*das Kind*	*einen Blumenstrauß.*

direct object	verb	subject	indirect object
Einen Blumenstrauß	*schenkt*	*das Kind*	*der Mutter.*

Exercise 1.5

Change the word order of the sentences completed in exercise 1.4 so that the indirect object takes front position.

Example:

1. *Der Mutter schenkt das Kind einen Blumenstrauß.*
2. *Der Schülerin gibt ....*

Using adjectives

So far we have talked about nouns, verbs and articles and the way they are used in a sentence. We have learnt that nouns and their respective articles depend very much on their function in the sentence, whether the noun is used as subject, direct object or indirect object. In other words the nouns always depend on the case they are used in.

Now let us take a closer look at how we can make a sentence even more elaborate. **Adjectives** are very useful when you want to give more information about a noun. While nouns and verbs form the structural core of a sentence, adjectives are used to make a sentence more colourful. They help us to describe persons or things.

Adjectives are usually placed in front of a noun (*das **kleine*** Kind – the *small* child) or after a form of the verb *sein* (to be), as in: *Das Kind ist **klein***. – The child is *small.* The sentence used in the last exercise (*Das Kind schenkt der Mutter einen Blumenstrauß.* – The child gives the mother a bouquet of flowers as a present.) can be made more interesting and colourful by adding adjectives to it:

subject noun group	**verb**	**indirect object** noun group	**direct object** noun group
*Das **kleine** Kind*	*schenkt*	*der **lieben** Mutter*	*einen **bunten** Blumenstrauß.*

An article, an adjective and a noun, as used in the example above, form a **noun group**. Since adjectives are dependent on the noun they describe, they are also dependent on the case this noun is used in and on the gender of the noun. The effect of this is that adjectives also change their endings, as opposed to their English counterparts which manage without a grammatical gender and without a case marking.

To demonstrate this effect we want to compare the example above to a very similar sentence. We have only changed a noun group from the nominative case (subject) to the dative case (indirect object) and vice versa:

subject noun group	**verb**	**indirect object** noun group	**direct object** noun group
***Das** kleine Kind*	*schenkt*	***der** lieb**en** Mutter*	***einen** bunten Blumenstrauß.*
***Die** liebe Mutter*	*schenkt*	***dem** klein**en** Kind*	*eine bunte Bluse.*

As these two sentences show, German adjectives reflect **gender** and **case** and consequently change their endings. The basic forms such as *klein* (little), *lieb* (dear), *bunt* (colourful) must be followed by a particular ending which marks a particular gender and case. Consider the following table and note how the articles and the endings of the adjectives change:

	subject (nominative)			indirect object (dative)			direct object (accusative)		
masc.	***der***	*liebe*	*Vater*	***dem***	*lieben*	*Vater*	***den***	*lieben*	*Vater*
femin.	***die***	*liebe*	*Mutter*	***der***	*lieben*	*Mutter*	***die***	*liebe*	*Mutter*
neuter	***das***	*liebe*	*Kind*	***dem***	*lieben*	*Kind*	***das***	*liebe*	*Kind*

Of course, the words of a noun group are also dependent on **number**, as you can see in the following table, which lists the plural forms of the words used in the preceding table. Note the change of the noun endings in the *dative case:*

	subject (nominative)			indirect object (dative)			direct object (accusative)		
masc.	*die*	*lieben*	*Väter*	*den*	*lieben*	*Vätern*	*die*	*lieben*	*Väter*
fem.	*die*	*lieben*	*Mütter*	*den*	*lieben*	*Müttern*	*die*	*lieben*	*Mütter*
neuter	*die*	*lieben*	*Kinder*	*den*	*lieben*	*Kindern*	*die*	*lieben*	*Kinder*

Exercise 1.6

Complete the following tables by filling in the given articles, adjectives and nouns. Be careful with case and gender.

	subject			indirect object (dative)			direct object (accusative)		
masc.	*der*	*alte*	*Mann*	*dem*	_____	*Mann*	*den*	_____	*Mann*
fem.	*die*	*junge*	*Frau*	*aer*	_____	*Frau*	*die*	_____	*Frau*
neuter	*das*	*treue*	*Tier*	*dem*	_____	*Tier*	*das*	_____	*Tier*

	subject			indirect object (dative)			direct object (accusative)		
masc.	___	*große*	*Baum*	*dem*	*großen*	_____	*den*	_____	_____
femin.	*die*	_____	*Schülerin*	*der*	_____	*Schülerin*	*die*	_____	*Schülerin*
neuter	*das*	_____	*Brot*	___	_____	_____	___	_____	_____

Exercise 1.7

Make the sentences completed in exercise 1.4 more colourful by adding adjectives to the noun groups used as subjects or objects. Be careful with case and gender markings!

Examples:

1. *Das **liebe** Kind schenkt der **kranken** Mutter einen **großen** Blumenstrauß.*
2. *Der **erfahrene** Lehrer gibt der **jungen** Schülerin einen **weisen** Rat.*

The use of pronouns

Personal pronouns of the third person

Pronouns represent nouns or a noun group, that is why they are called pronouns, **pro**-nouns. *Pro* is a Latin word and means 'for'. Pronouns often have a stylistic function. You do not want to use a noun too often, so you replace the noun or the noun group that you have mentioned earlier in a sentence by a pronoun, as you can see in the following examples:

- *Das liebe Kind schenkt der kranken Mutter einen großen Blumenstrauß.* ***Es*** (replacing *das Kind*) *liebt die Mutter.*
- *Das Kind liebt die Mutter.* ***Es*** (replacing *das Kind*) schenkt ***ihr*** (replacing *die Mutter*) einen großen Blumenstrauß.

Like the words (articles, adjectives and nouns) in a noun group, pronouns also depend on case, gender and number (singular or plural); in other words the personal pronoun must agree in case, number and gender with the noun it represents:

	subject		**indirect object** (dative)		**direct object** (accusative)	
	singular	plural	singular	plural	singular	plural
masc.	*der Vater* ***er***	*die Väter* ***sie***	*dem Vater* ***ihm***	*den Vätern* ***ihnen***	*den Vater* ***ihn***	*die Väter* ***sie***
fem.	*die Mutter* ***sie***	*die Mütter* ***sie***	*der Mutter* ***ihr***	*den Müttern* ***ihnen***	*die Mutter* ***sie***	*die Mütter* ***sie***
neuter	*das Kind* ***es***	*die Kinder* ***sie***	*dem Kind* ***ihm***	*den Kindern* ***ihnen***	*das Kind* ***es***	*die Kinder* ***sie***

Exercise 1.8

Replace the nouns or noun groups of the sentences completed in exercise 1.4 with pronouns.

Example:

1. ***Es*** *schenkt* ***ihr*** *einen Blumenstrauß.*
2. ***Er*** *gibt* ***ihr*** ...

Personal pronouns of the first and second person

So far we have only looked at the personal pronouns in the third person. These pronouns refer to people and things you are talking about. Of course personal pronouns also refer to yourself, i.e. the first person, or to the people you are talking *to*, i.e. the second person. Study the following sentences:

person	S subject	V verb (ditransitive)	objects: indirect object (dative)	direct object (accusative)
1st	***Ich***	*schenk**e***	*der Mutter/**ihr***	*einen Blumenstrauß.*
2nd	***Du***	*schenk**st***	*der Mutter/**ihr***	*einen Blumenstrauß.*
3rd	***Er/Sie/Es***	*schenk**t***	*der Mutter/**ihr***	*einen Blumenstrauß.*

> ***Note***: the verb changes its ending. This ending is called the **personal ending** of the verb since it depends on the person the verb is used in. The personal endings of the verb will be dealt with more thoroughly in chapter two. The following table shows you the various personal pronouns:

pers.	subject		indirect object (dative)		direct object (accusative)	
	singular	plural	singular	plural	singular	plural
1st	*ich*	*wir*	*mir*	*uns*	*mich*	*uns*
2nd	*du*	*ihr*	*dir*	*euch*	*dich*	*euch*
3rd	*er/sie/es*	*sie*	*ihm/ihr/ihm*	*ihnen*	*ihn/sie/es*	*sie*

Using possessive adjectives

If you want to indicate that something or someone belongs to someone else or is associated with them, you use a **possessive adjective**. Possessive adjectives are often used in a noun group and replace the article, which becomes obvious in the following table. The possessive adjectives are in bold type:

pers.	subject	verb	objects: indirect obj. (dative)	direct obj. (accusative)
1st	***Mein*** *Kind*	*schenkt*	***meiner*** *Mutter*	***meinen*** *Blumenstrauß.*
2nd	***Dein*** *Kind*	*schenkt*	***deiner*** *Mutter*	***deinen*** *Blumenstrauß.*
3rd	***Sein/Ihr*** *Kind*	*schenkt*	***seiner/ihrer*** *Mutter*	***seinen/ihren*** *Blumenstrauß.*

The following table shows the possessive pronouns that refer to words whose gender is **masculine**, such as ***der Hut*** (the hat).

pers.	Subject (my/our/your/his/her/their)		indirect obj. (dative) (my/our/your/his/her/their)		direct obj.(accusative) (my/our/your/his/her/their)	
1st	*mein Hut*	*unser Hut*	*meinem Hut*	*unserem Hut*	*meinen Hut*	*unseren Hut*
	meine Hüte	*unsere Hüte*	*meinen Hüten*	*unseren Hüten*	*meine Hüte*	*unsere Hüte*
2nd	*dein Hut*	*euer Hut*	*deinem Hut*	*eurem Hut*	*deinen Hut*	*euren Hut*
	deine Hüte	*eure Hüte*	*deinen Hüten*	*euren Hüten*	*deine Hüte*	*eure Hüte*
3rd	*sein/ihr Hut*		*seinem/ihrem Hut*		*seinen/ihren Hut*	
	seine/ihre Hüte		*seinen/ihren Hüten*		*seine/ihre Hüte*	
3rd pl.	*ihr Hut*		*ihrem Hut*		*ihren Hut*	
	ihre Hüte		*ihren Hüten*		*ihre Hüte*	

This table shows the possessive adjectives that refer to words whose gender is **feminine**, e.g. ***die Kur*** – the (health) cure:

pers.	**Subject** (my/our/your/his/her/their)		**indirect obj.** *(dative)* (my/our/your/his/her/their)		**direct obj.***(accusative)* (my/our/your/his/her/their)	
1st	*meine Kur*	*unsere Kur*	*meiner Kur*	*unserer Kur*	*meine Kur*	*unsere Kur*
	meine Kuren	*unsere Kuren*	*meinen Kuren*	*unseren Kuren*	*meine Kuren*	*unsere Kuren*
2nd	*deine Kur*	*euere Kur*	*deiner Kur*	*eurer Kur*	*deine Kur*	*eure Kur*
	deine Kuren	*eure Kuren*	*deinen Kuren*	*euren Kuren*	*deine Kuren*	*eure Kuren*
3rd	*seine/ihre Kur*		*seiner/ihrer Kur*	*seine/ihre Kur*		
	seine/ihre Kuren		*seinen/ihren Kuren*		*seine/ihre Kuren*	
3rd pl.	*ihre Kur*		*ihrer Kur*		*ihre Kur*	
	ihre Kuren		*ihren Kuren*		*ihre Kuren*	

The table below shows the possessive adjectives that refer to words whose gender is **neuter**, e.g. ***das Rad*** – the bike:

pers.	**Subject** (my/our/your/his/her/their)		**indirect obj. (dative)** (my/our/your/his/her/their)		**direct obj.(accusative)** (my/our/your/his/her/their)	
1st	*mein Rad*	*unser Rad*	*meinem Rad*	*unserem Rad*	*meinen Rad*	*unseren Rad*
	meine Räder	*unsere Räder*	*meinen Rädern*	*unseren Rädern*	*meine Räder*	*unsere Räder*
2nd	*dein Rad*	*euer Rad*	*deinem Rad*	*eurem Rad*	*deinen Rad*	*euren Rad*
	deine Räder	*eure Räder*	*deinen Rädern*	*euren Rädern*	*deine Räder*	*eure Räder*
3rd	*sein/ihr Rad*		*seinem/ihrem Rad*		*seinen/ihren Rad*	
	seine/ihre Räder		*seinen/ihren Rädern*		*seine/ihre Räder*	
3rd pl.	*ihr Rad*		*ihrem Rad*		*ihren Rad*	
	ihre Räder		*ihren Rädern*		*ihre Räder*	

Exercise 1.9

Rewrite the sentences completed in exercise 1.4 using possessive adjectives in front of the indirect object.

Examples:

1. *Das Kind schenkt* ***seiner*** *Mutter einen Blumenstrauß.*
2. *Der Lehrer gibt* ***seiner*** *Schülerin einen Rat.*

Using adverbs

Most commonly adverbs serve to modify:

- a verb (*Sie fährt* ***langsam****.* – She drives **slowly.**)
- another adverb (*Sie fährt* ***sehr*** *langsam.* – She drives **very** slowly.)
- an adjective (*Sein Deutsch ist* ***sehr*** *gut.* – His German is **very** good.)
- or a whole sentence (***Glücklicherweise*** *ist er nicht verletzt.* – **Fortunately**, he isn't hurt.).

In English many adverbs are formed by adding '-ly' to an adjective (quiet → quietly, bad → badly). In German, on the other hand, many adverbs are simply adjectives used as adverbs. Certain words are always adverbs, such as *jetzt* (now), *nie* (never), *nur* (only), *dort* (there), *bald* (soon) or *hier* (here). Very often the adverb describes the verb and gives more information about how something is being done or how something happens. The most common adverbs refer to manner, place and time.

The position of the adverb within a sentence differs from the English word order. In German most adverbs follow the verb, so do English adverbs of manner or place providing the sentence does not have an object:

- *Ein Baum wächst* ***langsam.*** – A tree grows **slowly**.
- *Sie fährt* ***vorsichtig.*** – She drives **carefully**.
- *Er arbeitet* ***dort.*** – He works **there**.

If the sentence has an object, you put the English adverb of manner or place after the object, but in German the adverb again follows the verb:

- *Wir machten* ***schnell*** *unsere Hausaufgaben.* – We did our homework **quickly**.
- *Andrea hilft* ***gerne*** *ihren Eltern.* – Andrea helps her parents **gladly**.
- *Wir spielen* ***draußen*** *Tennis.* – We play tennis **outside**.

In English adverbs of time and frequency precede the verb. In German, again, they follow the verb:

- *Holz schwimmt* ***immer.*** – Wood **always** floats.
- *Thomas lacht* ***häufig.*** – Thomas **often** laughs.

If the sentence has an object, the German object follows the adverb, whereas in English the adverb of frequency must not be put in between the verb and the object:

- *Männer spielen* ***häufig*** *Karten.* – Men **often** play cards.
- *Der Lehrer hilft* ***manchmal*** *den Schülern.* – The teacher **sometimes** helps the pupils.

As in English in German you can also put the adverb in front position. The effect is that the word order in German changes. In contrast to English, the verb must be placed in second position followed by the subject of the sentence:

- ***Langsam*** *wächst der Baum.* – **Slowly** the tree grows.
- ***Häufig*** *spielen Männer Karten.* – **Often** men play cards.
- ***Manchmal*** *hilft der Lehrer.* – **Sometimes** the teacher helps.

Exercise 1.10

Form sentences from the following. Put the subject in front position.

1. *zügig/sie/läuft/nach Hause*
2. *häufig/nach Berlin/fahren/wir*
3. *spielt/gut/sie/sehr/Gitarre*
4. *leise/er/spricht/sehr*
5. *kommt/zu spät/häufig/Herr Müller*

Exercise 1.11

Form sentences from the following. Put the adverb in front position.

1. *er/müde/geht/ins Bett*
2. *fährt/der Zug/schnell*
3. *ihre Arbeit/sie/macht/konzentriert*
4. *auf die Arbeit/geht/fröhlich/er*
5. *ich/manchmal/gehe/ins Kino*

The use of prepositions

The **preposition** is very useful and almost indispensable for creating elaborate and meaningful sentences. It **indicates the place** where an action occurs or the place where someone or something is. Furthermore, the preposition refers to the place someone is going to or coming from **or the direction** somebody is moving in.

Prepositions often stand in front of a noun, a pronoun or a noun group. The preposition and the noun group form a prepositional phrase. The noun group that follows the preposition must be put into a case, as shown in the following sentences:

	S	**V**	**prepositional phrase**	
	subject	**verb**	**preposition**	**noun group**
1.	*Das Kind* The child	*läuft* runs	***über*** **across**	*die breite Straße.* (accusative) the wide street.
2.	*Hans* Hans	*fährt* drives	***zu*** **to**	*seinem älteren Bruder.* (dative) his elder brother.
3.	*Der Baum* The tree	*wächst* grows	***in*** **in/into**	*die Höhe.* (accusative) the air.

The object that follows a preposition must be put into either a dative, an accusative or a genitive case. It always depends on the preceding preposition.

Here are some of the most common **prepositions taking the dative case:**

> *aus* (out of, from), *außer* (except), *bei* (at, near), *gegenüber* (opposite), *mit* (with), *nach* (after, to, according to), *seit* (since, for), *von* (from, about, by), *zu* (to, for)

The most common prepositions followed by the **accusative case** are:

> *durch* (through), *entlang* (along), *für* (for), *gegen* (against, towards), *ohne* (without), *um* (around, at, about), *wider* (contrary to, against)

Movement and position – the change of cases

Some prepositions can either take a dative or an accusative case. If the prepositional phrase involves **movement towards** a different place, the preposition takes the **accusative**. But it takes the **dative** when **position (or location)** is described as opposed to movement:

S subject	V verb	prepositional phrase preposition	 noun group	
Der Baum The tree	*wächst* grows	***in*** in	***die** Höhe.* the air.	**accusative** case, since **movement** is involved
Der Baum The tree	*wächst* grows	***in*** in	***dem** Urwald.* the jungle.	**dative** case, since **position** (location) is described

The most common prepositions that can take either the dative or the accusative case are:

> *an* (on, at, to), *auf* (on, in, to, at), *hinter* (behind), in (in, into, to), *neben* (next to, beside), *über* (over, across, above), *unter* (under, among), *vor* (in front of, before), *zwischen* (between)

The following prepositions take the genitive case:

> *außerhalb* (outside), *beiderseits* (on both sides of), *diesseits* (on this side of), *hinsichtlich* (with regard to), *infolge* (as a result of), *statt* (instead of), *trotz* (in spite of), *während* (during), *wegen* (on account of)

Exercise 1.12

Form complete sentences with the following sentence parts. The columns of the verbs and the prepositional phrases are not in the right order and have to be changed:

Pronoun, noun or noun group as subject	verbs	noun, pronoun or noun group as object	prepositional phrases
1. *Der gute Vater*	*untersucht*	1. *seinen Sohn*	*auf den Mund.*
2. *Er*	*bittet*	2. *sich*	*in die Schule.*
3. *Der erfahrene Arzt*	*bringt*	3. *das Kind*	*unter den Baum.*
4. *Der Professor*	*stellt*	4. *die Studentin*	*um Ruhe.*
5. *Der Lehrer*	*lobt*	5. *die lauten Schüler*	*im Krankenhaus.*
6. *Sie*	*verlässt*	6. *das Fahrrad*	*mit einem teuren Shampoo.*
7. *Die Urlauberin*	*stellt*	7. *die Region*	*gegen die Wand.*
8. *Ich*	*küsst*	8. *dieses Haus*	*trotz des guten Wetters.*
9. *Er*	*wäscht*	9. *seine Freundin*	*wegen ihrer guten Leistungen.*
10. *Die junge Frau*	*bewohne*	10. *ihre langen Haare*	*seit fünf Jahren.*

Example:

1. *Der gute Vater* ***bringt*** *seinen Sohn* ***in die Schule.***
2. *Er* ***stellt*** *sich ...*

The use of conjunctions

To **connect** one clause to another we need **conjunctions**. Not only do they connect clauses, they also join phrases and words. In German as in English we have to differentiate between **coordinating** conjunctions and **subordinating** conjunctions.

A **coordinating conjunction joins words, expressions or clauses of the same grammatical type**. The most common coordinating conjunctions are: *aber* (but), *denn* (for), *oder* (or), *sondern* (but), *und* (and). In the following example the coordinating conjunction *aber* links two main clauses.

- *Der Hund versucht eine Katze zu fangen,* ***aber*** *die Katze ist zu flink.* – The dog tries to catch a cat, **but** the cat is too quick.

Subordinating conjunctions link a subordinate clause to a main clause. A subordinate clause is a clause which cannot normally be a complete sentence on its own. The most common subordinating conjunctions are: *als* (when), *bis* (until), *bevor* (before), *da* (as, since), *damit* (so that), *ob* (whether), *obwohl* (although), *während* (while), *weil* (because), *wenn* (if, whenever, when). **The finite part of the verb (i.e. the conjugated verb) is always at the end of a subordinate clause:**

main clause				subordinate clause			
subject	verb	indirect object	direct object	**conj.**	subj.	dir. obj.	**finite verb**
Das Kind	*schenkt*	*seiner Mutter*	*einen Blumenstrauß,*	***weil***	*es*	*sie*	***liebt.***

The subordinate clause may precede the main clause. When this is the case, **the verb and subject of the main clause are inverted,** as shown in the following example:

subordinate clause				main clause			
conj.	subj.	dir. obj.	verb	verb	subject	indir. obj.	direct obj.
Weil	*es*	*die Mutter*	*liebt,*	***schenkt***	***das Kind***	*ihr*	*einen Blumenstrauß.*

Exercise 1.13

Join the following clauses using one of the following conjunctions: *weil, als, wenn, und, bevor, aber, während, obwohl, damit, bis.*

Example: *Das Tor war gefallen. Wir verließen das Stadion. –* ***Nachdem*** *das Tor gefallen war, verließen wir das Stadion.*

1. *Er konnte nach Hause gehen. Ich musste leider bleiben.*
2. *Wir fahren mit dem Bus nach Hause. Es regnet in Strömen.*
3. *Du rufst an. Ich fahre sofort los.*
4. *Sie ging in die Schule. Sie war krank.*
5. *Mein Bruder ist Lehrer. Meine Schwester studiert Jura.*
6. *Wir öffnen immer das Garagentor. Vater kann das Auto in die Garage fahren.*
7. *Wir wollten ins Kino gehen. Wir bekamen keine Karten mehr.*
8. *Das Glas fiel um. Ich stand auf.*
9. *Es dauert noch etwas. Der Zug fährt ab.*
10. *Die Schauspieler verneigten sich. Sie verließen die Bühne.*

Chapter 2: Choosing the Right Form of the Verb

One-minute overview

In this chapter we are going to focus on the different forms of the verb and the major tenses the verb is used in. The personal form of a verb is marked by its ending. These endings pose a special difficulty for native-speakers of English since the endings of the German verbs are more complex than their English equivalents. Basically, the personal forms of a verb depend on person, number and tense. As in English, the subject determines the first, the second and the third person as well as the singular and the plural forms of the verb. The complete set of the different forms of a given verb including its different endings is called **conjugation.** A verb which is put into one of the personal forms is called the conjugated or finite verb as opposed to the infinitive of a verb. This chapter will show you:

- the most important German tenses and their personal endings;
- the difference between strong and weak verbs;
- the formation of compound tenses;
- the most important auxiliary verbs and their usage;
- the difference between transitive and intransitive verbs.

The regular endings of the present tense

In English there exists only one personal ending to the present tense form of the verb, i.e. the third person singular *-s*, as in: He/She/It plays. Whereas in German the present tense is formed by adding ***-e, -st, -t, -en, -t, -en*** to the ***infinitive stem*** of the verb. The infinitive stem of the verb is derived by cutting off ***-en*** from the infinitive, so, for the infinitive: *spiel**en*** (to play), cut off ***-en***, giving the infinitive stem ***spiel-***.

	singular	*plural*
1st person	*ich spiel**e***	*wir spiel**en***
2nd person	*du spiel**st***	*ihr spiel**t***
3rd person	*er, sie, es spiel**t***	*sie spiel**en***

> ***Note***: there are infinitives that end in ***-eln, -ern, -n***, like ***handeln*** (to act), ***wandern*** (to hike) or ***tun*** (to do). Here the infinitive stem is derived by dropping the ***-n***, e.g. the infinitive stem of *handeln* is *handel-*. Also note that in informal conversation German the ***-e*** of the first person singular is often dropped: *Ich spiel' gern Fußball.* (I love to play football.)

> ***Note:*** the third person plural form of the verb (nominative: **Sie sprechen** sehr gut Deutsch. – **They speak** German very well.) is also used for the formal address in its singular and its plural form of the verb:
>
> Singular: *Herr Müller,* **Sie sprechen** sehr gut Englisch. – Mr Müller, **you can speak** English very well.
>
> Plural: *Meine Damen und Herren,* **Sie leisten** gute Arbeit. – Ladies and gentlemen, **you do** a very good job.

The formal *Sie* is used when you talk or write to a person you are not very close to. Usually, you would address these people by their last name.

The pronouns of the formal address are always capitalized. The forms for the dative and the accusative (singular and plural) are as follows:

Dative (*Ihnen*): *Wir wollen* **Ihnen**, Frau Müller, ein Geschenk machen. – We want to give **you**, Mrs Müller, a present.

Accusative (*Sie*): Wir freuen uns auf **Sie** alle. – We are looking forward to **you** all.

Exercise 2.1

Complete the following sentences by filling in the appropriate forms of the present tense of the verb in brackets.

1. *Wann ____________ das Fußballspiel? (beginnen)*
2. *Der Mann ________________ gerade. (telefonieren)*
3. *Ich ________________ in Köln. (studieren)*
4. *Du ________________ zu Hause. (bleiben)*
5. *Was ________________ ihr? (trinken)*
6. *Das Baby ________________ sehr laut. (schreien)*
7. *Ich ______________ an Gott. (glauben)*
8. *Die Frau ______________ ihren Mann. (lieben)*
9. *Du ______________ gute Aufsätze. (schreiben)*
10. *Wann ________________sie uns? (besuchen)*

Variants in personal endings

The additional *e* sound

When the infinitive stem ends in *-d, -t, -m, -n* preceded by a consonant other than *-l, -r,* the endings in the second and third person singular and the second person plural receive an *-e-* before the personal endings. Thus, for the verb *arbeiten* (to work):

	singular	*plural*
1st person	*ich arbeite*	*wir arbeiten*
2nd person	*du arbeitest*	*ihr arbeitet.*
3rd person	*er, sie, es arbeitet*	*sie arbeiten*

Here are some of the most important verbs which are expanded by adding an *-e-* before the personal endings:

antworten (to reply)	*atmen* (to breathe)
begegnen (to meet)	*beobachten* (to watch)
bitten (to ask)	*finden* (to find)
öffnen (to open)	*rechnen* (to calculate)
reden (to talk)	*retten* (to save)
schneiden (to cut)	*senden* (to send)
warten (to wait)	*zeichnen* (to draw)

Exercise 2.2

Complete the following sentences by filling in the appropriate forms of the present of the verb in brackets.

1. *Ich ____________ in einem Supermarkt. (arbeiten)*
2. *Seine Nase ____________ sehr stark. (bluten)*
3. *Wie ____________ du den Weg? (finden)*
4. *Wir ____________ gerade die Tiere. (beobachten)*
5. *Auf wen ____________ ihr? (warten)*
6. *Ich ____________ ihm regelmäßig. (begegnen)*
7. *Du ____________ sehr schöne Portraits. (zeichnen)*
8. *Das Mädchen ____________ das Buch. (öffnen)*
9. *Er ____________ sehr schwer. (atmen)*
10. *Die Mädchen ____________ sehr viel. (reden)*

No additional *s* sound

When the infinitive stem ends in *-s, -ss, -ß, -x, -z,* the personal ending for the second person singular is *-t* (rather than *-st*). Consequently the forms of the second and third person singular are the same. Take the verb *grüßen* (to greet) for an example:

	singular	*plural*
1st person	*ich grüße*	*wir grüßen*
2nd person	*du grüß**t***	*ihr grüßt*
3rd person	*er grüßt*	*sie grüßen*

Other verbs that belong to this group are:

hassen (to hate) *reisen* (to travel) *tanzen* (to dance)
heißen (to be called) *setzen* (to set)
mixen (to mix) *sitzen* (to sit)

Exercise 2.3

Complete the following sentences by filling in the appropriate forms of the present of the verb in brackets.

1. *Wie ____________ du? (heißen)*
2. *Warum ____________ du hier? (sitzen)*
3. *Wieso ____________ du nicht diesen Mann? (grüßen)*
4. *Du ____________ gut. (tanzen)*
5. *Warum ____________ du diese Frau? (hassen)*

Infinitives ending in *-eln*, *-ern*

When the infinitive ends in ***-eln***, the ***e*** preceding the ***-ln*** must be dropped in the first person singular. The other forms of the verb keep the ***e***. When the infinitive ends in ***-eln*** or ***-ern*** the endings in the first and third person plural do not end in ***-en***. The endings are identical to the infinitives, which means they end in ***–n***, as you can see for the verbs in the following table, *samm**eln*** (to collect) and *änd**ern*** (to change):

	singular	plural	
1st person	*ich **sammle***	*wir sammel**n***	*wir änder**n***
2nd person	*du sammelst*	*ihr sammelt*	*ihr ändert*
3rd person	*er sammelt*	*sie sammel**n***	*wir änder**n***

In addition to *sammeln* and *ändern* these exceptions to the rules must be applied to the following verbs:

behandeln (to treat) *klingeln* (to ring)
bewundern (to admire) *lächeln* (to smile)
füttern (to feed) *wandern* (to hike)
klettern (to climb)

Exercise 2.4

Complete the following sentences by filling in the appropriate forms of the present tense of the verb in brackets.

1. *Ich ____________ Briefmarken. (sammeln)*
2. *Wir ____________ in den Alpen. (klettern)*
3. *Das Kind ____________ die Vögel. (füttern)*
4. *Die Touristen ____________ die alte Kirche. (bewundern)*
5. *Ich stehe vor der Haustür und ____________. (klingeln)*
6. *____________ ihr am Sonntag? (wandern)*
7. *Ich ____________ meine Patienten mit großer Fürsorge. (behandeln)*
8. *Du ____________ ihn an. (lächeln)*
9. *Ich ____________ seine Ausdauer. (bewundern)*
10. *Wir ____________ den Plan. (ändern)*

The vowel change in the stem of strong verbs

There are many verbs that have a ***vowel change*** in the stem of the present tense in the ***second*** and ***third person singular***. These verbs are called ***strong verbs***.

Changes from ***a***, ***au*** to ***ä***, ***äu***, as in the verbs *schlafen* (to sleep) and *laufen* (to walk, to run):

	singular	*plural*	*singular*	*plural*
1st person	*ich schlafe*	*wir schlafen*	*ich laufe*	*wir laufen*
2nd person	*du schl**ä**fst*	*ihr schlaft*	*du l**äu**fst*	*ihr lauft*
3rd person	*er schl**ä**ft*	*sie schlafen*	*er l**äu**ft*	*sie laufen*

The following verbs change their stem vowel from ***a*** to ***ä***: *empfangen* (to receive), *fahren* (to drive), *fallen* (to fall), *fangen* (to catch), *halten* (to hold, to keep), *lassen* (to allow, to let), *schlagen* (to hit), *tragen* (to carry, to wear), *wachsen* (to grow), *waschen* (to wash). The verb *saufen* (to drink – in excess; and of animals) follows the same pattern as *laufen*.

Changes from *e* to *i*, as in the verb *essen* (to eat):

	singular	*plural*
1st person	*ich esse*	*wir essen*
2nd person	*du **i**sst*	*ihr esst*
3rd person	*er **i**sst*	*sie essen*

The following verbs change their stem vowel from ***e*** to ***i***: *brechen* (to break), *geben* (to give), *helfen* (to help), *sprechen* (to speak), *sterben* (to die), *treffen* (to meet), *vergessen* (to forget), *werfen* (to throw).

> ***Note***: the important verbs *gehen* (to go) and *stehen* (to stand) do not change their stem vowel from ***e*** to ***i*** as described above: ***du gehst, er geht; du stehst, er steht.***

Changes from ***e*** to ***ie*** as in the verb *sehen* (to see):

	singular	***plural***
1st person	*ich sehe*	*wir sehen*
2nd person	*du siehst*	*ihr seht*
3rd person	*er sieht*	*sie sehen*

The following verbs follow the same pattern as *sehen* and change their stem vowel from ***e*** to ***ie***: *empfehlen* (to recommend), *geschehen* (to happen), *lesen* (to read), *stehlen* (to steal).

Note: the verb *nehmen* (to take) does not follow the pattern above:

	singular	***plural***
first person	*ich nehme*	*wir nehmen*
second person	*du nimmst*	*ihr nehmt*
third person	*er nimmt*	*sie nehmen*

Exercise 2.5

Rewrite the following sentences by changing the plural to the singular form of the verb.

Example: *Wohin* ***laufen*** *die Frauen?* → *Wohin* ***läuft*** *die Frau?*

1. *Sie schlagen den Hund.*
2. *Wo schlaft ihr?*
3. *Was esst ihr?*
4. *Die Männer tragen einen Mantel.*
5. *Welches Buch empfehlt ihr mir?*
6. *Die Einbrecher stehlen Juwelen.*
7. *Was lest ihr?*
8. *Wunder geschehen in dem Dorf.*
9. *Wie weit werfen die Sportler?*
10. *Sie geben ihm etwas zu trinken.*

Important irregular verbs

The following irregular verbs need to be given closer consideration. The conjugation of these verbs does not go along any rule or pattern. Therefore their full conjugation needs to be mentioned here specifically. They are very important verbs. Three of them – *sein* (to be), *haben* (to have) and *werden* (to get, become) – are used to form other verb forms, such as the passive voice (*werden* + past participle) or other tenses like the perfect (*sein* or *haben* + past participle) or the future tense (*werden* + infinitive). That is the reason why these three verbs are also called ***auxiliary verbs*** (Latin: *auxiliaris* = helpful); they ***help*** you to form other verb forms.

sein (to be)	*haben* (to have)	*werden* (to get, to become)	*wissen* (to know)	*tun* (to do)
ich bin	*ich habe*	*ich werde*	*ich weiß*	*ich tue*
du bist	*du hast*	*du wirst*	*du weißt*	*du tust*
er ist	*er hat*	*er wird*	*er weiß*	*er tut*
wir sind	*wir haben*	*wir werden*	*wir wissen*	*wir tun*
ihr seid	*ihr habt*	*ihr werdet*	*ihr wisst*	*ihr tut*
sie sind	*sie haben*	*sie werden*	*sie wissen*	*sie tun*

Exercise 2.6

Complete the following sentences with the present tense of the verb in brackets.

1. *Sie _______ nicht zuhause. (sein)*
2. *Ich _______ ein Auto. (haben)*
3. *Du _______ ganz rot. (werden)*
4. *Er _______ sehr viel. (wissen)*
5. *_______ Sie auch Lehrer? (sein)*
6. *Wir _______ eine Familie. (sein)*
7. *Die Kinder _______ Durst. (haben)*
8. *Ich _______ nur meine Pflicht. (tun)*
9. *Ihr _________ gute Sportler. (sein)*
10. *Du _______ schöne Haare. (haben)*
11. *Was _______ ihr mir an?(tun)*
12. *Dem Kind _______ kalt. (werden)*
13. *Die Schüler _____ Ferien. (haben)*
14. *Ihr _____ wieder gesund. (werden)*
15. *Woher _______ du das? (wissen)*
16. *______ ihr zwei Hunde?(haben)*

The past tenses – imperfect (or preterite)

In German there exist various tenses that are used to describe events that happened in the past – the most important ones are the imperfect and the perfect tense. The imperfect tense is also called preterite and the perfect tense is often referred to as present perfect tense. While the perfect is mainly used in conversation, the imperfect is used for narrative purposes and in formal language: it is employed to narrate events or a chain of events that took place in the past. It is often used in written materials and in stories, novels, or any other forms of narrative prose. That is also the reason why it is often referred to as the narrative past. In practice, however, the perfect and imperfect are often interchangeable; in spoken German a mixture of both tenses is common.

The regular endings of the imperfect – weak verbs

The simple form of the weak verbs is formed by adding *-te-* plus the imperfect personal endings to the stem of the infinitive. Thus the conjugation of the imperfect of *spielen* (to play) is as follows:

	singular	*plural*
1st person	*ich spiel-**te*** (no ending)	*wir spiel-**te**-n*
2nd person	*du spiel-**te**-st*	*ihr spiel-**te**-t*
3rd person	*er spiel-**te*** (no ending)	*sie spiel-**te**-n*

Exercise 2.7

Rewrite the following sentences in the imperfect.

1. *Er spielt gerne Fußball.*
2. *Ich bezahle mit Kreditkarte.*
3. *Wir brauchen ein Auto.*
4. *Du entdeckst eine völlig neue Welt.*
5. *Ich bestelle ein Bier.*
6. *Ihr besucht eure Großmutter.*
7. *Sie danken ihrer Gastfamilie.*
8. *Sie hört gerne klassische Musik.*
9. *Er lernt Deutsch.*
10. *Ihr wohnt in Frankfurt.*

Exceptions

The additional e

When the stem of the infinitive ends in *-d*, *-t*, or in *-m*, *-n* preceded by a consonant other than *-l*, *-r*, an additional *-e-* must be inserted. If you did not have an inserted ***e***, it would be impossible to hear this tense marker and to distinguish it clearly from the present tense form of the verb. The pattern for these classes of verbs, some of which have already been mentioned above, is as follows:

	singular	*plural*
1st person	*ich arbeit-**e**-te* (no ending)	*wir arbeit-**e**-te*-n
2nd person	*du arbeit-**e**-te-st*	*ihr arbeit-**e**-te-t*
3rd person	*er arbeit-**e**-te* (no ending)	*sie arbeit-**e**-te-n*

Stem vowel change in weak verbs

There exist some weak verbs that have a stem vowel change in the imperfect, such as:

brennen → *brannte* (to burn) *kennen* → *kannte* (to know)
bringen → *brachte* (to bring) *nennen* → *nannte* (to call)
denken → *dachte* (to think) *wissen* → *wusste* (to know)

Exercise 2.8

Rewrite the following sentences in the imperfect.

1. *Der Junge blutet sehr stark.*
2. *Er antwortet auf ihre Frage.*
3. *Du kennst das Mädchen.*
4. *Das Mädchen zeichnet gern.*
5. *Er badet im See.*
6. *Ich öffne die Tür.*
7. *Er weiß es nicht.*
8. *Ihr kennt diese Straße.*
9. *Ich weiß von nichts.*
10. *Die Häuser brennen lichterloh.*
11. *Du nennst mich einen Lügner.*
12. *Sie ordnet die Akten.*
13. *Denkst du an ihn?*
14. *Der Jäger beobachtet die Rehe.*
15. *Er bringt ihr das Essen.*
16. *Sie weiß über uns Bescheid.*

The imperfect of strong verbs

Instead of the tense marker ***-te*** as used in the imperfect of the ***weak verbs***, the imperfect of the ***strong verbs*** are marked by a ***stem vowel change***. There are also some predictable patterns for the vowel change, but it is best to study and to learn the imperfect forms of the strong verbs by heart. As far as the endings are concerned, they are very similar to those of the weak verbs. Take for example the imperfect forms of *laufen* (to walk, to run):

	singular	*plural*
1st person	*ich lief (no ending)*	*wir lief-**en***
2nd person	*du lief-**st***	*ihr lief-**t***
3rd person	*er lief* (no ending)	*sie lief-**en***

Note that the only difference between weak and strong verbs, as far as the endings are concerned, is that the first and third person plural ending is ***-n*** for weak and ***-en*** for strong verbs.

The auxiliary verbs – *sein, haben, werden*

The imperfect forms of the auxiliary verbs mentioned earlier do not only refer to past events and are not only used in narrative texts, they are also used in conversation. Their irregular forms are as follows:

sein (to be)	***haben (to have)***	***werden (to get, to become)***
ich war	*ich hatte*	*ich wurde*
du warst	*du hattest*	*du wurdest*
er war	*er hatte*	*er wurde*
wir waren	*wir hatten*	*wir wurden*
ihr wart	*ihr hattet*	*ihr wurdet*
sie waren	*sie hatten*	*sie wurden*

Exercise 2.9

Rewrite the following sentences in the imperfect.

1. Wo bist du?
2. Hast du Ferien?
3. Ich werde krank.
4. Er hat Hunger.
5. Sie ist in der Schule.
6. Die Tiere werden unruhig.
7. Er ist Lehrer von Beruf.
8. Die Kinder sind in der Schule.
9. Ich habe wenig Zeit.
10. Du wirst müde.
11. Seid ihr böse auf uns?
12. Er hat eine Schwester.
13. Die Frau ist schwanger.
14. Sie hat eine schwere Krankheit.
15. Ich bin kaputt.
16. Du wirst ganz blass.

The past tenses – perfect tense

Unlike the imperfect, which is used mainly in writing and for narrative purposes, the perfect tense is chiefly used in conversation and refers to actions that have a link to the present. It is also called the conversational past or the present perfect.

The ***perfect tense*** is formed with the ***present tense of haben*** (to have) ***or sein*** (to be) ***plus the past participle*** of the main verb, as in the following examples:

- *Ich habe geschlafen.* – I have slept./I slept.
- *Er ist gekommen.* – He has come./He came.

The formation of the past participle – weak verbs and strong verbs

The past participle of most ***weak verbs*** is formed by placing the prefix ***ge-*** in front of the infinitive stem and adding ***-t*** or ***-et*** at the end of the stem.

Examples:

- *sagen* (to say): ***ge*** + *sag* + ***t*** = *gesagt*
- *arbeiten* (to work): ***ge*** + *arbeit* + ***et*** = *gearbeitet*

There are also some ***weak verbs*** that have a ***stem vowel change*** in the past participle, such as *brennen – gebrannt, denken – gedacht, kennen – gekannt, nennen – genannt.*

The past participle of most ***strong verbs*** is formed by placing the prefix ***ge-*** in front of the past participle stem and adding ***-en*** at the end of the stem. ***Note***: there are many strong verbs which change their stem vowel in the past participle.

Examples:

- *singen* (to sing): ***ge*** + *sung* + ***en*** = *gesungen*
- *bleiben* (to stay): ***ge*** + *blieb* + ***en*** = *geblieben*

Since there is no basic rule or pattern to predict the stem vowel of a past participle, neither for strong nor for weak verbs, you must learn and memorize the principal parts for each verb.

Exceptions

Verbs ending in ***-ieren*** do not have a ***ge-*** prefix: *agieren* (to act) → *agiert, probieren* (to taste, to try) → *probiert, studieren* (to study) → *studiert, telefonieren* (to telephone) → *telefoniert.*

Moreover, verbs with the following inseparable prefixes do not take the *ge-* prefix: ***be-***, ***emp-***, ***ent-***, ***er-***, ***ge-***, ***ver-***, ***zer-***.

Weak verbs
bestellen (to order) → ***bestellt; erklären*** (to explain) → ***erklärt; gehören*** (to belong) → ***gehört; verkaufen*** (to sell) → ***verkauft.***

Strong verbs
bestehen (to pass) → ***bestanden***; ***entnehmen*** (to take out) → ***entnommen***; ***erfahren*** (to learn) → ***erfahren***; ***gefallen*** (to please, to like) → ***gefallen.***

Transitive verbs – the position of the object

When a ***transitive verb*** is used in the perfect tense, its past participle is connected to the auxiliary verb *haben*. The object is placed between the conjugated form of *haben* and the past participle of the transitive verb, as in the ensuing example. ***Note*** that in English the object takes end position:

- *Er hat* **ein Lied** (= object) *gesungen.* – He sang ***a song***.
- *Sie haben* **ein Haus** *gebaut.* – They built ***a house***.

In the perfect tense the verb *singen* must be linked to the conjugated forms of the auxiliary *haben*. Thus the verb *singen* linked to the object *Lied* is conjugated as follows:

singular	***plural***
Ich habe ein Lied gesungen.	*Wir haben ein Lied gesungen.*
Du hast ein Lied gesungen.	*Ihr habt ein Lied gesungen.*
Er hat ein Lied gesungen.	*Sie haben ein Lied gesungen.*

Exercise 2.10

Form complete sentences with the following words in the perfect tense, using the auxiliary verb *haben*.

Example:
Ich / kaufen / ein Boot. → Ich ***habe*** ein Boot ***gekauft***.

1. Er / studieren / Medizin.
2. Der Chor / singen / viele Lieder.
3. Ich / probieren / den Kuchen.
4. Der Student / lernen / den Stoff.
5. Du / sagen / die Wahrheit.
6. Ich / bestellen / ein Bier.
7. Die Frau / kennen / diesen Mann.

8. Er / rauchen / eine Zigarette.
9. Ihr / schenken / Blumen.
10. Die Schüler / bestehen / den Test.
11. Der Film / gefallen / dem Mädchen.
12. Ich / verkaufen / mein Auto.
13. Sie / erzählen / eine Geschichte.
14. Er / spielen / Karten.
15. Du / lieben / deinen Mann.
16. Ich / öffnen / den Brief.

When an ***intransitive verb*** is used in the perfect tense, its past participle is connected to the auxiliary verb *sein*. Those verbs often describe a movement or a change of location, such as *klettern* (to climb), *reisen* (to travel), *rennen* (to run), *wandern* (to hike). ***Note*** the ***vowel change*** in the verb *rennen*. The past participle is *gerannt*.

Used in the perfect tense intransitive verbs are conjugated as follows:

singular	*plural*
Ich bin gewandert.	*Wir sind gewandert.*
Du bist gewandert.	*Ihr seid gewandert.*
Er ist gewandert.	*Sie sind gewandert.*

When the verb takes a prepositional phrase or an adjunct (such as an adverb or any other adjunct expressing direction, time, place or manner), the past participle is placed at the end of the sentence. ***Note*** that in English adjuncts take end position:

- *Ich bin* ***nach Deutschland*** *gereist.* – I travelled ***to Germany*** (= prepositional phrase).
- *Du bist* ***sehr schnell*** *gerannt.* – You ran ***very fast*** (= adverb).

Exercise 2.11

Form complete sentences with the following words in the perfect tense. Use the auxiliary verb *sein*.

Example: *Wir / reisen / um die Welt.* → *Wir sind um die Welt gereist.*

1. Die Katze / klettern / auf den Baum.
2. Wir / wandern / gestern.
3. Die Läufer / rennen / schnell.
4. Der Kanzler / reisen / nach Italien.
5. Ich / rennen / in die Schule.
6. Ihr / klettern / auf den Gipfel.

Strong verbs – the past participle with and without vowel change

Past participles with no vowel change

The perfect tense of most strong verbs is formed with the present tense of *haben* and the past participle of the main verb. A number of strong verbs do not change their stem vowel in the past participle. Accordingly the past participle of those strong verbs consists of the prefix ***ge-*** and the infinitive stem plus the suffix ***-en***, as in the following example:

- *Ich habe einen Kuchen* ***gebacken***. – I have baked a cake.

Verbs belonging to this group include: *essen* (to eat; note the extra **g** in ge**g**essen), *fahren* (to drive, to go), *geben* (to give), *halten* (to hold), *kommen* (to come), *lassen* (to let), *laufen* (to run), *lesen* (to read), *schlafen* (to sleep), *sehen* (to see), *treten* (to step), *vergessen* (to forget), *wachsen* (to grow), etc.

Remember that the past participles of verbs that begin with ***be-***, ***emp-***, ***ent-***, ***er-***, ***ge-***, ***ver-***, ***zer-*** do not take the ***ge-*** prefix.

Exercise 2.12

Form complete sentences with the following strong verbs in the perfect tense. Remember that the perfect of most strong verbs is formed with *haben*, and that most intransitive verbs and those verbs expressing movement or change of location take the auxiliary *sein*.

Example: *Ich / schlafen / gut.* → *Ich habe gut geschlafen.*

1. Er / essen / den Apfel.
2. Wir / kommen / nach Hause.
3. Ich / sehen / die Königin.
4. Ihr / laufen / sehr schnell.
5. Er / schlagen / sein Kind.
6. Ich / vergessen / mein Geld.
7. Die Polizisten / fangen / ihn.
8. Das Kind / fallen / in den Dreck.
9. Er / graben / ein Loch.
10. Ihr / backen / Plätzchen.
11. Die Frau / tragen / ein Kleid.
12. Du / treten / auf meinen Fuß.
13. Das Mädchen / lesen / das Buch.
14. Der Baum / wachsen / schnell.
15. Sie / waschen / die Hose.
16. Ich / fahren / nach Hamburg.

The past participle with vowel change

Many ***strong verbs*** change their ***stem vowel*** in the past participle. As noted earlier, there is no basic pattern to predict the stem vowel of a past participle and therefore it is necessary lo learn and to memorize the principal forms of the verb, i.e. the infinitive, the imperfect and the past participle. But on the other hand there are certain patterns of vowel changes which recur again and again and which can be grouped accordingly:

***Changes from* ei *to* ie *and* i:**

- *bleiben* (to stay) → *geblieben*
- *schreiben* (to write) → *geschrieben*
- *schreien* (to scream) → *geschrien*
- *beißen* (to bite) → *gebissen*
- *leiden* (to suffer) → *gelitten*
- *schneiden* (to cut) → *geschnitten*

***Changes from* ie *to* o:**

- *fliegen* (to fly) → *geflogen*
- *fliehen* (to flee) → *geflohen*
- *frieren* (to freeze) → *gefroren*
- *riechen* (to smell) → *gerochen*
- *schießen* (to shoot) → *geschossen*
- *schließen* (to shut) → *geschlossen*
- *verlieren* (to lose) → *verloren*
- *ziehen* (to pull) → *gezogen*

> *Note*: the past participle of the verb *liegen* does not fit into the category above. Its past participle is *gelegen*.

***Changes from* i *to* u, o, e:**

- *binden* (to bind) → *gebunden*
- *finden* (to find) → *gefunden*
- *singen* (to sing) → *gesungen*
- *springen* (to jump) → *gesprungen*
- *trinken* (to drink) → *getrunken*
- *beginnen* (to begin) → *begonnen*
- *gewinnen* (to win) → *gewonnen*
- *schwimmen* (to swim) → *geschwommen*
- *bitten* (to ask) → *gebeten*
- *sitzen* (to sit) → *gesessen*

***Changes from* e *to* o:**

- *brechen* (to break) → *gebrochen*
- *empfehlen* (to advise) → *empfohlen*
- *helfen* (to help) → *geholfen*
- *nehmen* (to take) → *genommen*
- *sprechen* (to speak) → *gesprochen*
- *sterben* (to die) → *gestorben*
- *treffen* (to meet) → *getroffen*
- *werfen* (to throw) → *geworfen*

Note: the past participle of *gehen* does not fit into the category above. Its past participle is *gegangen*.

Exercise 2.13

Rewrite the following sentences in the perfect tense.

Example: *Ich finde den Mann.* → *Ich habe den Mann gefunden.*

1. *Er spricht mit ihm.*
2. *Ich schließe die Tür.*
3. *Die Männer singen ein Lied.*
4. *Der Sträfling flieht.*
5. *Der Hund beißt einen Mann.*
6. *Wir verlieren das Spiel.*
7. *Ihr trefft meinen Freund.*
8. *Ich empfehle Ihnen ein Steak.*
9. *Die Frauen trinken Wein.*
10. *Du nimmst das Schnitzel.*
11. *Er leidet an einer Krankheit.*
12. *Ich schreibe eine Postkarte.*
13. *Die Lehrerin hilft dem Kind.*
14. *Wir finden das Hotel.*
15. *Meine Großmutter stirbt.*
16. *Du brichst den Rekord.*

The past participle of the auxiliary verbs *sein, haben* and *werden*

Again, special consideration must be given to the auxiliary verbs *sein*, *haben* and *werden*. The full conjugation of these verbs in the perfect tense is as follows:

sein	*haben*	*werden*
ich bin gewesen	ich habe gehabt	ich bin geworden
du bist gewesen	du hast gehabt	du bist geworden
er ist gewesen	er hat gehabt	er ist geworden
wir sind gewesen	wir haben gehabt	wir sind geworden
ihr seid gewesen	ihr habt gehabt	ihr seid geworden
sie sind gewesen	sie haben gehabt	sie sind geworden

Chapter 3: Word Order

One-minute overview

As we have seen in the first chapter, being able to form German sentences requires a sound knowledge of word order. Your ability to speak German fluently depends very much on your capacity for joining the words and the sentence parts discussed in the first chapter. German word order often differs greatly from English word order. Since the German language consists of more grammatical markers such as cases, gender or verb endings, the language is much more flexible and permits a more intricate sentence structure. This chapter will show you:

- the standard word order in declarative sentences, questions and commands;
- the word order with compound tenses;
- how to change the word order when an object or an adjunct is in front position;
- the word order with separable prefix verbs and compound verbs.

Declarative sentences

The regular German word order used in declarative sentences corresponds more or less to the English word order. They consist of a subject, an object and a transitive verb and form the basic **SVO** sentence structure. Study the following sentences:

- *Herr Müller kaufte einen Mercedes.* – Mr Müller bought a Mercedes.
- *Frau Schmidt liebt ihren Mann.* – Mrs Schmidt loves her husband.
- *Der Junge füttert seinen Hund.* – The boy is feeding his dog.
- *Das kleine Mädchen wäscht ihren blauen Rock.* – The little girl is washing her blue skirt.

The German word order and the English word order used in standard declarative sentences are identical. In the German sentence the position of each word corresponds to its position in the English sentence:

subject	conjugated verb	direct object
Herr Müller	*kaufte*	*einen Mercedes.*
Mr Müller	bought	a Mercedes.
Das kleine Mädchen	*wäscht*	*ihren blauen Rock.*
The little girl	is washing	her blue skirt.

The object in front position

In German you can exchange object and subject. The object can be put in front position:

- *Einen Mercedes kaufte Herr Müller.*
- *Ihren blauen Rock wäscht das kleine Mädchen.*

Exercise 3.1

Put the following words in the right order forming complete and sensible sentences. Put the subject in first position.

Example: *einen / Drachen / bastelte / er.* → *Er bastelte einen Drachen.*

1. *einen Kuchen / backte / er*
2. *half / der Notarzt / dem Verletzten*
3. *grüßen / ihren Lehrer / die Schüler*
4. *er / Geige / spielt*
5. *befragte / sie / den Zeugen.*
6. *fleißige Schüler / unterrichtet / der engagierte Lehrer*

Exercise 3.2

Change the sentences completed in exercise 3.1 by putting the object in first position.
Example: *Er bastelte einen Drachen.* → *Einen Drachen bastelte er.*

Word order with compound tenses

As in English, certain German tenses consist of more than one verb. They are called **compound tenses.** A compound tense consists of a conjugated (or finite) form of an auxiliary verb (e.g. *sein* or *haben*) and a non-finite form of a verb such as an infinitive or a past participle. They are called non-finite because they do not have a conjugated or finite personal ending.

The **perfect tense** is an important compound tense (see also chapter 2). It consists of a conjugated form of the auxiliary verb *haben* or *sein* plus the past participle: *Ich habe gesiegt.* – I have won. / *Ich bin gelaufen.* – I have run.

Another important compound tense is the **future tense**, which is formed with a conjugated form of *werden* plus the infinitive: *Sie werden siegen.* – They will win.

When an **object** or any other sentence part – such as a **prepositional phrase** or an **adverb** – becomes part of the sentence, **the second part of the compound verb**, i.e. the past participle or the infinitive, **is placed in final position.** Compare the following sentence structures:

tense	subject	conjugated verb	**adverb**	past participle or infinitive
perfect	*Ich*	*habe*	***überlegen***	*gesiegt.*
future	*Sie*	*werden*		*siegen.*

tense	subject	conjugated verb	past participle or infinitive	**adverb**
present perfect	I	have	won	**convincingly.**
future	They	will	win	

In German the adverb is placed between the conjugated verb and the past participle or the infinitive, while in English the adverb is placed in final position.

When the verb is connected with an **object**, in German the object takes the same position as the adverb:

tense	subject	conjugated verb	**object**	past participle or infinitive
perfect:	*Herr Müller*	*hat*	***einen Mercedes***	*gekauft.*
future:		*wird*		*kaufen.*

When the **object** is used in first position the **subject** is placed **between the conjugated verb and the finite verb:**

tense	**object**	conjugated verb	**subject**	past participle or infinitive
perfect	*Einen Mercedes*	*hat*	*Herr Müller*	*gekauft.*
future		*wird*		*kaufen.*

In English, on the other hand, the object always takes end position. Here the conjugated verb and the non-finite verb form a unit which does not permit the insertion of an object or a subject:

tense	subject	conjugated verb	past participle or infinitive	**object**
present perfect	Mr Müller	has	bought	**a Mercedes.**
future		will	buy	

The same rule must be applied when a passive voice or when other modal auxiliaries are used in connection with an infinitive. The most important modal auxiliaries are *dürfen* (to be allowed to, may), *können* (can, to be able to), *müssen* (to have to, must), *sollen* (ought to, should), *mögen* (to like to) and *wollen* (to want to).

Exercise 3.3

Put the following words in the right order to form complete and sensible sentences. Start with the subjects.

1. *hat / er / eine Reise / gebucht*
2. *eine Firma / gegründet / hat / sie*
3. *gemietet / er / hat / eine Wohnung*
4. *die meiste Arbeit / hat / sie / gemacht*
5. *angerufen / seinen Chef / er / hat*
6. *zu schnell / er / gefahren / ist*
7. *den Artikel / hat / geschrieben / sie*
8. *die Rechnung / er / bezahlen / wird*
9. *müssen / wir / das Haus / verkaufen*
10. *gespielt / gut / hat / er*

Exercise 3.4

Put the following words in the right order forming complete and sensible sentences. Start with the object.

1. *hat / das Hotel / angerufen / den Herrn*
2. *man / ihn / beraubt / hat*
3. *kaufen / das Haus / sie / werden*
4. *Arsenal / besiegt / hat / den FC Bayern*
5. *hat / er / das Bier / getrunken*
6. *sie / eine Hose / gekauft / hat*
7. *gemalt / das Kind / hat / das Bild*
8. *mein Chef / mich / entlassen / hat*
9. *das Auto / sie / hat / ausgeliehen*
10. *hat / der Mann / besessen / ein kleines Geschäft*

Placing an adjunct in front position

In German it is not only an object that can be placed in first position. As in English you can start a sentence with an adverb, a prepositional phrase or any other adjuncts which give more information about time, place, manner or any other circumstances. **When this is the case, the verb always takes second position. The verb must be followed by the subject of the sentence.** Study the following German sentence and compare it to its English translation:

prepositional phrase	**conjugated verb**	**subject**	**object**	**non-finite verb**
In Frankfurt	*hat*	*Herr Müller*	*einen BMW*	*gekauft.*
In Frankfurt	Mr Müller	has	bought	a BMW.
prepositional phrase	**subject**	**verb** (conjugated + non-finite verb)	**object**	

Here the English sentence structure, which retains its regular word order – SVO (Subject – Verb – Object), differs greatly from the German sentence structure, which permits the inversion of subject and verb. Study the following examples and compare them to their English translation. The subjects are put in bold type and the verbs are put in italics:

1. Gestern *hat* **Herr Müller** seiner Frau einen BMW *gekauft.* – Yesterday **Mr Müller** *bought* a BMW for his wife.
2. Selbst nach 30 Ehejahren *liebt* **sie** noch ihren Mann. – Even after 30 years of marriage **she** still *loves* her husband.
3. Mit viel Liebe *füttert* **der Junge** seinen Hund. – With much love **the boy** *feeds* his dog.
4. Trotz der Hitze *sind* **sie** den Marathon *gelaufen.* – Despite the heat **they** *ran* the marathon.
5. Weil er müde war, *ist* **er** nicht das Auto *gefahren.* – Because he was tired, **he** *didn't drive* the car.
6. Unglücklicherweise *konnte* **er** seine Arbeit nicht *beenden.* – Unfortunately, **he** *wasn't able to finish* his work.
7. Glücklicherweise *kann* **sie** noch ihre Beine *fühlen und bewegen.* – Fortunately **she** *is able to feel and to move* her legs.
8. Um mehr Geld zu verdienen, *hat* **er** seinen Arbeitsplatz *gewechselt.* – In order to earn more money, **he** *has changed* his job.

The German sentences above possess the following word order:

adjuncts	conjugated verb	subject	indirect object (other sentence parts)	direct object (other sentence parts)	non-finite verb (other sentence parts)
Gestern	*hat*	*Herr Müller*	*seiner Frau*	*einen BMW*	*gekauft.*

The German word order follows four simple rules:

1. In main clauses the conjugated verb always takes second position.
2. Whenever an adjunct (or even a subordinate clause) is in first position, subject and verb are inverted.
3. The non-finite verb, whether it be a past participle or an infinitive, always takes end position.
4. When the other sentence parts consist of a direct and an indirect object, the indirect object always precedes the direct object.

Exercise 3.5

Study the following sentences and underline the subject and the verb (conjugated and non-finite verb) of the main clauses.

1. *Hinter dem Haus steht ein großer Baum.*
2. *In den Ferien schläft er gewöhnlich sehr lange.*
3. *Vor den Prüfungen nimmt sie immer eine Beruhigungstablette.*
4. *Morgen werden wir nach München fahren.*
5. *In der kommenden Woche muss ich meine Prüfungen ablegen.*
6. *Da ich keine Zeit habe, kann ich nicht in den Urlaub fahren.*
7. *Trotz ihrer Höhenangst ist sie auf den Turm gestiegen.*
8. *Aufgrund einer Erkältung kann sie nicht an der Wanderung teilnehmen.*
9. *Nach dem Mittagessen macht er seine Hausaufgaben.*
10. *Mit ihrem Mann will sie in die Schweiz fahren.*

Exercise 3.6

Put the following sentence parts in the correct order to form complete and sensible sentences. Start with the underscored element.

Example: *können übernachten / Sie / sehr billig / in diesem Hotel.* → *In diesem Hotel können Sie sehr billig übernachten.*

1. *musst gehen / du / wieder in die Schule / nächste Woche*
2. *pünktlich in Hamburg / mit diesem Zug / ihr / werdet sein*
3. *den Berggipfel / können erreichen / wir / in zwei Stunden*
4. *einmal täglich / er / geht joggen / um sich fit zu halten*
5. *geht essen / sie / regelmäßig / in die Mensa*
6. *in Amerika / will studieren / nach ihrem Examen / sie*
7. *sind gefahren / trotz des schlechten Wetters / wir / an die Küste*

8. *er / mit dieser Aufgabe / wurde betraut / wegen seiner guten Qualifikation*
9. *haben Fußball gespielt / die Menschen / in Deutschland / schon immer gerne*
10. *man / einen wunderschönen Sonnenuntergang / über den Bergen / sieht*

Objects in front position with complex sentences

Note that it is impossible to put an adjunct plus a subject or an object in front position. The second place is always reserved for the conjugated verb. If you want to put an object – whether it be a direct or an indirect object – in front position, the adjunct (e.g. an adverb) must be placed after the subject. If an indirect object is used the adjunct precedes the indirect object:

direct object	**conjugated verb**	subject	**adjunct**	indirect object	non-finite verb
Einen BMW	***hat***	*Herr Müller*	***gestern***	*seiner Frau*	*gekauft.*

It is of course also possible to put an indirect or a prepositional phrase in front position. If this is the case, the indirect and direct objects change places:

indirect object	conjugated verb	subject	adjunct	**direct object**	non-finite verb
Seiner Frau	*hat*	*Herr Müller*	*gestern*	***einen BMW***	*gekauft.*

Exercise 3.7

Rewrite the sentences given above by putting an object in front position.

Examples:

1. *Gestern hat Herr Müller seiner Frau* ***einen BMW*** *gekauft.* → ***Einen BMW*** *hat Herr Müller gestern seiner Frau gekauft.* (direct object in front position)

   Alternatively (indirect object in front position):
   Seiner Frau *hat Herr Müller gestern einen BMW gekauft.*

2. *Selbst nach 30 Ehejahren liebt sie noch* ***ihren Mann.*** → ***Ihren Mann*** *liebt sie noch selbst nach 30 Ehejahren*

Verbs with separable prefixes

Certain German verbs can be used with prefixes in front of them. These prefixes are usually prepositions. Take for example the verb *nehmen* (to take) and study the following infinitives:

***ab**nehmen* (to lose weight, to decrease)
***zu**nehmen* (to increase, to put on weight)
***auf**nehmen* (to take up, to record)
***durch**nehmen* (to do in class)
***an**nehmen* (to take on, to accept)
***weg**nehmen* (to take away).

It becomes obvious that the prefixes slightly change or give a totally new meaning to the verb. When these verbs are used in simple tenses – such as the present tense or the imperfect – these prefixes must be separated from the verb. Study the following examples:

- present tense: *Sie **nimmt** das Kind **auf**.* – She takes up the child.
- imperfect: *Dann **nahm** er etwas Gewicht **ab**.* – Then he lost a bit of weight.

Here the prefix must be separated from the verb and be placed in final position. Other important separable verbs with prefixes are:

- ***ab**fahren* (to leave, to depart)
- ***ab**fliegen* (to depart)
- ***ab**holen* (to pick up)
- ***ab**sagen* (to cancel/to call off)
- ***an**kommen* (to arrive)
- ***an**sehen* (to take a look at, to view)
- ***an**ziehen* (to put on clothes)
- ***auf**machen* (to open)
- ***aus**gehen* (to go out)
- ***aus**steigen* (to get off – bus, etc.)
- ***bei**bringen* (to teach)
- ***ein**laden* (to invite)
- ***ein**steigen* (to get on – bus, etc.)
- ***fort**gehen* (to go away)
- ***heim**kommen* (to return home)
- ***mit**bringen* (to bring)
- ***mit**nehmen* (to take along)
- ***statt**finden* (to take place)
- ***um**tauschen* (to change)
- ***um**ziehen* (to move house)
- ***vor**ziehen* (to prefer)
- ***weg**fahren* (to drive off)
- ***zu**machen* (to close)
- ***zu**senden* (to send to)

Exercise 3.8

Put the following words in the right order to form complete and sensible sentences. Use the present tense and/or the imperfect.

Example:

der Zug / um 10.00 Uhr / abfahren. → Der Zug fährt um 10.00 Uhr ab.

1. ich / das Fenster / zumachen
2. sie / immer spät / heimkommen
3. du / etwas zu essen / mitbringen
4. wir / heute Abend / ausgehen
5. ich / meinen Bruder / mitnehmen
6. du / das Auto / wegfahren
7. er / sie / ansehen
8. wir / morgen früh / ankommen
9. ich / einen Mantel / anziehen
10. ihr / eure Freunde / einladen.

Note that the prefix must **always** be placed in final position even if you lengthen the sentence by adding other sentence parts such as adverbs of time or place. Study the following examples:

- *Der Zug **fährt** um 10.00 Uhr von Bahnsteig 3 **ab**.* – The train **leaves** from platform 4 at 10 o'clock.
- *Wenn ich heimkomme, **bringe** ich ihm immer ein Geschenk aus Spanien **mit**.* – On returning home, I always **bring** him a present from Spain.

Note: the indirect object (= *ihm*) precedes the direct object (= *ein Geschenk aus Spanien*).

Compound verbs

What we have just said about separable prefix verbs is also true for **compound verbs that consist of a verb and another word** (noun, preposition or another verb), for example a verb–verb- or a noun–verb combination such as *spazieren gehen* (to go for a walk) or *Rad fahren* (to go by bike). The second part of the compound verb has to be put in final position. Study the following examples:

- *Sie **geht** heute Nachmittag **spazieren**.* → This afternoon she **is going** for a walk.
- *Ich **fahre** gerne **Rad**.* → I enjoy **riding on my** bike.

When a compound verb consists of two verbs, the verb in final position (the infinitive) must be conjugated; e.g:

spazieren ***gehen*** *– Ich* ***gehe*** *spazieren.*
kennen ***lernen*** *– Er* ***lernte*** *sie dort kennen.*

Other important compound verbs are:

- *etwas schneiden lassen* (to have something cut)
- *jemanden arbeiten lassen* (to make or to let someone work)
- *jemanden Auto fahren lassen* (to let someone drive one's car)
- *Auto/Bahn/Rad fahren* (to go by car/train/bike)
- *jemandem Bescheid sagen* (to let someone know)
- *kennen lernen* (to get to know)
- *sitzen bleiben* (to have to repeat a year)
- *Halt machen* (to stop)
- *etwas liegen lassen* (to leave something behind)
- *verloren gehen* (to get lost)
- *getrennt schreiben* (to be written as two words)
- *etwas geschenkt bekommen* (to get something as a present)
- *zu Ende gehen* (to come to an end)
- *zustande (zu Stande) kommen* (to come about, to be achieved)
- *zustande (zu Stande) bringen* (to achieve something)

Exercise 3.9

Rewrite the following sentences in the present tense and/or the imperfect.

Example:
Ich habe gestern meine Haare ***schneiden lassen****. → Ich* ***ließ*** *gestern meine Haare* ***schneiden****.*

1. *Er ist gerne Auto gefahren.*
2. *Wir haben an der Raststätte Halt gemacht.*
3. *Ihr habt euch in Deutschland kennengelernt.*
4. *Sie hat mir Bescheid gegeben.*
5. *Du hast dieses Wort getrennt geschrieben.*
6. *Ich habe meine Tasche hier liegen lassen.*
7. *Ihr habt ein Auto geschenkt bekommen.*
8. *Wir haben ihn Auto fahren lassen.*
9. *Er ist mit der Bahn gefahren.*
10. *Sie ist letztes Jahr sitzen geblieben.*

Separable verbs and compound verbs in subordinate clauses

When separable verbs or compound verbs are used in a subordinate clause, they are not separated and are placed at the end of the subordinate clause, whatever tense is used. Study the following examples and note the differences in the English word order:

main clause	subordinate clause			
Ich studierte an der Uni,	*als* conjunction	*ich* subject	*ihn* direct object	***kennen lernte.*** **compound verb**
I was studying at university,	when conjunction	I subject	**got to know** **compound verb**	him. direct object

main clause	subordinate clause			
Der Zug fuhr sehr schnell,	*sodass* conjunction	*ich* subject	*rechtzeitig* adjunct	***ankam.*** **separable verb**
The train went very fast,	so that conjunction	I subject	**arrived** verb	in time. adjunct

Exercise 3.10

Continue the following subordinate clauses by putting the given words in the correct order. Make sure you use a tense which fits to the main clause of the sentence.

Example:
Ich war im Stress, sodass / liegen lassen / meine Geldbörse / ich → Ich war im Stress, sodass ich meine Geldbörse liegen ließ.

1. Die Frau war sehr glücklich, als / einen Blumenstrauß / sie / geschenkt bekommen
2. Peter legte sich gleich ins Bett, nachdem / er / übermüdet / heimkommen
3. Er hält sich auch im hohen Alter noch fit, indem / sehr viel/ Rad fahren / er
4. Es wurde sehr kalt im Zimmer, nachdem / das Fenster / aufmachen / sie
5. Das Kind freute sich, weil / ihm / der Vater / ein Geschenk / mitbringen
6. Seine Mutter informierte ihn, bevor / Bescheid geben / ihm / der Vater
7. Die Wanderer waren so müde, dass / Halt machen / sie / am nächsten Rastplatz
8. Er kam zu spät, weil / nicht rechtzeitig / das Flugzeug / abfliegen
9. Sie war sehr erstaunt, als / sie / er / mit ungläubigen Augen / ansehen

10. Sie kam rechtzeitig an, weil / sie / statt Auto / Bahn fahren

Yes–no questions

In German it is possible to turn any statement into a **yes–no question** (sometimes referred to as an **alternative question**) simply by inverting the word order. The conjugated verb must be placed in front position. The subject usually takes second position, while the object of the sentence is in final position preceded by other sentence parts. Study the following statements and questions. The conjugated verb is in bold type:

conjugated verb	subject	other sentence parts (here: adverb)	object
Fliegt	*er*	*gerne?*	
Kaufte	*Herr Müller*	*gestern*	*einen Mercedes?*

Study the following examples and note the differences in English.

Present tense

- *Er **fliegt** gerne.* – He likes to fly.
- ***Fliegt** er gerne?* – Does he like to fly?
- *Sie **sprechen** Deutsch.* – You speak German.
- ***Sprechen** Sie Deutsch?* – Do you speak German?

Imperfect

- *Herr Müller **kaufte** gestern einen Mercedes.* – Mr Müller bought a Mercedes yesterday.
- ***Kaufte** Herr Müller gestern einen Mercedes?* – Did Mr Müller buy a Mercedes yesterday?
- *Frau Schmidt **buchte** einen Flug.* – Mrs Schmidt booked a flight.
- ***Buchte** Frau Schmidt einen Flug?* – Did Mrs Schmidt book a flight?

Perfect

- *Herr Müller **ist** zu schnell gefahren.* – Mr Müller has driven too fast/ drove too fast.
- ***Ist** Herr Müller zu schnell gefahren?* – Did Mr Müller drive too fast?/Has Mr Müller driven too fast?
- *Frau Schmidt **hat** eine Reise gebucht.* – Mrs Schmidt booked/has booked a flight.
- ***Hat** Frau Schmidt eine Reise gebucht?* – Did Mrs Schmidt book a flight?/Has Mrs Schmidt booked a flight?

Note that the object may precede the noun subject, when the object is a pronoun object, as in the following examples:

- *Herr Meyer suchte seinen Sohn.* – Mr Meyer was looking for his son.
- *Suchte Herr Meyer seinen Sohn?* – Was Mr Meyer looking for his son?/Did Mr Meyer look for his son?

Pronoun object

- *Suchte Herr Meyer **ihn*** (= pronoun object)? *Hat Herr Meyer **ihn*** (= pronoun object) *gesucht?* – Did Mr Meyer look for ***him***?

Preceding pronoun object

- *Suchte **ihn** Herr Meyer?/Hat **ihn** Herr Meyer gesucht?* – Did he look for **him**?

Note: verbs with **separable prefixes** as well as **compound verbs** must also be separated in questions, when they are used in the present tense or in the imperfect:

- *Das Konzert **findet** im Park **statt**.* – The concert is held in the park.
- ***Findet** das Konzert im Park **statt**?* – Is the concert held in the park?

Exercise 3.11

Change the following declarative sentences into questions by putting the conjugated verb in front position.

Example: *Sie sind Engländer.* → *Sind Sie Engländer?*

1. Du bist aus Deutschland.
2. Sie haben noch ein Zimmer frei.
3. Ihr studiert in Berlin.
4. Du lebst in einer Kleinstadt.
5. Du gehst in die zehnte Klasse.
6. Sie kennen diese Stadt.
7. Sie können mich anrufen.
8. Der Zug fährt von Bahnsteig 2 ab.
9. Er ist gestern nach Düsseldorf gefahren.
10. Man schreibt das Wort „spazieren gehen" getrennt.
11. Der Zug kommt heute Abend um 19.00 Uhr an.
12. Er lernte sie an der Universität kennen.

13. Du hast in München Betriebswirtschaft studiert.
14. Sie ziehen bald nach Berlin um.
15. Er hat in Frankfurt eine Wohnung gekauft.
16. Sie möchte in England Politik studieren.

Questions with interrogative words

If you need some more specific information about something, you use questions that are introduced by an interrogative word or phrase. These type of questions are sometimes referred to as informational questions. The most common and most important interrogative words (also called interrogative adverbs) are the following:

wer? – who?
was? – what?
wem? – who/whom?
wessen? – whose?
wann? – when?
wo? – where?
wohin? – where to?
warum? – why?
wieso? – why?
weshalb? – why?
wie? – how?
wie viele? – how many?
wie viel? – how much?
was für? – what kind of?

When an interrogative word introduces a question, the inverted word order must also be used. The subject is preceded by the conjugated verb. Study the following sentences:

interrogative adverb	conjugated verb	subject	other sentence parts
	Fliegt	*er*	*gerne?*
Wohin	*fliegt*	*er*	*gerne?*

- *Fliegt er gerne?* – Does he like to fly?
- ***Wohin** fliegt er gerne?* – **Where** does he like to fly **to**?
- *Sprechen Sie Deutsch?* – Do you speak German?
- ***Warum** sprechen Sie so gut Deutsch?* – **Why** do you speak German so well?

Exercise 3.12

Translate the following questions into German.

Example: When does my train leave? (*Zug / abfahren*) → *Wann fährt mein Zug ab?*

1. How old are you? (*alt / sein*)
2. How much is a ticket? (*eine Fahrkarte / kosten*)

3. How do I get into the city centre? (*in das Stadtzentrum / kommen*)
4. What is the policeman doing there? (*der Polizist / machen / da*)
5. When are you visiting us in England? (*besuchen / uns / in England*)

Exercise 3.13

Form questions from the following words using the present tense. Be careful with the separable verbs and the compound verbs.

Example: *Wann / ankommen / du / in Frankfurt? → Wann kommst du in Frankfurt an?*

1. *Wie / Ihre Telefonnummer / lauten?*
2. *Was / Sie / können empfehlen?*
3. *Wo / sein / das WC / bitte?*
4. *Wie viel / die Hose / kosten?*
5. *Welcher / Bus / fahren / in die Innenstadt?*
6. *Wo / die nächste Bushaltestelle / sein?*
7. *Wie / ich / am schnellsten / kommen / zum Bahnhof?*
8. *Wie viele / Sie / Kinder / haben?*
9. *Wessen / fahren / du / Auto?*
10. *Wo / die Konferenz / stattfinden?*

Exercise 3.14

Form questions from the following words using the imperfect.

1. Warum / Sie / studieren / in England?
2. Wie / dich / kennen lernen / dein Mann?
3. Weshalb / du / das Treffen / absagen?
4. Wann / zustande kommen / dieser Beschluss?
5. Wie / deine Karriere / zu Ende gehen / an der Universität?

Exercise 3.15

Form questions from the following words using the perfect. Note that as a general rule you have to use the auxiliary *sein* for verbs that involve movement, and the auxiliary *haben* for transitive verbs (verbs that take an object).

1. *Warum / mit dem Zug fahren / du?*
2. *Wann / in Frankfurt / Sie / eine Wohnung / kaufen?*
3. *Wie / Sie / die Aufgabe / lösen?*
4. *Wo / die Tagung / stattfinden?*
5. *Wen / treffen / du / heute Vormittag?*

Commands

While the English language manages with only one imperative verb – it has the same form as the infinitive – there are basically three different forms of the imperative verb to express a command in German. We have to differentiate between the **two informal commands**, in the singular (***du***) as well as the plural (***ihr***), and the formal command (***Sie***), which is used for singular and plural alike. Commands are usually indicated by an exclamation mark. Study the following examples:

Informal commands in the singular

- ***Ruf(e)*** *mich morgen* ***an!*** – **Call** me tomorrow!
- ***Nimm*** *das Geld!* (vowel change) – **Take** the money!
- ***Sei*** *lieb!* – **Be** good!

Informal commands in the plural

- ***Fahrt*** *die Autobahn A5!* – **Take** the motorway A5!
- ***Seid*** *vorsichtig!* – **Be** careful!

The informal singular command is formed by adding an ***-e*** to the stem of the verb. The ***-e*** is often dropped. If there is a vowel change in the present tense of a strong verb, no ***-e*** is added in its singular imperative form (*Nimm das Geld!*). The informal plural command is formed by adding a ***-t*** to the stem of the verb (*Nehmt das Geld!*). As in English the subject is not expressed in the informal commands.

Study the following formal commands:

- *Bitte* ***kommen Sie*** *sofort in mein Büro!* – Please **come** to my office immediately!
- ***Seien Sie*** *immer nett zu Ihren Kollegen!* – Always **be** nice to your colleagues!

The formal command is formed by adding ***-en*** to the stem of the verb followed by the formal personal pronoun ***Sie***.

The imperative forms of ***sein*** (to be) are irregular:

– informal singular: *Sei !*
– informal plural: *Seid ...!*
– formal command: *Seien Sie ...!*

Word order

The **imperative forms** of the verb must always be placed in **front position**; it may only be preceded by the word *bitte* (please). In formal commands the subject *Sie* follows directly after the imperative verb. Note that separable prefixes have to be placed in final position.

Exercise 3.16

Complete the following sentences using the correct informal command as indicated.

Example: ____ *bitte in die Küche!* (*gehen*, singular) = ***Geh(e)*** *bitte in die Küche!*

1. ________ *mir Bescheid, wenn ihr kommen könnt!* (*sagen*, plural)
2. ________ *mich bitte in Ruhe! Ich möchte alleine sein.* (*lassen*, plural)
3. ________ *den Lehrer! Er weiß Bescheid.* (*fragen*, singular)
4. ________ *das Auto!* (*verkaufen*, singular)
5. ________ *euren Gästen ein guter Gastgeber!* (*sein*, plural)
6. ________ *dir das an! Welch eine Überraschung!* (*sehen*, singular)
7. ________ *mir bitte zwei Tüten Milch, wenn du einkaufen gehst!* (*holen*, singular)
8. ________ *nicht so viel Unfug im Urlaub!* (*machen*, plural)
9. ________ *mir bitte etwas zu trinken!* (*geben*, singular)
10. ________ *nicht immer so schlecht gelaunt!* (*sein*, singular)

Exercise 3.17

Write formal commands.

Example: *den 12-Uhr-Zug nehmen. = Nehmen Sie den 12-Uhr-Zug!*

1. *mit der Straßenbahn fahren*
2. *eine bestandene Prüfung feiern*
3. *diesen Text übersetzen*
4. *einen Aufsatz schreiben*
5. *nach Deutschland gehen*
6. *eine Fahrkarte am Schalter kaufen*
7. *mit meinem Chef sprechen*
8. *einen Polizisten fragen*
9. *die U-Bahn nehmen*
10. *für jeden Test lernen*

Chapter 4: Mastering Reflexive Verbs

One-minute overview

A reflexive verb is a transitive verb whose object, the reflexive pronoun, refers to the subject of the sentence. The effect of which is – in contrast to the ordinary transitive verbs – that the subject and object of a reflexive verb are the same person or thing. The object of a reflexive verb is called a reflexive pronoun because it reflects back to the subject of the sentence or clause. Reflexive verbs pose a difficulty for speakers of English because there are many reflexive verbs in German whose counterparts in English are non-reflexive. Additionally, there is a difference between English and German as far as the position of the reflexive pronoun is concerned. This chapter will show you:

- how and when to use reflexive verbs and their pronouns;
- the position and function of the reflexive pronoun;
- the use of reflexive pronouns in the accusative and the dative cases;
- how to complain about hotel facilities;
- how to ask someone to sit down;
- how to order a meal in a restaurant.

The reflexive pronoun *sich* – *-self/-selves (3rd person)*

Consider the following reflexives verbs *sich schneiden* (to cut oneself) and *sich verletzten* (to hurt oneself):

- *Sie hat **sich** geschnitten.* – She has cut **herself**.
- *Die Kinder haben **sich** verletzt.* – The children have hurt **themselves**.

Here, the third person reflexive pronoun *sich*, which also precedes the infinitive of a reflexive verb, reflects back to the subjects ***sie*** (she) and ***die Kinder*** (the children). Reflexive pronouns in German correspond to the English pronouns ending in *–**self*** (sing.) or *–**selves*** (pl.).

In German reflexive verbs are used quite often, whereas in English this relationship is often implied. Many verbs whose German equivalent are reflexive are non-reflexive in English, for example:

- *Sie **treffen sich** jeden Morgen im Büro.* – They **meet** every morning in the office.
- ***Wenden** Sie **sich** bitte an die Rezeption.* – **Turn to** the reception, please.
- *Wir **beklagten uns** über unser Hotelzimmer.* – We **complained** about our hotel room.
- ***Setzen** Sie **sich** bitte!* – Please **sit down.**

The same is true for the following words:

sich anmelden – to register
sich anstecken – to catch a disease
sich beeilen – to hurry
sich beklagen – to complain
sich beteiligen – to participate
sich bewegen – to move
sich einbilden – to imagine
sich entscheiden – to decide
sich entschuldigen – to apologize
sich erholen – to recover
sich ereignen – to happen
sich erinnern – to remember
sich freuen – to rejoice
sich freuen auf – to look forward to
sich fühlen – to feel
sich fürchten – to be afraid, to fear
sich grämen – to grieve
sich hinlegen – to lie down
sich (hin)setzen – to sit down
sich interessieren für – to be interested in
sich irren – to be wrong, to be mistaken
sich konzentrieren – to concentrate
sich kümmern – to look after
sich Mühe geben – to take trouble
sich nähern – to approach
sich öffnen – to open
sich treffen – to meet
sich umziehen – to change clothes
sich übergeben – to be sick, vomit

sich (ver)ändern – to change
sich verlassen auf – to rely on
sich verlaufen – to get lost
sich verlieben – to fall in love
sich verspäten – to come late, to be late
sich vertun – to make a mistake

A number of German reflexive verbs can be used in English with or without a reflexive pronoun, such as:

sich vorbereiten – to prepare (oneself); *sich anziehen* – to dress (oneself); *sich waschen* – to wash (oneself); *sich rasieren* – to shave (oneself); *sich verstecken* – to hide (oneself); *sich ergeben* – to surrender (oneself).

Position and function of the reflexive pronoun

German and English reflexive pronouns do not have the same position in a sentence:

subject	conjugated verb	**reflexive pronoun**	past participle
Sie	*hat*	***sich***	*geschnitten.*
She	has	cut	**herself.**
subject	*conjugated verb*	*past participle*	**reflexive pronoun**

> *Note*: all reflexive verbs are conjugated with the auxiliary ***haben***.

1. In a **main clause** with a regular word order the reflexive pronoun is usually placed right after the conjugated (finite) verb. When the **imperative** is used, the reflexive pronoun is preceded by the imperative verb:
   - *Setz'* ***dich, bitte!*** – Sit down, please.
   - *Erholt* ***euch*** *gut im Urlaub!* – Have a good rest on your holidays.
2. When the **formal address** *Sie* is used in the imperative, the reflexive pronoun comes after the *Sie*:
   - *Setzen Sie* ***sich****, bitte!* – Sit down, please!
   - *Bereiten Sie* ***sich*** *gut auf Ihre Prüfungen vor!* – Prepare yourselves well for your tests.
3. In **questions** the reflexive pronoun is placed after the subject of the sentence:
   - *Wann treffen wir* ***uns*** *wieder?* – When do we meet again?
   - *Für was interessieren Sie* ***sich****?* – What are you interested in?

4. When a **compound tense** (with an auxiliary verb or a modal verb) is used, the reflexive pronoun is placed after the conjugated auxiliary or modal verb (such as *müssen* – must, or *können* – can), while the infinitive is in final position:
   - *Er hat* ***sich*** *das Bein gebrochen.* – He has broken his leg.
   - *Wir werden* ***uns*** *wegen der schlechten Betten beschweren.* – We are going to complain about the uncomfortable beds.
   - *Du musst* ***dich*** *im Keller verstecken.* – You have to hide (yourself) in the basement.

The reflexive pronoun in the accusative case

Looking at the following table it also becomes obvious that the reflexive pronoun has the same function as an object. It is possible to replace the pronoun by an adequate object, thereby giving the sentence an ordinary sentence structure with a subject, verb and a regular direct object:

subject	conjugated verb	refl. pronoun object	past participle
Sie	*hat*	***sich***	*geschnitten.*
Sie	*hat*	***das Brot***	*geschnitten.*
She	has	cut	**the bread.**
She	has	cut	**herself.**
subject	**conjugated verb**	**past participle**	**refl. pron./object**

Since reflexive pronouns take the position of objects, they must also reflect case. When the reflexive pronoun functions as a direct object, the **accusative case** is usually used. The following table shows you the accusative reflexive pronouns. They are identical with the accusative personal pronouns except for the third person singular and plural and for the formal address *Sie*:

accusative case		
personal pronouns	**reflexive pronouns**	
mich	*mich*	myself
dich	*dich*	yourself
ihn	*sich*	himself
sie	*sich*	herself
es	*sich*	itself
uns	*uns*	ourselves
euch	*euch*	*yourselves*
sie	*sich*	themselves
Sie	*sich*	yourself/yourselves

Exercise 4.1

Complete the following sentences with the appropriate reflexive pronoun.

Example: *Du interessierst* ______ *für Kunst.* → *Du interessierst* ***dich*** *für Kunst.*

1. *Es bewegt* _______ *dort etwas.*
2. *Ich habe* _______ *am Bein verletzt.*
3. *Wir haben* _______ *amüsiert.*
4. *Er rasiert* _______ *jeden Morgen.*
5. *Ihr habt* _______ *verändert.*
6. *Dann wende ich* _______ *an die Polizei.*
7. *Die Studenten bereiten* _______ *auf ihr Examen vor.*
8. *Du erinnerst* _______ *doch auch an den Gast.*
9. *Bitte beklagen Sie* _______ *beim Chef!*
10. *Bitte gebt* ______ *doch Mühe beim Lernen!*

Exercise 4.2

Put the following sentence parts in the right order to form complete and sensible sentences (1–10), questions (11–15) and imperatives (16–20). Use the correct personal form of the verb. Start with the subject of the sentence. Be careful with the separable verbs.

Example: *sich freuen auf / die Ferien / ich.* → *Ich freue mich auf die Ferien.*

1. *sich rasieren / Männer*
2. *gerade / sie / sich anziehen*
3. *sich interessieren für / ich / Kunst*
4. *sich vorbereiten / ich / auf den Vortrag*
5. *der Grenze / sich nähern / er*
6. *haben / sich erinnern / die Frau / an den Vorfall*
7. *sich treffen / wir / im Konferenzzimmer*
8. *haben / sich verletzten / ich / bei dem Unfall*
9. *sich bewegen / müssen / im Freien / du*
10. *sich schneiden / haben / ihr.*

Questions:

11. *sich verletzen / das Kind / haben / wie?*
12. *sich vorbereiten / wann / du?*
13. *sich treffen / wollen / wir?*
14. *ihr / haben / sich erholen?*
15. *können / sich verlassen auf / dich / ich?*

Imperatives:

16. *auf die Prüfung / sich vorbereiten / Sie!* (formal)
17. *sich waschen / mit Seife!* (plural, informal)

18. *sich verstecken / im Schrank!* (singular, informal)
19. *sich hinlegen / Sie / bitte / auf die Liege!* (formal)
20. *auf den Urlaub / sich freuen!* (plural, informal)

The reflexive pronoun in the dative case

1. A few reflexive verbs do not require the accusative but the **dative case** such as *sich einbilden* (to imagine), *sich etwas vorstellen* (to imagine something), *sich weh tun* (to hurt oneself). Study the following sentences:

   - *Du bildest* ***dir*** *viel ein.* – You imagine a lot of things.
   - *Ich habe* ***mir*** *weh getan.* – I have hurt **myself.**

2. The reflexive pronouns in the dative case are also used if a direct object is used in the sentence. Examples:

   - *Ich kaufe* ***mir*** *eine Wohnung.* – I am buying a flat *for* **myself.**
   - *Er hat* ***sich*** *ein Steak bestellt.* – He has ordered a steak *for* **himself.**

   Here, the reflexive pronouns ***mir*** and ***sich*** have the function of an indirect object, therefore the reflexive pronouns have to be put in the dative case. In English the dative is expressed by the preposition 'for' plus the reflexive pronouns ending in '-self' or '–selves'.

3. In a sentence with a **regular word order** (**SVO**), the dative reflexive pronouns are placed immediately after the conjugated verb. Moreover, they usually precede the direct object:

subject	conjugated verb **(dative)**	**reflexive pronoun**	direct object	past participle
Ich	*kaufe*	***mir***	*eine Wohnung.*	
Er	*hat*	***sich***	*ein Steak*	*bestellt.*

4. In a sentence in which the direct object is in first position the reflexive pronoun comes after the subject of the sentence:

direct object	conjugated verb	subject	**reflexive pronoun (dative)**	past participle
Eine Wohnung	*kaufe*	*ich*	***mir.***	
Ein Steak	*hat*	*er*	***sich***	*bestellt.*

5. In a **question** the dative reflexive pronouns are placed right after the subject. As in a regular main clause, they always precede the direct object:

interrogative word	conjugated verb	subject (dative)	**reflexive pronoun**	direct object	past participle
Wo	*hast*	*du*	***dir***	*eine Wohnung*	*gekauft?*
Wann	*kauft*	*ihr*	***euch***	*ein Auto?*	

6. When the subject used in the third person of the verb is not a pronoun, but the name of a person, the dative reflexive pronoun precedes the subject:

interrogative word	conjugated verb	**reflexive pronoun (dative)**	subject	direct object	past participle
Wann	*hat*	***sich***	*Hans*	*eine Wohnung*	*gekauft?*
Warum	*kauft*	***sich***	*Lisa*	*ein Auto?*	

7. In the **informal address** the dative reflexive pronoun comes after the imperative verb. When the **formal address** is used, the dative reflexive pronoun ***sich*** is placed right after the pronoun ***Sie***. Study the following sentences:

   - *Nimm* ***dir*** *bitte einen Stuhl!* – Please, take a seat.
   - *Nehmen* **Sie** *sich bitte einen Stuhl!* – Please, take a seat.

8. The direct object may precede the reflexive pronoun, if a pronoun is used as a direct object:

   - *Bestell es* ***mir****, bitte!* – Order it for me, please.
   - *Nehmen* **Sie es sich***, bitte!* – Please, take it for yourself.

The dative reflexive pronoun is often used with verbs that can have an indirect and a direct object (the so-called **ditransitive verbs**), such as *sich kaufen* (to buy), *sich holen* (to get, to fetch), *sich bestellen* (to order), *sich machen* (to make), *sich nehmen* (to take), *sich gönnen* (to treat to).

The dative reflexive pronoun used with articles of clothing and parts of the body

Moreover, the dative reflexive pronoun is used when you want to express that someone does or has done something to his or her body or to his or her articles of clothing, such as *sich etwas* (*die Füße/die Haare, etc.*)

waschen (to wash one's feet/hair, etc.), *sich etwas brechen* (to break something), *sich etwas verrenken* (to dislocate something), *sich etwas anziehen* (to put on something), etc. To express this in English you do not need an indirect object, you just use the possessive adjectives, as in the following sentences:

- *Du hast* **dir** *das Bein gebrochen.* – You have broken **your** leg.
- *Ich habe* **mir** *die Haare gewaschen.* – I have washed **my** hair.
- *Die Kinder ziehen* **sich** *gerade die Schuhe an.* – The children are just putting on **their** shoes.

The following table shows you the dative reflexive pronouns. They are identical with the dative personal pronouns except for the third person singular and plural and for the formal address *Sie*:

dative case

personal pronouns	**reflexive pronouns**	
mir	*mir*	(for) myself
dir	*dir*	(for) yourself
ihm	*sich*	(for) himself
ihr	*sich*	(for) herself
ihm	*sich*	(for) itself
uns	*uns*	(for) ourselves
euch	*euch*	(for) yourselves
inhen	*sich*	(for) themselves
Inhen	*sich*	(for) yourself/yourselves

Exercise 4.3

Complete the following sentences with the appropriate reflexive pronoun.

Example: *Ich habe ____ in den Finger geschnitten.* → *Ich habe* **mir** *in den Finger geschnitten.*

1. *Wir holen ______ ein Eis.*
2. *Ich bestelle ______ ein Bier.*
3. *Wir machen es ______ hier gemütlich.*
4. *Er hat ______ die Haare gewaschen.*
5. *Ihr habt ______ einen freien Tag gegönnt.*
6. *Du hast ______ die Haare schneiden lassen.*
7. *Sie haben ______ Urlaub genommen.*
8. *Ich schneide ______ gerade die Fingernägel.*
9. *Bitte nehmen Sie ______ ein Glas Wein.*
10. *Ihr habt ______ ein Haus in Deutschland gekauft.*

Exercise 4.4

Put the following sentence parts in the right order to form complete and sensible sentences in the perfect tense. Start with the subject of the sentence.

Example: *in den Finger / sich schneiden / ich* → *Ich habe mir in den Finger geschnitten.*

1. *sich nehmen / ein Glas Wein / ich*
2. *sich machen / ihr / das Frühstück*
3. *sich gönnen / wir / jeden Sommer / einen Urlaub in Deutschland*
4. *sich bestellen / ein Schnitzel / er*
5. *sich verrenken / den Hals / ich.*

Exercise 4.5

Form questions with the following sentence parts. Use the tense given in brackets.

Example: *sich kaufen / wann / Hans / ein Haus?* (perfect tense) → *Wann hat sich Hans ein Haus gekauft?*

1. *sich bestellen / was / du?* (perfect tense)
2. *sich vorbereiten / wie / ihr / auf die Prüfungen?* (present tense)
3. *sich verrenken / wann / Sie / den Hals?* (perfect tense)
4. *sich vorstellen / wie / Sie / Ihre Arbeit?* (present tense)
5. *sich kaufen / was / du?* (perfect tense)

Chapter 5: Verb and Stress – Separable and Inseparable Verbs

One-minute summary

In this chapter we are going to cover pairs of verbs which outwardly look the same, but due to a different word stress take on a completely new meaning (compare in English, the words 'present' and 'present', or blackbird' and 'black bird') The verbs discussed in this chapter consist of two parts, a prefix (most commonly a preposition) plus the verb stem. If the prefix is stressed, the verb belongs to the separable verbs, which means prefix and verb stem can be separated. But if the verb stem is stressed, the word takes on a new meaning, and the prefix can no longer be separated from the verb stem. This chapter will show you:

- how word stress can bring about a change of meaning with certain verbs;
- the most commonly used verbs with change of word stress and their usage;
- the grammatical differences between separable and inseparable verbs;
- how to enquire for information about ferry departure times;
- words and phrases in translation;
- what to say if you want to transfer a booking or an amount of money from one account to another;
- classroom language (understanding, paraphrasing, repeating).

Durchschauen and *durchschauen*

The separable verb *durchschauen* (to look through)

If you give the primary stress to the prefix *durch-*, it means 'to look through', for example:

- *Die Fenster sind so schmutzig, man kann kaum noch durchschauen.* – The windows are so dirty, it's almost impossible **to look through** them.

- *Du musst / Sie müssen hier **durchschauen**.* – You must **look through** here.

Since the prefix is stressed, ***durchschauen*** must be used as a separable verb. So if it is not used with the infinitive, as with the examples above, the prefix must be separated from the verb stem, and verb stem and prefix be placed in different positions:

Present tense
- Er ***schaut*** gerade ***durch*** mein Fernglas. – He's just **looking** *through* my binoculars.

When an **infinitive** and a **direct object** are used, the infinitive is split into two parts consisting of prefix and verb stem, and the object is placed between the prefix and the verb stem (see also chapter 2):

- *Ich würde gerne **durch** dein/Ihr Fernglas* (= direct object) ***schauen***! – I would like **to look through** your binoculars!

Imperfect
- *Er **schaute** gestern **durch** meine Akten.* – Yesterday he **looked through** my files.

Present perfect
(= present tense of ***sein*** or ***haben*** + past participle)

- *Er **hat** gestern meine Akten **durch**geschaut.* (Variant: *Er **hat** gestern **durch** meine Akten **ge**schaut.*) – Yesterday he **looked through** my files.

Imperative
- ***Schauen** Sie **durch** mein Fernglas!* – **Look through** my binoculars!

The inseparable verb *durchschau*en (to understand, to see through.)

If you give primary stress to the verb stem *–schauen*, and secondary stress to the prefix *durch-*, the verb *durchschauen* means 'to understand' or 'to see through', for example:

Infinitive
- *Ich kann dich/Sie nicht **durchschauen**.* – I can't **see through** you.
- *Versuche/Versuchen Sie mich zu **durchschauen**!* – Try to **see through** me!

Since the stem of the infinitive is stressed, *durchschauen* must be used as an inseparable verb. Prefix and verb stem form an inseparable unit, whether the verb is used in its past tense form, present perfect tense or in the imperative. *Durchschauen* is hardly used as an imperative; it is most commonly used in the perfect tense, for example:

- *Ich **habe** deinen/Ihren Plan **durchschaut**.* – I can **see through** your scheme.

Present

- *Ich **durchschaue** dich/Sie.* – I can **see** right **through** you.

Perfect

- *Ich habe die Grammatik **durchschaut**.* – I **have understood** the grammar.
- *Sie hat die Aufgabenstellung **durchschaut**.* – She **has understood** the assignment.

> *Note*: the inseparable verb ***durchschauen*** does not take the **ge-** prefix. This is the case for all the other inseparable verbs.

Imperfect

- *Er **durchschaute** ihren Plan. – He* **saw** right **through** their scheme.

Durchdringen and *durchdringen*

The separable verb *durchdringen* (to penetrate, to come through.)

Infinitive and direct object

- *Die Sonne konnte noch nicht **durch** die dicken Wolken (= direct object) **dringen**.* – The sun couldn't yet **penetrate** the thick clouds.

Present

- *Das Wasser **dringt** nicht durch die Kleidung **durch**.* – The water is not **penetrating** the clothing.

Perfect

- *Die Sonne **ist** heute kaum **durchgedrungen**.* – The sun **has** hardly **come through** today.

Imperfect

- *Der Regen **drang** durch die Decke **durch**.* – The rain **came through** the ceiling.

The inseparable verb ***durchdringen***
(To pass through, to pervade, to penetrate, to grasp.)

Infinitive
- *Röntgenstrahlen können feste Körper* ***durchdringen****.* – X-rays can **pass through** solid material.

Present
- *Der Kaffeegeruch* ***durchdringt*** *die Markthalle.* – The smell of coffee **pervades** the market.

Perfect
- *Der Student* ***hat*** *das Problem* ***durchdrungen****.* – The student **has grasped** the problem.

Imperfect
- *Ein Licht* ***durchdrang*** *die Dunkelheit.* – A light **penetrated** the darkness.

> Note that *durchdringen* and *durchdringen* are strong verbs and undergo a vowel change.

Durchlaufen and ***durchlaufen***

The separable verb ***durchlaufen***
(To run through or to go through [e.g. streets, or big pipes], to wear through [e.g. shoes or socks].)

Infinitive
- *Der Kaffee muss langsam* ***durchlaufen****.* – The coffee must **run through** slowly.

Present
- *Der Fluss* ***läuft durch*** *dieses Tal.* – The river **runs through** this valley.
- *Der Mann* ***läuft*** *gerade* ***durch*** *das Tor.* – The man **is running** through the gate.

Perfect
- *Seine Schuhe* ***sind*** *an den Sohlen* ***durchgelaufen****.* – His shoes **have worn** through at the soles.
- *Die ersten Marathonläufer* ***sind*** *schon* ***durch*** *den Tunnel gelaufen.* – The first marathon runners **have** already **run** through the tunnel.

Imperfect

- *Er **lief durch** die Absperrung.* – He **ran through** the barrier.

The inseparable verb *durchlaufen*

(to pass through, to go through [period of time at school or any other educational institution], to run through, to walk through [an area or region] to spread through or run through [of feelings, emotions]).

Infinitive

- *Er will die Wüste alleine **durchlaufen**.* – He wants **to walk through** the desert on his own.

Present

- *Ein Schauder der Angst **durchläuft*** ihn. – A shiver of fear **is running through** him.
- *Jeder Student **durchläuft** diesen Teil seiner Ausbildung.* – Every student **goes through** this part of his education.

Perfect

- *Sie hat die Schule gerade **durchlaufen**.* – She **has** just **passed** *through* school.
- *Wir haben den ganzen Wald kreuz und quer **durchlaufen**.* – We **ran** all over the forest.

Imperfect

- *Er **durchlief** eine Ausbildung an der Militärakademie.* – He **went through** a training at the military academy.

Übersetzen and *übersetzen*

The separable verb *übersetzen*

(To take a ferry, to go across (by ferry) or to take someone (to the other side).)

Infinitive

- *Wissen Sie, wann die nächste Fähre nach Hamburg **übersetzen** wird?* Do you know, when the next ferry **goes across** to Hamburg?

Present

- *Die Fähre **setzt** an dieser Stelle **über** den Fluss.* – The ferry **goes across** the river at this point.

Perfect

- *Die Fähre* ***hat*** *uns ans andere Ufer* ***übergesetzt****.* – The ferry **has taken** us **to** the other side.

Imperfect

- *Wir* **setzten** *mit der Fähre* ***über****.* – We **took** the ferry.

The inseparable verb *übersetzen*

(To translate.)

Infinitive

- *Könntest du / Könnten Sie diesen Brief für mich* ***übersetzen****?* – Could you **translate** this letter for me?

Present

- *Ich* ***übersetze*** *gerade diesen Artikel.* – Right now I'*m translating* this article.
- *Sie verdient ihr Geld damit, dass/indem sie Romane* ***übersetzt****.* – She makes her living **by translating** novels.

Perfect

- *Sie* ***hat*** *schon viele Gedichte* ***übersetzt****.* – She **has** already **translated** many poems.

Imperfect

- *Sie* ***übersetzte*** *viele Bücher ins Deutsche.* – She **translated** many books into German.

Umgehen and *umgehen*

The separable verb *umgehen*

(To treat or to handle someone or something, to be about, to be around [of an illness, fears], to haunt [of ghosts haunting a place].)

Infinitive

- *Wie soll ich nur mit diesem Schüler* ***umgehen****?* – But how should I **treat** this pupil?

Present

- *Dieser Arzt* ***geht*** *mit seinen Patienten sehr sanft* ***um****.* – This doctor **treats** his patients very gently.
- *In unserer Familie* ***geht*** *die Grippe* ***um****.* – The flu **is going round** in our family.

- *Hier in diesem Schloß* ***gehen*** *Gespenster* ***um***. – This castle here **is haunted** by ghosts.

Perfect

- *Ich* ***bin*** *immer sehr behutsam mit meinen Kindern* ***umgegangen***. – I **have** always **treated** my children very gently.
- *Wie* ***bist*** *du / sind Sie mit dem Problem* ***umgegangen***? – How **did** you **handle** this problem?

Imperfect

- *Nach dem Mord* ***ging*** *in der Stadt die Angst* ***um***. – After the murder there **was** fear **around** the town.

The inseparable verb *umgehen*

(To go round, to bypass [traffic], to avoid, to evade something.)

Infinitive

- *Gibt es eine Möglichkeit die Baustelle/Straßenarbeiten zu* ***umgehen***? – Is there a possibility **to bypass** the roadworks?
- *Er versuchte dieses Treffen zu* ***umgehen***. – He tried **to avoid** this meeting.

Present

- *Ich* ***umgehe*** *immer dieses Problem, indem ich still bin.* – I always **evade** this problem by keeping quiet.

Perfect

- *Wie* ***hast*** *du /* ***haben*** *Sie die Frage* ***umgangen***? – How did you **evade** the question?

Imperfect

- *In seiner Rede* ***umging*** *er diesen kritischen Punkt.* – In his speech he **evaded** this critical point.

Umschreiben and *umschreiben*

The separable verb *umschreiben*

(To rewrite, to transfer [money, booking, mortgage, etc.], to change, to adapt [e.g. a novel for a film].)

Infinitive

- *Könntest du/Können Sie diesen Artikel* ***umschreiben***? – Could you **rewrite** this article?

- *Du musst/Sie müssen diesen Aufsatz **umschreiben**.* – You have to **rewrite** this essay.
- *Können Sie diesen Betrag auf mein Konto in Luxemburg **umschreiben**?* – Could you **transfer** this amount to my account in Luxembourg?

Present

- *Er **schreibt** gerade den Artikel **um**.* – He **is rewriting** the article at the moment.
- *Er **schreibt** diese Buchung auf einen anderen Gast **um**.* – He **is transferring** this booking to some other guest.

Perfect

- *Er **hat** meinen Liedtext **umgeschrieben**.* – He **has rewritten** my lyrics.
- *Der britische Führerschein **ist** von den deutschen Behörden **umgeschrieben worden**.* – The British driving licence **has been changed** by the German authorities.

Imperfect

- *Sie **schrieb** ihr Theaterstück für einen Film **um**.* – She **adapted** her play for a film.

The inseparable verb *umschreiben*

(To paraphrase, to describe something in your own words, to describe something, to outline something, e.g. the facts of a matter, an idea, a plan.)

Infinitive

- *Wenn dir dieses Wort nicht einfällt, musst du es mit anderen Worten **umschreiben**.* – If this word doesn't come to mind, you must **paraphrase** it.
- *Versuche, diesen Begriff mit eigenen Worten **zu umschreiben**.* – Try to **use your own words** in order to describe this term.

Present

- *Immer wenn er ein Wort nicht weiß, **umschreibt** er es.* – Whenever he doesn't know the word, he **paraphrases** it.

Perfect

- *Der Schüler **hat** diesen Ausdruck ziemlich gut **umschrieben**.* – The pupil **has paraphrased** this expression quite well.

Imperfect

- *Der Richter **umschrieb** den Tatbestand in wenigen Worten.* – The judge **outlined** the facts of the case in a few words.

Umstellen and *umstellen*

The separable verb *umstellen* (1)

(To rearrange something [plan, furniture], to reorder something [sentence or words].)

Infinitive

- *Wir sollten die Möbel **umstellen**.* – We should **rearrange** the *furniture.*
- Wir müssen den Satz ***umstellen***. – We must **reorder** the sentence.

Present

- *Wir **stellen** gerade unseren Plan **um**.* – We **are rearranging** our plan at the moment.

Perfect

- *Wir haben unsere Möbel **umgestellt**.* – We **have rearranged** our furniture.

Imperfect

- *Gestern **stellten** wir den Wochenplan **um**.* – Yesterday we **rearranged** the weekly plan.

Imperative

- ***Stell(e)** doch das Subjekt **um**!* – **Reorder** the subject!

The separable verb *umstellen* (2)

(To switch over, to change, to alter, e.g. switch, TV, telephone, plan, factory, time.)

Infinitive

- *Vergessen Sie nicht die Zeit **umzustellen**, wenn Sie nach Deutschland fliegen.* – Don't forget **to alter** the time, when you fly to Germany.
- *Wir müssen unseren Reiseplan **umstellen**.* – We have **to change** our travel plan.

Present

- Wir ***stellen*** jeden Monat unsere Arbeitszeiten ***um***. – Every month we **alter** our working-hours.

Perfect

- ***Hast*** du den Schalter ***umgestellt***? – **Have** you **altered** the switch?
- ***Habt*** ihr schon eure Produktion auf Computer ***umgestellt***? – **Have** you already **computerized** your production?

Imperfect

- *Letzten Monat* ***stellten*** *wir unsere Produktion auf ein anderes System* ***um***. – Last month we **changed** our production to a different system.

The separable verb *umstellen* (3)

(To get used to a different lifestyle, habits, etc., to change; *sich umstellen*: to adapt or adjust to sth.)

Infinitive

- *Wenn Sie in Deutschland leben, sollten Sie manche Ihrer Lebensgewohnheiten (Essgewohnheiten)* ***umstellen***. – When you live in Germany, you should **change** some of your habits (eating habits).
- *In Deutschland muss man* ***sich*** *auf Rechtsverkehr* ***umstellen***. – In Germany you have **to adapt to** driving on the right.

Present

- *Ich* ***stelle*** *gerade meine Diät* ***um***. – I'm **changing** my diet.

Perfect

- *Ich* ***habe*** *meinen Lebensstil* ***umgestellt***. – I **have changed** my lifestyle.

Imperfect

- *In Deutschland* ***stellte*** *ich mich auf einen anderen Lebensstil* ***um***. – In Germany I **adapted to** a different lifestyle.

The inseparable verb *umstellen*

(To surround)

Infinitive

- *Die Polizisten wollen das Gebäude* ***umstellen***. – The policemen want **to surround** the building.

Present tense

- *Die Jäger* ***umstellen*** *den Tiger*. – The hunters **surround** the tiger.

Perfect tense

- *Die Polizei* ***hat*** *das Haus* ***umstellt***. – The police **have surrounded** the house.

Imperfect

- *Die Soldaten **umstellten** das Gebiet.* – The soldiers **surrounded** the area.

Imperfect (passive voice)

- *Das Gelände **wurde** von allen Seiten **umstellt**.* – The area **was surrounded** from all sides.
- *Der Hoteleingang **wurde** von Autos **umstellt**.* – The entrance to the hotel **was surrounded** by cars.

Unterstellen and *unterstellen*

The separable verb *unterstellen*

(To keep, to store; the reflexive verb *sich **unter**stellen* [non-reflexive in English] to take shelter, to take cover.)

Infinitive

- *Es regnet. Wo können wir **uns unter**stellen?* (reflexive verb) – It's raining. Where can we **take shelter**?
- *Du kannst das Fahrrad in unserer Garage **unterstellen**.* – You can **keep** your bicycle in our garage.

Present

- *Er **stellt** immer seinen Koffer bei **mir** unter.* – He always **stores** his suitcase at my place.

Perfect

- *Ich **habe** meine Möbel in der Garage **untergestellt**.* – I **have stored** my furniture in the garage.

Imperfect

- *Während es regnete, **stellte** sie **sich** unter den Bäumen **unter**.* (reflexive verb) – While it was raining, she **took shelter** under the trees.

The inseparable verb *unterstellen*

(To imply, to insinuate, to put something under someone's command, to put somebody in charge of something.)

Infinitive

- *Ich möchte dir / Ihnen keine Dummheit **unterstellen**.*– I don't wish **to imply** that you're stupid.

Present

- *Der Zeuge **unterstellt** mir, ich sei zu schnell gefahren.* – The witness **is implying** that I have driven too fast.

Perfect

- *Sie **hat** mir Nachlässigkeit **unterstellt**.* – She **insinuated** that I had been negligent.

Imperfect

- *Mein Vorgesetzter **unterstellte mir** die Produktion.* – My superior **put me in charge of** the production.

Imperfect (passive voice)

- *Es wurde ihm **unterstellt**, gelogen zu haben.* – He **was purported** to have lied.

Wiederholen* and *wiederholen

The separable verb wiederholen

(Means to fetch sth. back or to get sth. back.)

Infinitive

- *Ich muss mir den Titel **wiederholen**.* – I must **get** the title **back**.
- *Er sprang über den Zaun, um den Ball **wiederzuholen**.* – He jumped over the fence **to get** his ball **back**.

Present

- *Ich **hole** mir mein Kind **wieder**.* – I will **get** my child **back**.

Perfect

- *Sie **hat** sich den Ball **wiedergeholt**.* – She **fetched** her ball **back**.

Imperfect

- Die Mannschaft ***holte*** sich den Titel ***wieder (zurück)***. – The team **got** the title **back**.

The inseparable verb *wiederholen*

(To repeat, to do sth. again, to revise, to retake.)

Infinitive

- *Könnten Sie bitte Ihre Frage **wiederholen**?* – Could you please **repeat** your question?
- *Du musst die unregelmäßigen Verben **wiederholen**.* – You have **to revise** the irregular verbs.

Present

- *Ich **wiederhole** gerade die deutschen Vokabeln.* – **I'm repeating** the German vocabulary.

Present tense (passive voice)

- *Dieser Freistoß muss **wiederholt werden**.* – The free-kick must **be retaken.**

Perfect

- *Ich **habe** eben gerade die Lektion **wiederholt**.* – I **have** just **repeated** the lesson.

Imperfect:

- Ich ***wiederholte*** ein Schuljahr. – I **repeated** one year at school.

Exercise 5.1

Which part of the verbs in bold type has to be stressed?

1. *Nachdem er seinen entflohenen Kanarienvogel auf dem Baum gefunden hat, möchte er ihn nun* **wiederholen**.
2. *Diese Szene muss* **wiederholt** *werden.*
3. *Seine Frau und seine Kinder haben ihn* **durchschaut**.
4. *Könnten Sie mir bitte diese Broschüre zum* **Durchschauen** *geben?*
5. *Haben Sie das Buch* **übersetzt**?
6. *In der Deutschprüfung musste er einen kurzen Text* **übersetzen**.
7. *Wann wollen Sie mit der Fähre* **übersetzen**?
8. *Wo können wir die Möbel während unserer Abwesenheit* **unterstellen**?
9. *Er hat mir* **unterstellt,** *eine falsche Aussage gemacht zu haben.*
10. *Kann ich mein Gepäck bei Ihnen* **unterstellen**?
11. *Sein Professor hat ihm deutlich gemacht, dass er die Seminararbeit* **umschreiben** *müsse.*
12. *Ich habe diesen Ausdruck nicht verstanden. Könnten Sie ihn bitte mit anderen Worten* **umschreiben**?
13. *Der Bankangestellte muss jede Woche den Zugangscode* **umstellen**.
14. *Die Soldaten haben das Gebäude komplett* **umstellt**.
15. *Er hat die 800m in weniger als zwei Minuten* **durchlaufen**.
16. *Der Kaffee ist gerade am* **Durchlaufen**.

Exercise 5.2

Complete the following sentences with the appropriate past participle.

1. *Sie hat dieses mathematische Problem ______________. (durchschauen)*
2. *Hast du mir meinen Ball ____________________? (wiederholen)*
3. *Wollen Sie jetzt das Mikroskop benutzen? Ich habe gerade schon ______________. (durchschauen)*
4. *Er hat das Schuljahr __________________ . (wiederholen)*
5. *Der Dolmetscher hat für die ausländischen Gäste ________________. (übersetzen)*
6. *Die Autorin hat die Kurzgeschichte ____________________. (umschreiben)*
7. *Sein bester Freund hat seine Absichten ____________________. (durchschauen)*
8. *Wir sind mit der Fähre nach Fehmarn __________________. (übersetzen)*
9. *Mein Chef hat mir diese Aufgabe _____________________. (unterstellt)*
10. *Ich habe meine Fahrweise _______________________. (umstellen).*

Exercise 5.3

Change the sentences completed in exercise 5.2 into the imperfect.

Example:

Sie hat dieses mathematische Problem durchschaut. → *Sie durchschaute das mathematische Problem.*

Chapter 6:
Choosing the Right Noun – Finance, Business, Work

One-minute overview

In this chapter we will be taking a closer look at nouns that have to do with finance, business and work. As in every other language, there are nouns in English that can be translated by two or more words in German, e.g. the word 'account' (or its plural form 'accounts') can mean a written or spoken report, or the facility with a bank where you can deposit money, or a record of all the money that a person or business spends. The German language has three different nouns for these three meanings, which for speakers of English often causes difficulties in choosing the right one. This chapter gives a lot of help for those travellers to Germany who are on business or who have to deal with financial matters. It will show you how:

- to open a bank account;
- to ask how much credit is in your account;
- to enquire about business hours;
- to express that you have an appointment with someone;
- to ask someone to give you change for coins or notes of large denomination;
- to say in what line of business you work and how you earn your living.

Account(s): *der Bericht, die Darstellung/das Konto/die Einnahmen und Ausgaben*

der Bericht, die Darstellung

Written or spoken report of some event or occurrence

- *Darüber gab es* ***Berichte*** *im Fernsehen.* – There were **accounts** of it on television.

das Konto

A facility with a bank where you can deposit money or withdraw it when you need it.

- *Ich möchte gerne bei Ihrer Bank ein* ***Konto*** *eröffnen.* – I would like to open an **account** with your bank.

die Einnahmen und Ausgaben (pl.)

A detailed record of all the money which a person or business receives or spends.

- *Er musste die* ***Einnahmen und Ausgaben*** seinem Chef vorlegen. – He had to submit the **accounts** to his boss.

Exercise 6.1

Fill in the correct word.

1. *Wer ist in der Firma für die* ________________ *zuständig?*
2. *Bitte schreiben Sie einen* ________________ *über Ihre Erfahrungen in Deutschland!*
3. *Ich habe ein* ________________ *bei der Commerzbank.*

Affair: *die Sache, die Angelegenheit/das Verhältnis, die Affäre*

die Sache, die Angelegenheit

A matter, concern, an event or a series of events.

- *Die Beerdingung war eine stille und trostlose* ***Angelegenheit***. – The funeral was a quiet and dreary **affair**.
- *Die Art und Weise, wie er für diese Position ausgewählt worden ist, war überhaupt eine seltsame* ***Sache***. – The way he has been chosen for this position was an odd **affair** altogether.

das Verhältnis, die Affäre

Secret sexual relationship between two people.

- *Sie hatte ein außereheliches* ***Verhältnis*** *mit einem ihrer Arbeitskollegen.* – She had an extramarital **affair** with one of her colleagues from work.
- *Seine* ***Affäre*** *mit der jungen Frau dauerte nicht sehr lange.* – His **affair** with the young woman didn't last very long.

Exercise 6.2

Fill in the correct word.

1. *Dieser Professor hatte eine* ____________________ *mit einer Studentin.*
2. *Sie haben mit dieser* ____________________ *nichts zu tun. Das ist meine* ____________________.
3. *Ich komme in einer dienstlichen* ____________________ *zu Ihnen.*

Appointment: *die Verabredung, der Termin/die Ernennung, die Berufung/die Stelle*

die Verabredung, der Termin

A prearranged meeting (often concerning one's job).

- *Morgen habe ich einen Zahnarzt**termin**.* – Tomorrow I'm having an **appointment** with my dentist.
- *Heute Nachmittag hat sie eine* **Verabredung** *mit ihrem Chef.* – This afternoon she is having an **appointment** with her boss.

die Ernennung, die Berufung

The act or process of appointing someone to do a particular job, especially a post at a higher institution.

- *Sie gratulierten ihm zu seiner* **Ernennung** *zum Außenminister.* – They congratulated him on his ***appointment*** to the post of Foreign Secretary.
- *Seine Berufung zum Polizeipräsidenten steht kurz bevor.* – His *appointment* to the post of chief constable is imminent.

die Stelle

A job or position involving much responsibility; a post.

- *Nach reiflicher Überlegung nahm er **die Stelle** als Direktor an.* – After careful consideration he accepted the **appointment** of headmaster.

Exercise 6.3

Fill in the correct word.

1. *Der Professor hat die ____________________ an die Universität in München abgelehnt.*
2. *Er hat sich um die ____________________ als Botschafter beworben.*
3. *Um vier Uhr habe ich eine geschäftliche ____________________.*
4. *Ich muss die Sitzung auf einen späteren ____________________ verschieben.*

Business: *das Geschäft/die Branche/der Betrieb, das Geschäft/die Sache, die Angelegenheit*

das Geschäft, die Geschäfte (pl.)

Commerce in general, production, buying and selling of goods.

- *Diese Firma hat **Geschäfts**interessen in Deutschland.* – This company has **business** interests in Germany.
- *Wie laufen die **Geschäfte**?* – How's **business**?

die Branche

A certain line of business, the area in which you work in order to earn your living.

- *Er ist in der Hotel**branche** tätig.* – He is in the hotel **business**.

der Betrieb, das Geschäft

A company that produces and/or sells goods or that provides a service.

- *Mein Freund leitet einen großen Familien**betrieb** in Berlin.* – My friend runs a big family **business** in Berlin.
- *Sie hat ein kleines **Geschäft** am Rande der Stadt.* – She's got a small **business** on the edge of town.

die Sache, die Angelegenheit

Something that concerns only you and that other people have no right to ask you about. The words *Angelegenheit* and *Sache* are interchangeable.

- Das ist meine *Sache/Angelegenheit* und geht dich nichts an. – That's my *business* and none of yours.

Exercise 6.4

Fill in the correct word.

1. *Ich arbeite in der Autoindustrie. Und in welcher ________________ sind Sie tätig?*
2. *Er besitzt ein rentables ________________ in der Innenstadt.*
3. *Ich habe mit der ganzen ________________ nichts zu tun.*
4. *Ich halte mich in Deutschland auf um ________________ zu tätigen.*

Chance: *der Zufall/die Aussichten, die Chancen/die Chance, die Gelegenheit/das Risiko*

der Zufall

Coincidence, when two or more things happen at the same time unexpectedly.

- *Durch reinen **Zufall** habe ich gestern meinen ehemaligen Deutschlehrer getroffen.* – Just by sheer **chance** I met my former German teacher yesterday.

die Aussichten (pl.), *die Chancen* (pl.)

The extent to which something is likely to happen. In German the plural *Aussichten* is used quite often.

- *Wir haben gute **Aussichten/Chancen**, das Spiel zu gewinnen.* – We've got good **chances** to win the game.

die Chance, die Gelegenheit

The opportunity to do something.

- *Wir haben die einmalige **Gelegenheit/Chance**, den Präsidenten zu treffen.* – We won't get another **chance** to meet the President.

das Risiko

The possibility that something dangerous or unpleasant might happen.

- Sie geht kein ***Risiko*** ein. – She's not taking any **chances**.

Exercise 6.5

Fill in the correct word.

1. *Sie hat keine guten ________________ ein Stipendium zu bekommen.*
2. *Wenn ich an deiner Stelle wäre, würde ich kein ________________ eingehen.*
3. *Werde ich noch einmal die ________________ bekommen nach Berlin zu fahren?*
4. *Es war purer ________________, dass wir uns in Hamburg begegnet sind.*

Change: *die Veränderung, die Änderung/die Abwechslung/der Wechsel/das Wechselgeld, das Kleingeld*

die Veränderung, die Änderung

When something or someone becomes different.

- *Wir sind Zeugen einer Wetter**veränderung**.* – We are witnessing a **change** in the weather.

die Abwechslung

Something which is different, often in a pleasant or interesting way.

- *Ich bin so gestresst; jetzt wäre ein Urlaub eine nette **Abwechslung**.* – I'm so stressed out; now a holiday would make a nice **change**.
- *Du solltest **zur Abwechslung** mal mit Freunden verreisen.* – You should travel together with friends **for a change**.

der Wechsel

If one thing is replaced for something of a similar kind.

- *Ein Schul**wechsel** scheint unvermeidbar.* – A **change** of schools seems inevitable.

das Wechselgeld

The money you receive when you have paid with more than what is due; *das Kleingeld*: money of a smaller denomination.

- *Verkäufer: Und hier ist Ihr **Wechselgeld**.* – Shop-assistant: And here's your **change**.
- *Hast du/Haben Sie etwas **Kleingeld**?* – Have you got any **change**?
- *Können Sie mir einen Euro **wechseln**?* – Can you give me **change** for a euro?

Exercise 6.6

Fill in the correct word.

1. *Ich benötige etwas ________________ für den Zigarettenautomaten.*
2. *Das Leben in diesem Ort bietet keine ________________.*
3. *Verkäuferin: Bitte, warten Sie! Ich habe Ihnen noch nicht Ihr ________________ gegeben.*
4. *Im Sommer kommt es zu einem ________________ an der Spitze des Unternehmens.*
5. *Wir sehen zur Zeit eine drastische ________________ in der Arbeitsmoral.*

Company: *die Gesellschaft/der Besuch/die Firma, der Konzern/die Schauspieltruppe/die Kompanie*

die Gesellschaft

The state of having other people with you preventing you from feeling lonely.

- *Sie besuchte ihre Nachbarin, um etwas* ***Gesellschaft*** *zu haben.* – She visited her neighbour just for **company**.
- *Ich bin immer gern mit dir zusammen.* – I always enjoy your *company*.
- *Ich werde dir/Ihnen etwas* ***Gesellschaft*** *leisten.* – I'll keep you some **company**.

der Besuch

People who have gathered in someone's place for social purposes, usually a guest or guests.

- Ich muss leider unser Gespräch beenden, ich habe ***Besuch***. – Sorry, but I have to finish our conversation, I've got **company**.

die Firma, der Konzern

A business organization, a firm.

- Er *arbeitet als Ingenieur bei einem großen* ***Ölkonzern***. – He works as an engineer with a big oil **company**.
- *Sie fährt einen* ***Firmenwagen***. – She drives a **company** car.

die Schauspieltruppe

A group of actors or opera singers.

- *Eine englische* ***Schauspieltruppe*** *führt gerade in Frankfurt „Hamlet" auf.* – An English **company** is staging "Hamlet" in Frankfurt.

die Kompanie

A group of soldiers, which is divided into platoons.

- *Hauptmann Brendler kommandiert eine Infanterie**kompanie**.* – Captain Brendler commands a **company** of infantry.

Exercise 6.7

Fill in the correct word.

1. *Eine* ________________ *aus Deutschland führt morgen ein Theaterstück auf.*
2. *Er arbeitet an der Spitze eines großen deutschen* ________________.
3. *Wir können dir heute Abend etwas* ________________ *leisten.*
4. *Wie viele Soldaten haben Sie in Ihrer* ________________*?*
5. (On the phone:) *Hast du gerade* ________________*? Ich höre Stimmen im Hintergrund.*

Concern: *der Konzern/die Angelegenheit/die Sorge, die Besorgnis/die Bedeutung*

der Konzern

A company or business.

- *BASF in Ludwigshafen ist einer der größten Chemie**konzerne** in Europa.* – BASF in Ludwigshafen is one of the biggest chemical **concerns** in Europe.

die Angelegenheit

A matter or affair that you have a responsibility to be involved with.

- *Das ist die **Angelegenheit** des Direktors der Schule.* – That's the **concern** of the headmaster of the school.

die Sorge, die Besorgnis

A situation that causes a feeling of worry and anxiety.

- *Meine **Sorge** ist die hohe Quote von Schulabbrechern.* – My **concern** is the high rate of drop-outs.
- *Die gegenwärtige Situation auf dem Arbeitsmarkt ist **Besorgnis** erregend.* – The current situation of the job market is causing **concern**.

die Bedeutung

Something that is very important and about which a person thinks a lot.

- *Das ist eine Angelegenheit von großer nationaler* **Bedeutung**. – This is a matter of great national **concern**.

Exercise 6.8

Fill in the correct word.

1. *Die großen ________________ bauen zur Zeit viele Arbeitsplätze ab.*
2. *Seine größte ________________ war, dass sein Arbeitsplatz in Gefahr ist.*
3. *Das ist nicht meine ________________. Mein Kollege ist dafür zuständig.*
4. *Die Energieversorgung ist eine Angelegenheit von immenser ________________.*

Credit(s): *der Kredit/das Guthaben/die Ehre/der Glauben/der Nachspann/der Schein*

der Kredit

An amount of money that a bank makes available to a client.

- *Günstige langfristige* **Kredite** *würden den kleinen Betrieben helfen.* – Cheap long-term **credits** would help small businesses.

das Guthaben

The positive balance or amount remaining in a person's account.

- Wie hoch is das *Guthaben* auf meinem Konto? – How much **credit** is there on my account?

die Ehre

The respect you give to somebody who has achieved something good.

- *Sie macht ihrer Familie* **Ehre**. – She's a **credit** to her family.
- *Er macht seinen Eltern wenig* **Ehre**. – He does not do his parents any **credit**.

der Glauben

The belief that something is true.

- *Er möchte dieser Angelegenheit keinen* **Glauben** *schenken.* – He doesn't want to give **credit** to this matter.

der Nachspann

The list of people who helped to make a film or a television programme which is shown at the end of the film or the programme.

- *Ihr Name wurde im* **Nachspann** *aufgeführt.* – Her name was listed in the **credits**.

der Schein

A document that confirms your successful completion of a course at university.

- *Sie benötigt nur noch zwei* **Scheine** *für ihren Abschluss.* – She needs only two more **credits** for her degree.

Exercise 6.9

Fill in the correct word.

1. *Sie macht ihrer Heimatstadt alle* ________________ .
2. *Wie viele* ________________ *bis zum Examen musst du noch machen?*
3. *Die Namen aller Mitwirkenden wurden im* ________________ *des Films genannt.*
4. *Es tut mir Leid, aber ich kann dieser Sache nur wenig* ________________ *schenken.*
5. *Sie hat ein beachtliches* ________________ *auf der Bank.*
6. *Die Bank hat mir leider keinen* ________________ *gewährt.*

Demand: *die Forderung/die Nachfrage*

die Forderung

A firm request for something.

- *Sie diskutierten über die* **Forderung** *der Arbeiter nach besserer Bezahlung.* – They discussed the workers' **demand** for better pay.

Nachfrage

Willingness and ability to buy certain goods and services.

- *Zur Zeit gibt es eine große* **Nachfrage** *nach Handys.* – Currently there's a high **demand** for mobile phones.

Exercise 6.10

Fill in the correct word.

1. *Die* ________________ *nach besseren Arbeitsbedingungen bestimmte die Diskussion.*
2. *Die* ________________ *nach Fernsehgeräten geht zurück.*

Hours: *die Stunden/die Geschäftszeiten, die Öffnungszeiten*

die Stunden

The hours of a particular part of the day or night, the hours when you do a particular activity.

- *Seit zwei **Stunden** spielt er Tennis.* – He has been playing tennis for two **hours**.
- *Sie verließ die Stadt in den frühen Morgen**stunden**.* – She left the city in the very early **hours** of the morning.

die Geschäftszeiten (pl.), *die Öffnungszeiten* (pl.)

The actual period of time a business is open.

- *Wann sind Ihre **Geschäftszeiten**/Öffnungszeiten?* – When do you have your **business hours/opening hours**?

Exercise 6.11

Fill in the correct word.

1. *Viele unserer Kunden befürworten längere* ____________________.
2. *In den* ____________________ *der Einsamkeit wird sie sehr schnell melancholisch.*

Item: *der Punkt/der Posten, das Stück/der Bericht, die Nachricht*

der Punkt

One of a number of matters you are dealing with.

- *Das ist der wichtigste **Punkt** auf unserer Agenda.* – This is the most crucial **item** on our agenda.

der Posten, das Stück

A list of objects you are buying or selling.

- *Der Preis für den ersten* **Posten** *auf der Liste beträgt €5.* – The price for the first **item** on the list is €5.
- *Wir müssen bis Samstag noch einige Möbel***stücke** *bestellen.* – We have to order some more **items** of furniture by Saturday.

der Bericht, die Nachricht

A report in a newspaper or magazine; a short piece of news on radio or television.

- *Für eine Freundin sammelt sie* **Berichte** *aus Frauenzeitschriften.* – For a friend she collects **items** from women's magazines.
- *Die wichtigste* **Nachricht** *war der Sturz des Regimes.* – The main news **item** was the fall of the regime.

Exercise 6.12 (p.000)

Fill in the correct word.

1. *Wir müssen noch einen größeren ________________ Kochtöpfe bestellen.*
2. *Dieser ________________ über die Anhebung der Steuern erschien in der Stuttgarter Zeitung.*
3. *Die Partei muss die einzelnen ______________ ihres Wahlprogramms überarbeiten.*

Notice: *die Benachrichtigung, der Bescheid/das Plakat/die Kündigung/die Kritik, die Rezension*

die Benachrichtigung, der Bescheid

Usually a written piece of information about a future event, an announcement.

- *Gestern erhielt er* **eine Benachrichtigung/einen Bescheid** *von der Einwanderungsbehörde.* – Yesterday he received a **notice** from the immigration authorities.

das Plakat, die Notiz, die Mitteilung

A displayed announcement giving information, often about a future event.

- *Könntest du in der Schule ein* ***Plakat*** *aufhängen?* – Could you put up a **notice** at the school?
- *Unser Chef hat eine* ***Notiz*** *an der Eingangstür aufgehängt.* – Our boss put up a **notice** at the entrance.

die Kündigung

Notification of intent to end a contract, e.g. of employment or renting.

- Sie musste ihm die ***Kündigung*** erteilen. – She had to give him **notice**.

die Kritik, die Rezension

A review of a play, film or concert in a newspaper or magazine.

- *Der Film erhielt sehr gute* **Kritiken.** – The movie received very good *notices.*

Exercise 6.13

Fill in the correct word.

1. *Ich muss Ihnen leider eine ________________ erteilen.*
2. *Sie werden bald von Ihrer Krankenkasse einen ________________ erhalten.*
3. *Er ist bei einer Zeitung angestellt und schreibt vor allem ________________.*
4. *Könnten Sie bitte diese ________________ am schwarzen Brett aufhängen?*

Reason: *der Grund/der Verstand/die Vernunft*

der Grund

The cause of, or justification for, something.

- *Was sind Ihre* ***Gründe*** *für Ihren Arbeitsplatzwechsel?* – What are your **reasons** for changing your employment?
- *Aus gesundheitlichen* ***Gründen*** *bin ich in den Ruhestand gegangen.* – I have retired for health **reasons**.

der Verstand

Someone's mental faculty.

- Er verliert den *Verstand.* – He is losing his **reason**.

die Vernunft

A sensible attitude towards making decisions; common sense.

- *Höre immer auf die Stimme der* ***Vernunft****!* – Always listen to the voice of **reason!**

Exercise 6.14

Fill in the correct word.

1. Diese Entscheidung ist gegen alle Regeln der ________________.
2. Können Sie triftige ________________ für Ihre Kündigung vorlegen?
3. Mein ________________ sagt mir, dass ich diesen Beschluss nicht mittragen kann.

Chapter 7: Choosing the Right Noun – Education, School, Career

One-minute overview

In this chapter we are going to discuss nouns that have to do with education, school and career. As in the previous chapter on nouns the definitions, examples and exercises are meant to clarify words which possess more than one German translation. In this chapter you will find many phrases and expressions used by teachers and students during lessons ('classroom language') as well as words and sentences that are quite helpful if you need to talk or write about your past achievements at school or university, e.g. in writing a CV or a letter of application. The speech material shown in this chapter is therefore quite useful for those who want to go to a German-speaking country in order to attend a school or a university. This chapter will show you how:

- to formulate what university degree you have completed;
- to express what kind of education you have received;
- to enquire about tests and examinations;
- to talk about marks and test results;
- to discuss a piece of writing (essay, novel, play, etc.);
- to talk about someone's social and educational background;
- to ask the way to a doctor's practice.

Action: *das Handeln/die Handlung, die Action/die Tat*

das Handeln

Anything that you do in order to achieve something.

- *Jetzt ist die Zeit zum* ***Handeln*** *gekommen.* – Now is the time for *action.*

die Handlung

All the things that happen in a story, film or play; *die Action* on the other hand is a word borrowed from English and refers to the exciting and thrilling events of a film or movie, used mainly in colloquial German.

- *Die **Handlung** des Theaterstücks ist ziemlich langweilig.* – The **action** of the play is rather boring.
- *In dem Film gibt es keine **Action**.* – There's no **action** in this movie.

die Tat

A deed.

- *Seine erste **Tat** bestand darin, seine Frau anzurufen.* – His first **action** was to ring up his wife.
- *Er ist ein Mann der **Tat**.* – He is a man of **action.**

Exercise 7.1

Fill in the right word.

1. *Meiner Meinung nach fehlt diesem Hollywood-Streifen die* _______________.
2. *Wir müssen jetzt endlich diesen Plan in die* _______________ *umsetzen.*
3. *Die* _______________ *des Romans spielt in Alsfeld, einer Kleinstadt in Oberhessen.*

Background: *der Hintergrund/der Werdegang, die Verhältnisse, die Herkunft/die Zusammenhänge, die Hintergründe*

der Hintergrund

Things or people that you can see behind the main things, e.g. in a picture or photo.

- *Er zeichnete mehrere Pferde vor dem **Hintergrund** der untergehenden Sonne.* – He drew several horses against the **background** of the setting sun.
- *Während der Diskussion hielt er sich im **Hintergrund**.* – During the discussion he stayed in the **background.**

die Verhältnisse (pl.), *die Herkunft, der Werdegang*

The environment, the family you come from, the education you have.

- *Sie kommt aus ärmlichen **Verhältnissen**.* – She comes from a **background** of poverty.

- *Wir wissen nicht viel über ihre* ***Herkunft****.* – We don't know much about her **background.**
- *Als er sich um diese Stelle bewarb, schauten sie genau auf seinen* ***Werdegang****.* – When he applied for this post, they looked very closely into his **background**.

die Zusammenhänge (pl.), *die Hintergründe* (pl.)

The circumstances surrounding and leading up to an important event.

- *Die* ***Zusammenhänge*** *dieser Tat bleiben im Verborgenen.* – The **background** of this deed is not yet known.
- *Sie untersuchten die wirtschaftlichen* ***Hintergründe*** *zu der gegenwärtigen politischen Krise.* – They examined the economic **background** to the present political crisis.

Exercise 7.2

Fill in the correct word.

1. *Er stammt aus kleinen ____________________ und hat sich hochgearbeitet.*
2. *Wir müssen die ____________________ dieser Tat bis ins Detail aufdecken.*
3. *Die Handlung des Theaterstücks hat einen geschichtlichen ________________.*

Degree: *der Grad* (measurement)/*das Maß, der Grad/der akademische Grad, der Hochschulabschluss*

der Grad

A unit of measurement used to measure temperature, the angles in a circle or latitude or longitude.

- *Ich glaube, es sind draußen etwa 25* ***Grad****.* – I think it's about 25 **degrees** outside.

das Maß, das Ausmaß, der Grad

Extent to which something is done or to which something happens; here the words *Maß* and *Grad* are used interchangeably.

- *Der See ist in einem sehr hohen* ***Maß*** *verschmutzt.* – The lake is polluted to a very high **degree**.

- *Bis zu einem gewissen* **Grad** *hat er Recht.* – To a certain **degree** he is right.

der akademische Grad/der Hochschulabschluss

An academic title given by a college or university.

- *Ich werde meinen* ***akademischen Grad*** *im August des nächsten Jahres bekommen.* – I'll get my *degree* in August next year.
- *Er hat einen* ***Hochschulabschluss*** *in Ökonomie.* – He has a **degree** in economics.

Exercise 7.3

Fill in the correct word.

1. *Die Schüler müssen bis zu einem gewissen* ________________ *belastbar sein.*
2. *Um bei uns arbeiten zu können brauchen Sie einen*________________.
3. *Das Thermometer steigt im Laufe des Tages auf 30* ________________.

Education: *die Erziehung/die Ausbildung/die Bildung/die Pädagogik, die Erziehungswissenschaft*

die Erziehung

The influence you can have on young people as a teacher or parent by which you form and teach them, so that they become responsible and strong characters, esp. at school or college.

- *Die* ***Erziehung*** *der Kinder ist Aufgabe und Pflicht unserer Lehrer.* – The **education** of the children is the duty and the task of our teachers.
- *Die* ***Erziehung*** *der Schüler ist unseren Lehrern sehr wichtig.* – The **education** of the children is very important to our teachers.

die Ausbildung

The skill or training developed or gained through a systematic learning process.

- Eine gute **Ausbildung** ist die Grundlage für den beruflichen Erfolg. – A good **education** is the basis for success in your working life.
- Seine ***Ausbildung*** wurde unterbrochen. – His **education** was interrupted.

die Bildung

The shaping and moulding of a person's character, especially his or her intellectual and spiritual nature, which endows him or her with knowledge, critical judgement, fine manners and tactfulness.

- Die *Bildung* unserer jungen Menschen sollte jedem von uns am Herzen liegen. – The **education** of our children should be important to everyone of us.
- Das gehört zur allgemeinen *Bildung*. – This belongs to general **education**.

die Pädagogik, die Erziehungswissenschaft

The field of study that has to do with theories and methods of teaching and learning pedagogy.

- *Sie studiert **Pädagogik** an der Frankfurter Universität.* – She's studying **education** at Frankfurt University.

Exercise 7.4

Fill in the correct word.

1. *Nach meinem Abitur möchte ich gerne* ________________ *studieren.*
2. *Sie befindet sich noch in der* ________________.
3. *Er ist sehr belesen und verfügt über eine umfassende* ________________.
4. *In seiner Kindheit wurden Fehler in der* ________________ *gemacht.*

Examination: *das Examen, die Prüfung/die Prüfung/die Untersuchung* (medical)/*das Verhör*

das Examen, die Prüfung

An official test (written exercises, oral questions, etc.) which someone takes in order to show his or her knowledge.

- Er hat das *Examen* nicht bestanden. – He hasn't passed the **examination**.
- Wie lange dauert die schriftliche *Prüfung*? – How long does the written **examination** take?

die Prüfung

A check or an inspection of something, especially something of technical nature.

- *Eine **Prüfung** der Bremsen wird gerade durchgeführt.* – An **examination** of the brakes is being carried out at the moment.

die Untersuchung

A medical examination of a person or of parts of his or her body in order to diagnose a disease.

- *Morgen muss er sich einer **Untersuchung** der Lunge unterziehen.* – Tomorrow he has to undergo an **examination** of the lungs.

das Verhör

A formal interrogation, especially of an accused person or of a witness.

- *Das **Verhör** durch die Polizei dauerte drei Stunden.* – The **examination** by the police lasted three hours.
- *Der Zeuge wurde einem rigorosen **Verhör** unterzogen.* – The witness was subjected to a rigorous **examination**.

Exercise 7.5

Fill in the correct word.

1. *Morgen muss ich wegen einer _______________ zum Arzt gehen.*
2. *Sie müssen sich während der Verhandlung einem __________ unterziehen.*
3. *Eine gründliche _______________ Ihres Autos dauert bis zu drei Stunden.*
4. *Ihre mündliche _______________ ist am Freitag um 14.00 Uhr.*

Failure: *der Misserfolg/der Versager/der Ausfall, das Versagen*

der Misserfolg

Lack of success; if you haven't achieved the desired end.

- Die Aufführung des Dramas war ein *Misserfolg*. – The performance of the drama was a **failure**.

der Versager

An unsuccessful person.

- *In seinem Beruf ist er ein völliger* ***Versager****.* – He is a complete **failure** in his job.
- *Nach der Niederlage betrachtete er sich als* ***Versager****.* – After the defeat he considered himself a **failure.**

der Ausfall, das Versagen

If something stops working and a proper functioning is no longer possible.

- *Der Orkan verursachte einen Strom****ausfall****.* – The storm caused a power **failure.**
- *Sie starb an Herz****versagen****.* – She died of heart **failure.**

Exercise 7.6

Fill in the correct word.

1. *Das Nichterreichen des Viertelfinals muss als ______________ gewertet werden.*
2. *Nach der nichtbestandenen Prüfung fühlte er sich als ______________.*
3. *Durch den ______________ der Heizung bekamen die Kinder schulfrei.*

Faith: *das Vertrauen/der Glaube/das Bekenntnis, der Glaube*

das Vertrauen

Strong feeling of confidence in and optimism about a person or thing.

- *Ich habe großes* ***Vertrauen*** *in seine Fähigkeiten.* – I have great **faith** in his capabilities.

der Glaube

Strong religious belief in a particular deity.

- Mein *Glaube* an Gott ist mir sehr wichtig. – My **faith** in God is very important to me.

das Bekenntnis, der Glaube

A particular religion such as Christianity or Islam.

- *Er gehört dem katholischen* **Bekenntnis** *an.* – He belongs to the Catholic **faith.**
- *Der protestantische* **Glaube**/*Das protestantische* **Bekenntnis** *geht auf Martin Luther zurück.* – The Protestant **faith** goes back to Martin Luther.

Exercise 7.7

Fill in the correct word.

1. *Der __________________ kann Berge versetzen.*
2. *Welchem __________________ gehören Sie an?*
3. *Der jüdische und der christliche __________________ haben gemeinsame Wurzeln.*
4. *Nach diesem Vorfall hat sie ihr __________________ in ihn verloren.*

Figure: *die Zahl, die Ziffer/die Figur/die Gestalt/die Persönlichkeit*

die Zahl, die Ziffer

A number, the written symbols from 0 to 9 that are used to represent a number.

- *Es gibt eine Unstimmigkeit in den* **Zahlen**. – There's a mistake in the **figures.**
- *Wir einigten uns auf eine* **sechsstellige Zahl**. – We decided on a six-**figure number.**

die Figur

The shape of your body.

- *Sie hat eine tolle* **Figur**. – She's got a fabulous **figure.**

die Gestalt

Someone you cannot see clearly.

- *In der Dunkelheit sah ich eine* **Gestalt** *auf uns zukommen.* – In the darkness I saw a **figure** approaching us.

die Persönlichkeit

A well-known and an important person.

- *Dieses Ereignis machte ihn zu einer nationalen* ***Persönlichkeit.*** – This incident made him into a national **figure**.

Exercise 7.8

Fill in the correct word.

1. *Er ist ein Mann von kleiner und untersetzter* ____________________.
2. *Es handelt sich bei diesem Herrn um eine hochgestellte* ________________.
3. *Im dichten Nebel konnte ich diese* __________________ *nur sehr schwer erkennen.*
4. *Haben Sie die* ___________________ *von diesem Jahr mit denen vom letzten Jahr verglichen?*

Mark: *der Fleck/der Kratzer, die Schramme/die Note/das Zeichen/die Züge*

der Fleck

A small part of the surface which is a different colour because something has been dropped on it; a stain.

- *Da ist ein* ***Fleck*** *auf deiner/Ihrer Hose.* – There's a **mark** on your trousers.

der Kratzer, die Schramme

A small part of the surface which has been damaged; a scratch.

- *Das Auto hat viele* ***Kratzer*** *auf der Motorhaube.* – This car has got a lot of *marks* on its bonnet.

die Note

A symbol used by the teacher to indicate how good or bad a pupil's or student's work is; a grade.

- *Die Studenten in diesem Kurs haben ziemlich schlechte* ***Noten.*** – The students on this course have got rather poor **marks**.
- *Was meinst du, welche* ***Note*** *hast du verdient?/Was meinen Sie, welche* ***Note*** *haben Sie verdient?* – What do you think, which *mark* do you deserve?

das Zeichen

An indication of quality; it also shows that a certain situation or emotion exists.

- *Als ein **Zeichen** des Respekts stehen die Schüler auf, wenn der Lehrer den Klassenraum betritt.* – As a **mark** of respect the pupils stand up when the teacher enters the classroom.

Exercise 7.9

Fill in the correct word.

1. *Er hat eine schlechte* ______________ *im Fach Deutsch.*
2. *Er hat eine blutige* ____________ *in seinem Gesicht.*
3. *Auf der Tischdecke ist ein dicker* ______________.
4. *Als ein* __________ *der Freundschaft überreichte er ihm ein Geschenk.*
5. *Nach dem Umzug hatten die Möbel mehrere* ______________.

Note: *das Briefchen, ein paar Zeilen/die Notiz/die Fußnote/die Note* (music)*/der Ton, der Klang*

das Briefchen, ein paar Zeilen

A rather brief, usually informal letter.

- *Sie schrieb **ein paar Zeilen** an ihren Kollegen.* – She wrote **a note** to her colleague.

die Notiz

Some information that you jot down for future reference.

- *Er machte sich eine **Notiz** davon.* – He made a **note** of it.

die Fußnote

A short explanatory statement in a book, which gives extra information about the main text; an annotation.

- *Die **Fußnoten** am Ende eines Kapitels sind für den Leser sehr hilfreich.* – The **notes** at the end of a chapter are quite helpful to the reader.

die Note

The sound made by a musical instrument or a voice as well as the written symbol that represents the sound.

- *Er kann keine* ***Noten*** *lesen.* – He is unable to read **notes.**

der Ton, der Klang

The quality in a person's voice that shows how he or she feels.

- *Den traurigen* ***Ton*** *in seiner Stimme konnte er nicht verbergen.* – He couldn't hide the **note** of sadness in his voice.

Exercise 7.10

Fill in the correct word.

1. *Im Musikunterricht müssen wir ______________ lernen.*
2. *Der ______________ in ihrer Stimme verriet mir, dass sie Angst hatte.*
3. *Machen Sie sich während der Vorlesung ____________________.*
4. *An ihre Freundin schrieb sie noch _________________ auf ein Blatt, welches sie an ihrer Zimmertür befestigte.*
5. *Sie müssen die _______________ an das Ende des Buches platzieren.*

Order: *die Reihenfolge/die Ordnung, die Systematik* (system)/*die Ordnung* (satisfactory state)/*die Ordnung* (in society), *die Disziplin* (in school or in a team)/*der Befehl, die Anweisung/die Bestellung*

die Reihenfolge

The way a set of things is arranged or done; a sequence.

- *Die Namen der Schüler stehen in alphabetischer* ***Reihenfolge.*** – The names of the pupils list are in alphabetical **order.**

die Ordnung

The state in which all parts related to each other are arranged.

- *Der zukünftige Präsident kündigte eine neue soziale* ***Ordnung*** an. – The future president announced a new social **order.**
- *Du solltest etwas mehr* ***Ordnung/Systematik*** *in deine Arbeit hineinbringen.* – You should introduce some more **order** into your work.

die Ordnung

A satisfactory or tidy state.

- Ihr Pass ist nicht in ***Ordnung***. – Your passport isn't in **order**.
- Du musst dein Leben in ***Ordnung*** bringen. – You have to put your life in **order**.

die Ordnung, die Disziplin

A peaceful and harmonious state when law rules and normal activities can take place, especially in society; discipline.

- *Ohne **Disziplin** und **Ordnung** kann man Kinder nicht unterrichten.* – Without **discipline** and **order**, you cannot teach children.

der Befehl, die Anweisung

An instruction given by someone in authority and which must be obeyed.

- Er erhielt die ***Anweisung*** seine Arbeit fortzusetzen. – He received **orders** to continue with his work.
- Dies ist ein ***Befehl***! – This is an **order**!

die Bestellung

Something that you ask to be made for you, brought or sent to you in return for payment.

- *Ich möchte bei Ihnen eine **Bestellung** aufgeben.* – I would like to place an **order** with you.
- *Ist meine **Bestellung** bei Ihnen eingegangen?* – Have you received my **order**?

Exercise 7.11

Fill in the correct word.

1. *Der Lehrer rief die Schüler zur* ____________________.
2. *Ich kann Ihnen dieses Produkt nur auf* ________________ *liefern.*
3. *Der Kapitän gab den* ____________________ *die Segel zu setzen.*
4. *Die Spieler müssen sich in der* ______________ *ihrer Platzierung aufstellen.*
5. *Sie müssen diese Angelegenheit in* ________________ *bringen.*
6. *Der Präsident betonte, dass die politische* ______________ *in Europa bewahrt werden soll.*

Practice: *die Gewohnheit/der Brauch, die Sitte/die Verfahrensweise, die Praktik/das Training, die Übung/die Praxis* (as opposed to theory)/*die Praxis*

die Gewohnheit

A regular activity or habit.

- *Das Rauchen ist zu seiner **Gewohnheit** geworden.* – It has become his **practice** to smoke.
- *Ich habe es mir zur **Gewohnheit** gemacht um sechs Uhr aufzustehen.* – I've made it a **practice** to rise at six.

der Brauch, die Sitte

A custom, a tradition.

- *Bei uns ist es (so) **Brauch** vor dem Essen ein Tischgebet zu sprechen.* – It is our **practice** to say grace before the meals.

die Verfahrensweise, die Praktik

The way of doing things within one specific institution; the procedure.

- *Das ist die normale **Verfahrensweise** in unserem Betrieb.* – This is the normal **practice** in our business.
- *Dies ist allgemeine **Praktik** im Geschäftsleben in Deutschland.* – This is normal business **practice** in Germany.

das Training, die Übung

The condition of having mastery of a certain skill.

- *Ich bin schon lange nicht mehr im **Training**.* – I've been out of **practice** for a long time.
- ***Übung** macht den Meister.* – **Practice** makes perfect.
- *Du bist/Sie sind nicht mehr in (der) **Übung**.* – You're out of **practice**.

die Praxis

The act of doing something according to your beliefs or theories.

- *Setze deine/Setzen Sie Ihre Ideen in die **Praxis** um!* – Put your ideas into *practice*!

die Praxis

The place where a lawyer or a doctor works.

- *Können Sie mir bitte den Weg zu Dr. Schmidts **Praxis** sagen?* – Could you tell me the way to Dr Schmidt's **practice**, please?

Exercise 7.12

Fill in the correct word.

1. *Seit Wochen trainiert er nur unregelmäßig. Er ist völlig aus der* ________________.
2. *Die theoretische Ausbildung stimmt oft nicht mit der* __________ *überein.*
3. *Wenn er mit seiner Facharztausbildung fertig ist, möchte er eine* __________ *aufmachen.*
4. *Wir haben bei uns im Betrieb eine andere* ______________.
5. *Ein warmes Abendessen ist bei uns (so)* ______________.
6. *Sie hat die* ____________ *nach dem Essen zu schlafen.*

Chapter 8: Choosing the Right Noun – Travelling

One-minute overview

In this chapter we are going to take a closer look at nouns that are often needed when you are on holiday or travelling in a German-speaking country. We will again focus on nouns that have more than one meaning and therefore can be translated by two or more words in German. This chapter will show you how:

- to talk about the matter of identification (e.g. passport);
- to inform yourself about board and lodging/vacancies;
- to ask for a city guide;
- to get some information about railway lines and bus routes;
- to ask for someone's address;
- to ask your doctor for some medicine.

Address: *die Adresse/die Ansprache*

die Adresse

The number of the house, the street and the town where you live.

- *Könnten Sie mir Ihre E-Mail-**Adresse** mitteilen?* – Could you please tell my your e-mail **address**?
- *Er hat seine **Adresse** bei uns hinterlassen.* – He has left his **address** with us.

die Ansprache

A formal speech, often on a special occasion.

- *Ich habe eine **Ansprache** vor der Deutschen Physikalischen Gesellschaften gehalten.* – I gave an **address** to the German Association of Physicists.

Exercise 8.1

Fill in the right word.

1. *Könnten Sie bitte Ihre ________________ auf einem Zettel notieren?*
2. *Er hält heute Abend eine ________________ vor dem Kongress.*

Board: *das Brett/die Tafel/die Kost, die Verpflegung/der Ausschuss, der Vorstand*

das Brett

A long, flat, rectangular piece of wood.

- *Die Maurer nahmen die* **Bretter** *und deckten damit den Beton ab.* – The bricklayers took the **boards** and covered the concrete with it.

die Tafel

A blackboard.

- *Der Lehrer schrieb die Namen an die* ***Tafel***. – The teacher wrote the names on the **blackboard**.

die Kost, die Verpflegung

The meals that are provided when you stay in a hotel or at a bed-and-breakfast.

- *Unterkunft und* ***Verpflegung*** *sind im Preis inbegriffen.* – The price includes **board** and lodging.
- ***Kost*** *und Logis sind nicht im Preis inbegriffen.* – The price doesn't include **board** and lodging.
- *Vollpension* – full **board**.
- *Halbpension* – half **board**.

der Ausschuss, der Vorstand

The management that controls and directs a company or an organization.

- *Gestern verabschiedete der* **Vorstand** *neue Richtlinien für die Firma.* – Yesterday the **board** passed new guidelines for the company.

Exercise 8.2

Fill in the correct word.

1. *Der Schüler rechnete die Aufgabe an der _______________.*
2. *Auf der letzten Mitgliederversammlung wurde ein neuer _______ gewählt.*
3. *Was hattest du in deinem Urlaub für Unterkunft und _____________ ausgegeben?*
4. *Um auf dem Gerüst arbeiten zu können, brauchen die Handwerker noch längere _____________.*

Capital: *die Hauptstadt/der Großbuchstabe, die Blockschrift/ das Kapital/das (menschliche) Kapital*

die Hauptstadt

The main city or town of a country where the government meets.

- *Die **Hauptstadt** von Frankreich ist Paris.* – The **capital** of France is Paris.

der Großbuchstabe

A letter used at the beginning of a sentence or a proper name; in German the nouns have a capital at the beginning of the word. When you write in capitals only, this is called *Blockschrift* in German.

- *Die englischen Wörter **God, Bible** und **Christian** beginnen mit einem **Großbuchstaben**.* – The English words **God**, **Bible** and **Christian** begin with a **capital**.
- *Bitte in **Blockschrift** schreiben!* – Please write in **capitals**!

das Kapital

Funds; money you use for investment to make more money or which you use to expand your business.

- ***Kapital** wird dringend benötigt um den Betrieb zu modernisieren.* – **Capital** is urgently needed in order to modernize the business.
- *Wir haben nur wenig verfügbares **Kapital**.* – We have only a small amount of available **capital**.

das (menschliche) Kapital

Human capital, the skills or knowledge a person has for a particular job.

- *Dr. Krönings umfangreiches Wissen im Bereich der Augenheilkunde ist sein **Kapital**.* – Dr Kröning's wide knowledge within the field of ophthalmology is his **capital**.

Exercise 8.3

Fill in the correct word.

1. *Substantive werden im Deutschen am Anfang mit einem ______ geschrieben.*
2. *Wir müssen unser gesamtes __________ in das Geschäft stecken.*
3. *Seine ganzes ____________ waren seine schnellen Beine.*
4. *Die _________ des Bundeslands Hessen ist Wiesbaden.*

Custom(s): *die Sitte, der Brauch/die Gewohnheit, die (An-)gewohnheit/die Kundschaft/der Zoll*

die Sitte, der Brauch

A tradition, often a festivity which takes place at the same time every year.

- *In Deutschland ist es* **Sitte** *einen Weihnachtsbaum aufzustellen.* – In Germany it is a **custom** to put up a Christmas tree.
- *Möchtest du/Möchten Sie mit dieser* **Sitte** *brechen?* – Do you want to break with this **custom**?

die (An-)Gewohnheit

Somebody's habit, something which someone does in a special situation or at a special time. The word *die Angewohnheit* has a negative connotation and is usually a bad habit.

- *Es war Ottmars* **Angewohnheit** *nach den Mahlzeiten eine Zigarette zu rauchen.* – It was Ottmar's **custom** to smoke a cigarette after meals.

die Kundschaft

The practice of regularly buying something from a special shop.

- *Wir bekommen sehr viel* **Kundschaft** *von Touristen.* – We get a lot of **custom** from tourists.

der Zoll

The place at a border where you have to declare goods.

- *Der* **Zoll***beamte kontrollierte meinen Koffer.* – The **customs'** officer checked my suitcase.
- *Er ist beim* **Zoll** *beschäftigt.* – He works at the **customs**.

Exercise 8.4

Fill in the correct word.

1. *Wie möchten Sie damit durch den ______________ kommen?*
2. *Während meines Aufenthaltes in Deutschland habe ich viele fremde ______________ und Gebräuche kennen gelernt.*
3. *Der Geschäftsinhaber hat seine __________ verärgert. Nun bleibt sie weg.*
4. *Sie hat die ________________ während des Essens fernzusehen.*

Gift: *das Geschenk/die Gabe*

das Geschenk

Something that you give someone as a present.

- *Wir müssen noch ein* **Geschenk** *für unsere Gastfamilie kaufen.* – We must buy a **gift** for our host family.

die Gabe

The natural ability for doing something.

- Sie besitzt die **Gabe** des Unterrichtens – *She has the* **gift** *for teaching.*

Exercise 8.5

Fill in the correct word.

1. *Ich möchte noch ein paar _________ für meine Eltern und Freunde kaufen.*
2. *Sie ist eine junge Frau mit vielen ____________.*

Guide: *der Führer/der Stadtführer (ein Buch)/das Handbuch*

der Führer, der Stadtführer

Someone who shows places such as cities or museums to tourists.

- *Unser* **Führer** *zeigte uns die Hauptattraktionen.* – Our **guide** showed us the main attractions.
- *Könnten wir einen* **Stadtführer** *bekommen?* – Can we get a city **guide**?

der Stadtführer, der Führer

A book giving information about a city, especially for tourists, a guidebook.

- *Wie viel kostet der **Stadtführer** für Berlin?* – How much is the **guide** to Berlin?

das Handbuch

A book giving instructions and advice to help you do or understand something; a handbook.

- *Haben Sie/Führen Sie Aerobic-**Handbücher**?* – Do you have any **guides** to aerobics?

Exercise 8.6

Fill in the correct word.

1. *Um darüber Bescheid zu wissen, sollten Sie sich ein ____________ zur Gartenkunde kaufen.*
2. *Wir haben uns mit mehreren Touristen einem ____________ angeschlossen.*
3. *Bevor wir mit dem Stadtrundgang beginnen, will ich mir noch schnell einen ____________ kaufen.*

---

idea: *die Idee, der Einfall/die Meinung, die Ansicht/die Vorstellung/die Ahnung*

die Idee, der Einfall

A plan, a proposal, or a suggestion.

- *Es war deine **Idee** nach Dänemark in den Urlaub zu fahren.* – It was your **idea** to go to Denmark on holiday.
- *Plötzlich hatte ich einen **Einfall**.* – Suddenly I had an **idea**.

die Meinung, die Ansicht

An opinion or a belief.

- *Manche Menschen haben schon merkwürdige **Ansichten** über die Bayern.* – Some people have really odd **ideas** about the Bavarians.

die Vorstellung

Your impression of what something is like, a conception of something.

- *Du hast eine falsche* **Vorstellung** *von dieser Angelegenheit.* – You have a wrong **idea** of that matter.
- *Macht euch mal eine* **Vorstellung**, *wie unser Aufenthalt in Berlin aussehen könnte.* – Form an **idea** of what our stay in Berlin might look like.

die Ahnung

What you know about something or someone.

- *Ich habe keine* **Ahnung**, *wovon du redest.* – I've no **idea** what you're talking about.
- *Hast du eine* **Ahnung**, *wo dein Sohn sein könnte?* – Do you have an **idea** where your son might be?

Exercise 8.7

Fill in the correct word.

1. *Das ist meine ______________ von einem schönen Urlaub.*
2. *Sie hat keine ____________________ , wie das passieren konnte.*
3. *Manche Deutsche haben etwas schräge __________ über die Engländer.*
4. *Hast du eine ____________ , was wir morgen Abend machen wollen?*

Identification: *die Identifizierung/die Ausweispapiere/die Identifikation*

die Identifizierung

The ability to name and to recognize a particular person or thing because you know them.

- *Die* **Identifizierung** *der Leichen dauerte sehr lange.* – The **identification** of the bodies took a long time.

die Ausweispapiere

Something that shows or proves who you are such as a passport or a driving licence.

- *Können Sie mir Ihre* **Ausweispapiere** *zeigen?* – Could you show me some **identification**?
- *Du musst (Sie müssen) deine (Ihre)* **Ausweispapiere** *mitnehmen.* – You have to take some **identification** with you.

die Identifikation

A feeling of support or sympathy for a particular person or group.

- *Ihm fehlt die* ***Identifikation*** *mit seinem Vater.* – He has no **identification** with his father.

Exercise 8.8

Fill in the correct word.

1. *Wenn Sie ins Ausland reisen, vergessen Sie nicht Ihre_______ mitzunehmen.*
2. *Junge Menschen sind auf der Suche nach __________.*
3. *Wir brauchen Sie zur __________ des Toten.*

Issue: *die Frage, die Angelegenheit/die Ausgabe*

die Frage, die Angelegenheit

An important subject people are discussing.

- *Das ist eine wichtige und ernste* ***Frage****.* – This is an important and serious **issue**.

die Ausgabe

A particular edition of a magazine or newspaper.

- *Haben Sie die letzte* ***Ausgabe*** *der ,,Frankfurter Allgemeinen"?* – Have you got the latest **issue** of the 'Frankfurter Allgemeine'?
- *Die gestrige* ***Ausgabe*** *war schnell vergriffen.* – Yesterday's **issue** was out-of-print soon.

Exercise 8.9

Fill in the correct word.

1. *Ich hätte gerne die heutige ______________ des „Daily Telegraph".*
2. *Diese ______________ wird uns auch noch in 100 Jahren beschäftigen.*

Line: *die Linie/die Grenze/die Reihe/die Gesellschaft, die Linie/die Linie* (public transport)*/die Bahnlinie/die Zeile*

die Linie

A long thin mark which is drawn or painted.

- *Er zeichnete eine gebogene* ***Linie****.* – He drew a curved **line**.

die Grenze

The boundary between two states or countries; borderline.

- *Diese Kinder erkennen* ***die Grenze*** *zwischen Recht und Unrecht.* – These children recognise the border**line** between right and wrong.

die Reihe

People or things standing one behind the other one or side by side; a row, a queue.

- *Du kannst/Sie können das Haus hinter dieser Baum**reihe*** erkennen. – You can see the house behind this **line** of trees.

die Gesellschaft, die Linie

A company that provides transport by sea, air, bus or rail.

- *Mit welcher Fähr**gesellschaft** reist du/reisen Sie?* – Which ferry **line** are you travelling with?
- *Diese* ***Linie*** *wird immer am stärksten befahren.* – This is always the busiest **line**.

die Linie

A route along which a train, coach, or bus service regularly operates.

- *Wohin fährt diese* ***Linie****?* – Where does this **line** go to?
- *Diese* ***Linie*** *endet am Bahnhof.* – This **line** ends at the station.

die Bahnlinie

A railway line.

- *Die Bahn**linie** nach Hamburg ist wegen Reparaturarbeiten geschlossen.* – The (railway) **line** to Hamburg is closed for repairs.

die Zeile

A group of words that are printed in a row.

- Du musst/Sie müssen zwischen den ***Zeilen*** lesen. – You have to read between the **lines**.
- Wir diskutierten über die letzten ***Zeilen*** des Gedichts. – We discussed the last **lines** of the poem.

Exercise 8.10

Fill in the correct word.

1. *Diese __________________ führt direkt nach Frankfurt.*
2. *Sie haben gerade eine ____________________ übersprungen.*
3. *Wenn Sie die ____________________ passiert haben, dürfen Sie nicht schneller als 130 km/h fahren.*
4. *Auf allen innerdeutschen _____________ werden die modernsten Flugzeuge eingesetzt.*
5. *Unsere _____________ bietet unseren Passagieren den besten Komfort.*
6. *Wie heißt die erste Ortschaft hinter der ___________________?*
7. *Stellen Sie sich bitte in einer ___________________ auf!*
8. *Er ist nicht in der Lage, eine gerade ____________________ zu zeichnen.*

Medicine: *die Arznei, die Medizin/die Medizin*

die Arznei, die Medizin

Medication.

- *Sie müssen Ihre* **Medizin** *regelmäßig nehmen.* – You have to take your **medicine** regularly.
- *Können Sie mir eine* **Arznei** *gegen meine Erkältung verschreiben?* – Could you prescribe a **medicine** for my cold?

die Medizin

The academic field that has to do with the treatment of illnesses.

- *Er studiert* **Medizin** *an der Frankfurter Universität.* – He is studying **medicine** at Frankfurt University.

Exercise 8.11

Fill in the correct word.

1. *Nach seinem Schulabschluss möchte er gerne _____________ studieren.*
2. *Ich muss jeden Abend meine __________________ schlucken.*

People: *die Menschen, die Leute/die Bevölkerung/das Volk* (the masses)/*das Volk* (ethnic group)

die Menschen (pl.), *die Leute* (used only as a plural)

Men, women and children; persons/people in general.

- *In Westeuropa nimmt die Zahl der dicken* **Menschen** *zu.* – In Western Europe the number of the fat **people** is increasing.

- *Etwa 50 000* **Menschen** *leben in dieser Stadt.* – About 50,000 **people** live in this town.
- *Was machen diese* **Leute** *dort unten am Flussufer?* – What are those **people** doing down there on the riverbank?

die Bevölkerung

The citizens of a nation or state; all people living in a particular region; the population.

- *Die* **Bevölkerung** *missbilligt die gegenwärtige Politik der Regierung.* – **The people** do not approve of the present government policy.
- *Bei der ländlichen* **Bevölkerung** *genießt er eine hohe Popularität.* – With the rural **people** he enjoys a high popularity.

das Volk

The common people as opposed to the rich and privileged people; the masses.

- *Das* **Volk** *plant einen Aufstand gegen das Regime.* – The **people** are planning a rebellion against the regime.
- *Er wiegelte das* **Volk** *zum Streik auf.* – He incited **the people** to go on strike.

***das Volk* (ethnic group)**

All the men, women and children of a particular country, nation or race.

- *Die europäischen* **Völker** *vereinigen sich.* – The European **peoples** are uniting.
- *Das deutsche* **Volk** *wählt ein neues Parlament.* – The German **people** are electing a new parliament.

Exercise 8.12

Fill in the correct word.

1. *Die ländliche __________ im Raum Nordhessen geht immer weiter zurück.*
2. *Der neue Präsident hat das ______________ auf seiner Seite.*
3. *Wir wollen versuchen, die einfachen ___________ auf der Straße zu erreichen.*
4. *Die Deutschen sind das _____________ der Dichter und Denker.*

Service: *der Dienst/die Dienstleistung/der Betrieb/der Militärdienst/die Bedienung/die Busverbindung, die Zugverbindung, der Busverkehr/der Gottesdienst*

der Dienst

The state or activity of working for a particular person or organization.

- *Jeder* **Dienst** *an der Gemeinschaft muss unterstützt werden.* – Any form of **service** to the community must be supported.
- *Er hat fünfzehn Jahre* **Dienst***zeit hinter sich.* – He has fifteen years' **service** behind him.
- *Ich habe ihm einen schlechten* **Dienst** *erwiesen.* – I've done him a dis**service**.

die Dienstleistung

All the jobs in which people are paid to do something for others rather than to make things.

- *Ich bin in der* **Dienstleistungs***branche tätig.* – I have got a job in the **service** industry.

der Betrieb

When something such as a machine or a form of transport is available for use by the public.

- *Ist dieser Fahrstuhl außer* **Betrieb***?* – Is this lift out of **service**?
- *Man wird diese Zuglinie bald in* **Betrieb** *nehmen.* – They will bring this railway line into **service** soon.

der Militärdienst

The work someone does in the army, navy or air force.

- *Vor zehn Jahren machte ich meinen* **Militärdienst***.* – Ten years ago I did my national service.

die Bedienung

The process of being served in a shop or restaurant.

- *Sie haben eine sehr nette* **Bedienung** *in diesem Restaurant.* – They have very good *service* in this restaurant.

die Bus-, die Zugverbindung, der Bus-, der Zugverkehr

Public transport by bus or train.

- *An Samstagen besteht kein* **Bus- oder Zugverkehr** *nach Hamburg.* – There's no **service** to Hamburg on Saturdays.
- *Gibt es* **Zug- oder Busverbindungen** *nach Frankfurt?* – Are there any **services** to Frankfurt?

der Gottesdienst

A formal religious ceremony, often held on a particular occasion.

- *Der Sonntagabend***gottesdienst** *beginnt um 19.00 Uhr.* – The Saturday evening **service** starts at seven o'clock.

Exercise 8.13

Fill in the correct word.

1. *Gibt es in diesem Restaurant denn keine* ______________________?
2. *Der* ______________ *in unserer Kirchengemeinde ist immer gut besucht.*
3. *Meinen* ________________________ *leistete ich bei der Luftwaffe ab.*
4. *Dieser Fahrkartenautomat ist zur Zeit leider nicht in* _______________.
5. *Er ist im* _______________ *der Weltgesundheitsorganisation unterwegs.*
6. *Aufgrund der geringen Zahl von Reisenden wurde der* _________ *an die Küste eingestellt.*
7. *Als eine der führenden Banken bieten wir Ihnen* ___________ *aller Art an.*

Vacancy: *das freie Zimmer/die offene Stelle, die freie Stelle*

das freie Zimmer

An unoccupied room in a hotel or boarding house.

- *Haben Sie ein* **freies Zimmer**? – Do you have any **vacancies**?

die offene Stelle, die freie Stelle

An unoccupied post or office.

- *Wir haben eine* **freie Stelle** *in der Buchhaltung.* – We have a **vacancy** in the accounts department.

Exercise 8.14

Fill in the correct word.

1. *Wir können Ihnen in unserer Pension noch ein* ________________ *anbieten. Es kostet €25 inklusive Frühstück.*
2. *In unserer Firma haben wir zur Zeit einige* ________________. *Wir suchen dringend Arbeitskräfte.*

Chapter 9: Choosing the Right Pronoun

One-minute overview

In this chapter we are going to take a closer look at pronouns. A pronoun is a word that is used to replace a noun or a noun group that has been mentioned earlier in a sentence or text. Like adjectives and nouns, pronouns are dependent on gender (masculine, feminine or neuter), number (singular or plural) and case (their function in the sentence). Since the English language does not differentiate between cases, pronouns pose a special problem. Where English manages with only one pronoun, there are often two different pronouns in German, e.g. one for the dative case and the other for the accusative case. And when it comes to reflexive pronouns, which are used when subject and object are identical, the English language provides a new set of words ending with '–self' (singular) or '–selves' (plural), whereas in German the pronouns used for reflexive and non-reflexive verbs are alike. This chapter will show you:

- when and how to use personal and reflexive pronouns;
- how to differentiate between the cases (accusative and dative) when using pronouns;
- how to ask the way;
- useful words and sentences needed at an airport or railway station (buying tickets, enquiring about times, etc.);
- how to ask someone to leave a message;
- how to apologize.

First person singular

The personal pronouns *mich* and *mir*

me – mich (accusative)

Mich is used for the accusative case of the first person singular. In English the equivalent of the accusative case is the **direct object** of a verb. The direct object is the person or thing directly affected by the verb, e.g. *Ich hasse Sport*. – I hate **sports** (= direct object).

- Seine Frau kennt ***mich***. – His wife knows **me**.
- Hast du ***mich*** gestern im Kino gesehen? – Did you see **me** in the cinema yesterday?
- Er hat ***mich*** in Köln besucht. – He visited **me** in Cologne.

The accusative case is also used after verb phrases that contain the prepositions ***an***, ***auf*** and ***über***:

- Sie hat ***an mich*** gedacht. – She thought of **me**.
- Bitte wartet/Bitte warten Sie ***auf*** *mich*! – Please wait for **me**!
- Deine Freunde haben ***über mich*** gesprochen. – Your friends have talked about **me**.
- Sie haben ***über mich*** gelacht. – They have laughed at **me**.

me – mir (dative)

Mir is used in the dative case of the first person singular. In English the equivalent of the dative case is the **indirect object** of the verb. The indirect object denotes a person who benefits from an action or receives something as a result, the so-called beneficiaries or recipients. In English the indirect object is often indicated by the use of the preceding prepositions '**to**' or '**for**', e.g.: Er hat ***mir*** ein Buch gekauft. – He bought a book **for me**./*Er gab es* ***mir***. – He gave it **to me**. Note that in English if you replace the pronoun of the direct object by a noun (here the pronoun **it**), the *to* is no longer needed: He gave **me** the book. – *Er gab* ***mir*** *das Buch*.

- *Kannst du/Können Sie* ***mir*** *den Weg zum Bahnhof zeigen?* – Could you show **me** the way to the railway-station?
- *Sie hat es* ***mir*** *gesagt.* – She said it **to me**.
- *Er hat* ***mir*** *einen Rat gegeben.* – He has given **me** a piece of advice.

Preposition + dative case

The dative case is also used after verb phrases that contain the prepositions ***von***, ***zu***, ***nach*** and ***vor***:

- *Plötzlich stand er* ***vor*** *mir.* – Suddenly he stood right in front of **me**.
- *Hat meine Frau* ***nach*** *mir gefragt?* – Has my wife asked about **me**?
- *Ich habe ihn* ***zu mir*** *eingeladen.* – I have invited him to **me**.

Exercise 9.1

Fill in the right pronoun using either *mich* or *mir*.

1. *Er hat ein Geschenk für ________ gekauft.*
2. *Die Katze legte sich auf ________.*
3. *Sie hat ________ das Auto gewaschen.*
4. *Nicola fährt in dem Auto vor ________.*
5. *Wilfried hat ________ beim Schach geschlagen.*
6. *Die Polizei hat im Wald nach ________ gesucht.*
7. *Bitte denkt an ________, wenn ich morgen in meine Prüfung gehe.*
8. *Komm, wir gehen einfach zu ________. Ich habe noch viel zu trinken im Kühlschrank.*
9. *Meine Freundin Riki hat ________ zum Abschied einen Kuss gegeben.*
10. *Kannst du ________ bitte die Butter reichen?*

Exercise 9.2

Translate the following sentences into German.

1. My son loves **me**.
2. My friends waited **for me**.
3. Give it **to me**, please!
4. She gave **me** a present.
5. This is a book **about me**.

The reflexive pronouns: *mich* and *mir*

Reflexive pronouns are used when the **subject** and the **direct object** of the verb are identical, e.g.: ***Ich** habe **mich** verletzt.* – I have hurt **myself**. Here the subject *ich* executes an action, i.e.: *jemanden verletzen* (to hurt someone), and performs the action upon him- or herself, which is ***mich***. Here the verb *verletzen* takes the accusative case. There are also reflexive verbs that take an **indirect object**. The indirect object is put in the dative case, e.g. *Ich habe **mir** ein Auto gekauft.* – I have bought **myself** a car (=I have bought a car **for myself**).

myself – mich (accusative)

- *Ich rasiere **mich** jeden Morgen.* – Every morning I shave (**myself**).
- *Ich muss **mich** waschen.* – I must wash **myself**.
- *Ich habe **mich** selbst geheilt.* – I've cured **myself**.

myself – mir (dative)

- *Ich habe **mir** eine Tasse Kaffee gemacht.* – I have made **myself** a cup of coffee.

- *Morgen werde ich* ***mir eine*** *Hose kaufen.* – Tomorrow I'm going to buy **myself** a pair of trousers.
- *Heute Morgen habe ich* ***mir*** *in die Hand geschnitten.* – This morning I have cut **myself** on the hand.
- *Wo kann ich* ***mir*** *eine Fahrkarte kaufen?* – Where can I buy (**myself**) a ticket?

Reflexive verbs which are non-reflexive in English

There are many reflexive verbs in German that are used without a reflexive pronoun in English (there is a long list in chapter 4):

- *Ich kann* ***mich*** *nicht auf den Text konzentrieren.* – I can't concentrate on the text.
- *Ich möchte* ***mich*** *für mein schlechtes Verhalten entschuldigen.* – I'd like to apologize for my bad behaviour.
- *Ich kann* ***mich*** *ziemlich gut an dich erinnern.* – I can remember you quite well.
- *Ich muss* ***mich*** *beeilen um rechtzeitig am Flughafen zu sein.* – I must hurry in order to be at the airport in time.

Exercise 9.3

Fill in the right pronoun using either *mich* or *mir.*

1. *Ich möchte ________ gerne vorstellen.*
2. *Ich habe ________ in eine sehr nette Frau verliebt.*
3. *Ich schneide ________ regelmäßig beim Kartoffelschälen in den Finger.*
4. *Nach der Arbeit auf der Baustelle habe ich ________ erst mal gewaschen.*
5. *Ich erinnere ________ an diesen Schüler.*
6. *Gestern habe ich ________ ein Auto gekauft.*
7. *Ich habe ________ für das Foul bei meinem Gegenspieler entschuldigt.*
8. *Ich fühle ________ gut.*
9. *Gestern habe ich ________ beim Fußballspielen verletzt.*
10. *Meine Mahlzeiten mache ich ________ immer selbst.*

Exercise 9.4

Translate the following sentences into German.

1. I want to buy (**for**) **myself** a tourist guide to Frankfurt.
2. I said **to myself**, this is the right time to act.
3. In order to catch the train I had to hurry.
4. Look, I've made (**for**) **myself** a beautiful skirt.
5. Yesterday, I cut **myself**.

Second person singular

The personal pronouns: *dich, dir* and the formal address *Sie* and *Ihnen*

You – dich

Dich is used in the accusative case:

- *Ich liebe* ***dich***. – I love **you**.
- *Er möchte* ***dich*** *kennen lernen.* – He would like to get to know **you**.
- *Sie braucht* ***dich*** *sehr.* – She needs **you** very much.

Preposition + accusative case

Dich is used in the accusative case after the prepositions ***an***, ***auf*** and ***über***:

- Er hat eine Postkarte ***an*** *dich* geschrieben. – He wrote a picture postcard to **you**.
- ***Auf*** *dich* können wir zählen. – We can count on **you**.
- Sie hat ein Buch ***über*** *dich* geschrieben. – She wrote a book about **you**.

You – dir

Dir is used in the dative case:

- *Gefällt* ***dir*** *dein Urlaub?* – Do **you** enjoy your holidays?
- *Deine Lehrerin hat* ***dir*** *eine schlechte Note gegeben.* – Your teacher has given **you** a bad mark.
- *Er hat* ***dir*** *gestern eine E-Mail geschrieben.* – Yesterday he wrote an e-mail to **you**.

Preposition + dative case

Dir is used in the dative case after the prepositions ***von***, ***zu***, ***nach*** and ***vor***:

- Sie hat den Brief ***von dir*** bekommen. – She's got the letter from **you**.
- Er möchte ***zu dir*** reisen. – He wants to travel to **you**.
- Sie ist hier um ***nach dir*** zu schauen. – She's here to look after **you**.
- Er hat Angst ***vor dir***. – He's afraid of **you**.

You – Sie

Sie is used in the **accusative case** for the formal address in the singular and the plural form. Remember that the pronouns *Sie* and *Ihnen* used for the formal address are always capitalized:

- *Wir möchten* ***Sie*** *gerne unterstützen.* – We would like to support **you**.

- *Ich möchte **Sie** gerne zu einer Tasse Kaffee einladen.* – I would like to invite **you** for a (cup of) coffee.

You – Ihnen

Ihnen is used in the **dative case** for the formal address in the singular and the plural form:

- *Ich möchten **Ihnen** einen Vorschlag machen.* – I want to make a suggestion to **you**.
- *Können wir **Ihnen** helfen?* – Can we help **you**?

Exercise 9.5

Fill in the right pronoun using either *dich* or *dir.*

1. *Uli hat _______ ein köstliches Essen zubereitet.*
2. *Dein Lehrer hat sich über ________ beschwert.*
3. *Max hat ________ fotografiert.*
4. *Er steht direkt vor _________ in der Schlange.*
5. *Ich habe ________ einen Hut aus Deutschland mitgebracht.*
6. *Wir verlassen uns auf ________.*
7. *Ich bin nach ________ an der Reihe.*
8. *Zu deinem Geburtstag möchten wir _________ herzlich gratulieren.*
9. *Sie hat mir einiges über _________ erzählt.*
10. *Ich habe _________ vermisst.*

Exercise 9.6

Translate the following sentences into German.

1. She hates *you.*
2. The dog follows *you* wherever you go.
3. I would like to visit *you* in May.
4. He has written *you* a letter.
5. I'll buy *you* a present.

Execise 9.7

Translate the following sentences into German using the formal address.

1. Mr Müller, can I ask *you* something?
2. Can I help *you,* Madam?
3. What can I do for *you*?
4. She wants to teach *you* German.
5. I have a great offer for *you.*

The reflexive pronouns: *dich, dir* and *sich*

yourself – dich (accusative)

- *Du hast* ***dich*** *bei dem Unfall verletzt.* – You have injured **yourself** in the accident.
- *Du musst* ***dich*** *häufiger waschen.* – You have to wash **yourself** more often.
- *Und plötzlich findest du* ***dich*** *im Krankenhaus wieder.* – And suddenly you find **yourself** in hospital again.

yourself – dir (dative)

- *Du hast* ***dir*** *selbst damit geschadet.* – You have hurt **yourself** with it.
- *Kaufst du* ***dir*** *eine Wohnung?* – Are you buying a flat **for** yourself?
- *Mache es* ***dir*** *bequem!* – Make **yourself** comfortable!

yourself/yourselves – sich (accusative and dative for the formal address – singular and plural)

- *Sie haben* ***sich*** *verletzt.* – You have injured **yourself**/yourselves.
- *Sie müssen* ***sich*** *häufiger waschen.* – You must wash **yourself**/ yourselves more often.
- *Kaufen Sie* ***sich*** *eine Wohnung?* – Are you buying **yourself**/yourselves a flat?
- *Machen Sie es* ***sich*** *bequem!* – Make **yourself**/yourselves comfortable!

Exercise 9.8

Fill in the right pronoun using either *dich, dir* or *sich.*

1. *Sie müssen ________ selbst entscheiden.*
2. *Würdest du ________ als Marxisten bezeichnen?*
3. *Wann kaufst du ________ ein Auto?*
4. *Sie dürfen ________ auf keinen Fall überanstrengen.*
5. *Bleib ruhig! Du regst ________ zu sehr auf.*
6. *Machen Sie ________ nicht so viele Gedanken!*
7. *Du kannst ________ hier im Badezimmer waschen.*
8. *Du musst ________ Zeit lassen.*
9. *Wie hast du ________ verletzt?*
10. *Du hast ________ gestern aber dumm verhalten.*

Exercise 9.9

Translate the following sentences into German. Use the formal and the informal address.

1. Behave **yourself**!
2. You must hurry!
3. You have to express **yourself** clearly.
4. Would you like to introduce **yourself**?
5. You can make **yourself** a cup of tea.

Third person singular masculine

The personal pronouns: *ihn* and *ihm*

him – ihn

Ihn is used in the **accusative** case:

- *Ich möchte **ihn** gerne sprechen.* – I would like to talk to **him**.
- *Kannst du **ihn** überzeugen?* – Can you persuade **him**?
- *Wann wirst du **ihn** treffen?* – When will you meet **him**?

With prepositions

Ihn is used in the **accusative** case after the prepositions ***an***, ***auf*** and ***über***:

- Dieses Paket ist ***an*** *ihn* adressiert. – This packet is addressed to **him**.
- Wir wollen ***auf ihn*** und sein erfolgreiches Examen anstoßen. – We want to drink to **him** and his successful exam.
- Was sagen die Leute ***über*** *ihn*? – What do people say about **him**?

Him – ihm

Ihm is used in the **dative** case:

- *Kannst du **ihm** etwas ausrichten?* – Can you give **him** a message?
- *Er hat **ihm** seine Frau vorgestellt.* – He introduced his wife to **him**.
- *Haben Sie es **ihm** schon gesagt?* – Have you already told **him** about it?

With prepositions

Ihm is used in the **dative** case after the prepositions ***von***, ***zu***, ***nach*** and ***vor***:

- ***Vor ihm** steht ein Polizist.* – A policeman is standing in front of **him**.
- *Die Tochter ist **nach ihm** gekommen.* – The daughter came after **him**.
- *Es wird viel **von ihm** gesprochen.* – They talk a lot about **him**.

Exercise 9.10

Fill in the correct pronoun using either *ihn* or *ihm*.

1. *Sie können ________ anrufen.*
2. *Könnten Sie ________ einen Gruß ausrichten?*
3. *Die Straße wurde nach ________ benannt.*
4. *Ich werde ________ eine E-Mail schicken.*
5. *Ich habe von ________ ein Fax erhalten.*
6. *Wir haben auf ________ gesetzt.*
7. *Du musst ________ die Wahrheit sagen.*
8. *Wir sind ________ gefolgt.*
9. *Wann werden Sie ________ sehen?*
10. *Die Leute werden über ________ reden.*

Exercise 9.11

Translate the following sentences into German.

1. I'll send **him** a postcard.
2. Just go to **him** and ask **him**!
3. Who gives the present to **him**?
4. Try to stop **him**.
5. I once taught **him**.

The third person singular feminine

The personal pronouns: *sie* and *ihr*

her – sie

Sie is used in the **accusative** case:

- *Willst du **sie** anrufen?* – Do you want to call **her**?
- *Wann willst du **sie** treffen?* – When do you want to meet **her**?
- *Ich werde **sie** morgen sehen.* – I will see **her** tomorrow.

With prepositions

Sie is used in the **accusative** case after the prepositions ***an***, ***auf*** and ***über***:

- *Es wird viel **über sie** geredet.* – They talk a lot about **her**.
- *Ich werde einen Brief **an sie** schreiben.* – I'm going to write a letter to **her**.
- *Es kommt alles **auf sie** an.* – It all depends on **her**.

Her – ihr

Ihr is used in the **dative** case:

- *Kannst du **ihr** das Frühstück machen?* – Can you make breakfast for **her**?
- *Wir werden es **ihr** heute sagen.* – We are going to tell **her** about it *today.*
- Er kann ***ihr*** *viel bieten.* – He can offer **her** much.

With prepositions

Ihr is used in the **dative** case after the prepositions ***von***, ***zu***, ***nach*** and ***vor***:

- *Du kommst **nach ihr dran.*** – It's your turn after **her**.
- *Ich habe Vertrauen **zu ihr**.* – I trust in **her**.
- *Du hast auch einen Brief **von ihr** bekommen.* – You've also got a letter from **her**.

Exercise 9.12

Fill in the right pronoun using either *sie* or *ihr*.

1. *Ich werde mich an ________ wenden.*
2. *Wir schenken ________ eine Reise nach Italien.*
3. *Du musst ________ jetzt helfen.*
4. *Wir wollen ________ freundlich begrüßen.*
5. *Ich werde ________ vermissen.*
6. *Fährst du zu ________ nach Hamburg?*
7. *Können Sie ________ die Bestellung zufaxen?*
8. *Du musst dich auf ________ einstellen.*
9. *Bitte richte ________ einen Gruß von mir aus!*
10. *Hast du diesen Brief von ________ erhalten?*

Exercise 9.13

Translate the following sentences into German.

1. When can I see **her** again?
2. Please, tell **her** to call me at the office!
3. What can I do for **her**?
4. Where can I find **her**?
5. Could you lend **her** some money?

The reflexive pronoun: *sich*

Himself, herself, itself – *sich*

The reflexive pronoun *sich* is used for the third person singular in the accusative as well as in the dative case; *sich* is used for masculine, feminine and neuter.

sich in the accusative case

- *Oliver streckt* ***sich*** *gewöhnlich auf dem Sofa aus.* – Usually Oliver stretches **himself** out on the sofa.
- *Andrea hat* ***sich*** *selbst vorgestellt.* – Andrea has introduced **herself.**
- *Deutschland muss* ***sich*** *auf den neusten Stand bringen.* – Germany has to bring **itself** up to date.

sich in the dative case

- *Stefan hat* ***sich*** *weh getan.* – Stefan has hurt **himself.**
- *Cornelia will* ***sich*** *ein Auto kaufen.* – Cornelia wants to buy **herself** a car.
- *Die Schildkröte baut* ***sich*** *gerade ein Nest.* – The tortoise is building **itself** a nest.

themselves – *sich*

Additionally *sich* is used for the **third person plural** in the **accusative** and the **dative** case.

Accusative case

- *Diese Jungen sollten* ***sich*** *schämen.* – These boys should be ashamed of **themselves.**
- *Die Kinder müssen* ***sich*** *waschen.* – The children have to wash **themselves.**

Dative case

- *Die Zwei wollen* ***sich*** *ein Haus kaufen.* – The two want to buy a house for **themselves.**
- *Sie dachten, sie gönnten* ***sich*** *mal etwas.* – They thought they'd give **themselves** a treat.

yourself, yourselves – *sich*

Sich is also used as the reflexive pronoun for the singular and plural form in the **accusative** and the **dative** case of the **formal address** *Sie.*

Accusative case (singular and plural)

- *Herr Weber, Sie müssen* **sich** *selbst fragen, ob dieses Benehmen angemessen war.* – Mr Weber, you have to ask **yourself** if this behaviour was appropriate.
- *Meine Damen und Herren, bitte benehmen Sie* ***sich***! – Ladies and gentlemen, please behave ***yourselves***!

Dative case (singular and plural)

- *Frau Müller, Sie sollten* **sich** *deswegen keine Vorwürfen machen.* – Mrs Müller, you shouldn't reproach **yourself** for that.
- *Meine Damen und Herren, bitte machen Sie es* **sich** *bequem!* – Ladies and gentlemen, please, make **yourselves** comfortable.

Exercise 9.14

Translate the following sentences into English. Be careful with the reflexive verbs whose English counterparts are non-reflexive.

1. *Sie haben* ***sich*** *verspätet.*
2. *Hier können Sie* ***sich*** *waschen, Herr Clemens.*
3. *Er hat* ***sich*** *geschämt.*
4. *Bitte, beeilen Sie* ***sich***!
5. *Der Vogel hat* ***sich*** *verletzt.*
6. *Sie machte es* ***sich*** *bequem.*
7. *Er will* ***sich*** *ein Zelt kaufen.*
8. *Liebe Kollegen, bringen Sie* ***sich*** *immer auf den neusten Stand!*
9. *Sie fühlt* ***sich*** *gut.*
10. *Sie stellte* ***sich*** *den Zuhörern kurz vor.*

Chapter 10: Adverbs and Adjectives

One-minute overview

In this chapter we are going to deal with adverbs and adjectives. While adjectives give some additional information about nouns or pronouns, adverbs serve to modify a verb, adjective, another adverb or even a whole sentence. In English adverbs are formed by adding '–ly' to adjectives (e.g. easily, happily). Some German adverbs are formed by adding *-weise* or *-sweise* to a noun (e.g. *beispielsweise* – for example, *zeitweise* – at times). As in English there are also adverbs that do not derive from other parts of speech (e.g. *oben* – above). In English some of these adverbs can also be used as adjectives, (e.g. 'only', 'then', or 'late'). For these adverbs and adjectives two different words are used in German whereas English manages with only one word (e.g. late (in time) – *spät*; late (dead) – *verstorben*). Consequently these words are easily mixed up and apt to cause problems for the English-speaking student of German. This chapter will show you:

- how to translate English words which can be either used as adjectives or as adverbs;
- how to use the German translation of these words in a sentence;
- useful words and sentences needed when travelling by plane, train, or coach;
- how to apologize when being late;
- words and sentences needed when talking about one's profession, plans for the future (studies), career;
- helpful sentences needed when talking about one's health (at the doctor's).

'Only' as an adverb: *erst/nur, bloß*

Only – *erst*

Erst is used to indicate that something only happened a short while ago.

- *Es ist doch* **erst** *zehn Uhr.* – But it's **only** ten o'clock.
- **Erst** *letzte Woche sind wir nach Berlin gefahren.* – **Only** last week we went to Berlin.

- *Der Reisebus ist gerade* ***erst*** *gekommen.* – The coach has **only** just arrived.

Only – *nur, bloß*

Nur and *bloß* are interchangeable and used to indicate that something is the one thing that is (to be) done or that happens.

- *Sie müssen* ***nur*** *den Schaffner in diesem Zug fragen.* – You **only** have to ask the guard on this train.
- *Er ist* ***bloß*** *an den Fakten interessiert.* – He's **only** interested in the facts.
- *Ich konnte* ***nur*** *eine Fähre nehmen, um die Insel zu verlassen.* – I could **only** take a ferry in order to leave the island.

'Only' as an adjective: *einzige(s)*

This adjective is used to describe a single example or occurrence of something or a group of something that is small in number. The adjective modifies the noun group that immediately follows it.

- *Er ist mein* ***einziges*** *Kind.* – He's my **only** child.
- *Sie war die* ***Einzige,*** *die geraucht hat.* – She was the **only one** who was smoking.
- *Sie waren die* ***einzigen*** *Ausländer in diesem Dorf.* – They were the **only** foreigners in this village.
- *Das ist das* ***einzige*** *Flugzeug nach München an diesem Abend.* – This is the **only** plane to Munich tonight.
- *Das ist der* ***einzige*** *Weg nach draußen.* – This is the **only** way out.

Exercises 10.1

Fill in the gaps using the correct adjective or adverb.

1. *Dies ist heute der _________ Bus nach München.*
2. *Sie müssen _____ die Straße hinuntergehen, bis Sie zum Postamt kommen.*
3. *Dieses Auto kostet ________€5000; Sie würden ein gutes Geschäft machen.*
4. *Wir sind doch ________ vor einer Viertelstunde hier angekommen.*
5. *________ in Mathematik hatte Ulrike eine schlechte Note.*
6. *Sie müssten mir _______ Ihre Bankverbindung geben.*
7. *John ist der ________ Engländer in dieser Touristengruppe.*
8. *Das Flugzeug ist _______ vor fünf Minuten gelandet.*
9. *Du musst dich _______ etwas mehr anstrengen; dann klappt es auch.*
10. *Ich bin der ________ Schüler, der eine Eins in Deutsch bekommen hat.*

Exercise 10.2

Translate the following sentences into German.

1. I'm the **only** son.
2. There's **only** one professor who teaches German linguistics.
3. We've **only** been here two months.
4. She's the **only** girl on this course.
5. You **only** have to push this button.

'Then' as an adverb: *dann/damals, da/dann, außerdem*

Then – *dann*

Dann is used when you are referring to what happens next or to what is done next in a procedure. Here the adverb modifies a complete sentence:

- *Erst fliegen wir nach Frankfurt;* ***dann*** *fahren wir mit dem Zug nach Stuttgart.* – First we are going to fly to Frankfurt; **then** we are going to take the train to Stuttgart.
- *Und wenn wir kein Bargeld mehr haben, was machen wir* ***dann****?* – And when we have run out of cash, what are we going to do **then**?
- *Die ersten zwei Jahre studierte er in England,* ***dann*** *setzte er sein Studium an einer deutschen Universität fort.* – He studied in England for the first two years, **then** he continued his studies at a German university.

Then – *damals, da*

Damals is used when you refer to a specific time in the past, whereas *da* is used when you refer to a specific time in the past or in the future; *damals* and *da* are often used together with the adverb *gerade* (just).

- ***Damals*** *dachte ich, er sei eine nette Person; und ich denke, er ist es immer noch.* – I thought he was a nice person **then,** and I think he still is.
- *Es war* **da** (***gerade***) *sieben Uhr.* – It was seven o'clock **then.**
- *Ich war* **da** (***gerade***) *in Griechenland im Urlaub/Ich werde da im Urlaub in Griechenland sein.* – I was/will be on holiday in Greece ***then.***

Then – *dann, außerdem*

You use *dann* or *außerdem*, which are interchangeable, at the beginning of a sentence – especially after *und* – to add another piece of information which is relevant to what you have been talking about:

- *Und **dann** ist da noch meine kleine Schwester.* – And **then** there's my little sister.
- *Und **außerdem** gibt es da noch die Möglichkeit die U-Bahn zu nehmen.* – And **then** there's the possibility of taking the underground.

'Then' as an adjective: *damalig, damalige(n)*

The adjective *damalig* is used when you talk about something which was true at a particular time in the past but is not true now, especially when you refer to an office.

- *Der **damalige** Kanzler hieß Helmut Kohl.* – The **then** Chancellor was Helmut Kohl.
- *Der **damalige** Bürgermeister wurde aus seinem Amt geworfen.* – The **then** Mayor was thrown out of office.
- *In der Innenstadt traf sie den **damaligen** Besitzer der Kneipe.* – In the city centre she met the **then** owner of the pub.

Exercise 10.3

Fill in the gaps using the correct adjective or adverb.

1. *Wir fuhren an Darmstadt vorbei; und _____ erreichten wir endlich Frankfurt.*
2. *Und ________ musst du dich fragen, warum du diesen Weg gegangen bist.*
3. *Ich war _________ gerade mal sechs Jahre alt, als dies passiert ist.*
4. *Der _________ Bürgermeister ließ eine neue Stadthalle bauen.*
5. *Und _________ ist da noch das Problem der hohen Jugendkriminalität.*
6. *Zuerst war er voller Zuversicht; ________ verließ ihn aber der Mut.*
7. *Die ________ Klassenkameraden ließen ihn im Stich.*
8. *Ich war _________ Student in Hamburg, als ich meine Frau kennen lernte.*
9. *Und ______ müssen wir uns noch über das bevorstehende Treffen unterhalten.*
10. *_______ glaubte ich noch, er würde mich lieben.*

Exercise 10.4

Translate the following sentences into German.

1. The **then** Secretary of State was James Baker.
2. First we are going to visit Munich and **then** we're planning to fly to Cologne.
3. And **then** you have to think of the high rate of unemployment.
4. I was in Germany **then**, together with my family.
5. And if they have no vacancies either, where are we going to sleep **then**?

'Well' ('as well') as an adverb: *gut/gründlich/ohne weiteres, gut, wohl, auch*

well – *gut*

You use *gut* to describe something which is done to a high standard or to a great extent:

- *Er spricht* ***gut*** *deutsch.* – He speaks German **well**.
- *Ich kenne dieses Land sehr* ***gut***. – I know this country very **well**.
- *Sie kommt* ***gut*** *voran in der Schule.* – She is doing **well** at school.

Well – *gründlich*

Gründlich is used to describe an action that is done thoroughly.

- *Du musst das Schweinefleisch* ***gründlich/gut*** *durchbraten.* – You have to cook that pork **well**.
- *Ich habe mich* ***gründlich/gut*** *auf die Prüfung vorbereitet.* – I'm **well** prepared for the exam.

If the adverb is used to describe something which contains a rather negative piece of information, particularly from the speaker's point of view, *gründlich* is not to be replaced by *gut*, since *gut* has only positive connotations:

- *Wir sind von der englischen Mannschaft* ***gründlich*** *geschlagen worden.* – We were **thoroughly** beaten by the English team.
- *Endlich ist auch er* ***gründlich*** *in seine Schranken verwiesen worden.* – Finally he too has been **well** put in his place.

Well – *ohne weiteres, gut, wohl*

Ohne weiteres, *gut* and *wohl* are used when you are talking about something which you believe is likely to happen. It is often used after an impersonal construction introduced by es (it) and a modal verb such as *könnte* (could) or *mag* (may), followed by a subordinate clause introduced by *dass*: *Es kann ohne weiteres/wohl/gut sein, dass …* or *Es mag ohne weiteres/wohl/gut sein, dass …* (This sentence structure also exists in English: It may well be that …)

- *Es mag/könnte* ***wohl/ohne weiteres/gut*** *sein, dass sich Ihr Gehör bessert.* – Your hearing may/could **well** improve.
- *Es ist* ***ohne weiteres/wohl/gut*** *möglich, dass er bald wieder laufen kann.* – It may **well** be that he will be able to walk again soon.
- Sie mögen *wohl* Recht haben. – You may **well** be right.

As well – *auch*

You use *auch* when mentioning something that happens in the same way as something else already mentioned:

- ***Auch** er ist einer der beliebtesten Professoren.* – *He* **as well** is one of the most popular professors.
- *Sie möchte **auch** ihr Examen im Frühjahr ablegen.* – She **as well** wants to take her exams in the spring.
- *Anna sagte mir, dass* **auch** *sie Kunst studieren will.* – Anna told me that she ***as well*** wants to study art.

'Well' as an adjective: *gesund/gut*

Well – *gesund;* to be well – *gut gehen*

'To be well' in the sense of healthy (as opposed to ill), can be translated with the adjective *gesund* as well as the **idiomatic expression** *gut gehen,* which is an impersonal construction in which the person who talks about his health or who people talk about is put in the dative case:

- *Ich bin kein* **gesunder** *Mann./Es geht mir* (= dative case) *nicht* **gut.** – I'm not a **well** man.
- ***Ihm*** (= dative case) *geht es sehr* **gut,** *danke.* – He's very **well**, thank you.
- *Aber du siehst überhaupt nicht* **gesund** *aus.* – But you don't look **well** at all.

Idiomatic expressions

When 'to be well' is used to describe a situation that is satisfactory or desirable, **idiomatic expressions** are often used in German. They are impersonal constructions in which the word *es* (it) is the subject, and consist of the adjectives *gut* (or its superlative form: *zum Besten*) or *leicht,* which are connected to certain verbs such as *nicht zum Besten stehen, gut aussehen, gut reden haben* or *leicht reden können.*

- In der Welt ***steht*** *es* nicht ***zum Besten.***/In der Welt ***sieht*** *es* nicht ***gut aus.*** – All is not **well** in the world.
- Es sieht ***gut*** aus. – All is **well**.
- Mit ihm ***sieht es*** im Moment nicht **gut** aus. – He's not ***well*** at the moment.
- Du ***hast gut reden***/Du ***kannst leicht reden***, du brauchst nicht zu laufen. – It's all very **well** for you, you don't have to walk.
- Ende ***gut***, alles ***gut***. – All's **well**, that ends **well**.

Exercise 10.5

Fill in the gaps using the appropriate adjective or adverb.

1. *Sie haben diese Aufgabe sehr ________ gelöst.*
2. *Dieser Mann dort nahm __________ an der Konferenz teil.*
3. *Schau dir seine Gesichtsfarbe an; ich finde, er sieht nicht sehr ________ aus.*
4. *Die Mannschaft hat sehr __________ Fußball gespielt.*
5. *Es kann _____ möglich sein, dass Sie in zwei Wochen wieder laufen können.*
6. *Die deutschen Fußballer wurden von dem starken Gegner aus England __________ in ihre Schranken verwiesen.*
7. *Sie möchte ________ mit nach Süddeutschland fahren.*
8. *Es könnte ________ sein, dass es bald anfängt zu schneien.*
9. *Das letzte Mal, als ich ihn traf, sah er recht __________ aus.*
10. *Ich werde mich auf das anstehende Examen ________ vorbereiten müssen.*

Exercise 10.6

Translate the following sentences into German.

1. I may **well** be that the conflict will be over by the end of the year.
2. Her grandfather is not **well**.
3. It's all very **well** for you; you can stay in bed.
4. She **as well** wants to buy a car.
5. My sister plays the violin very **well**.

'Late' as an adverb: *lange/länger*

Lange or its comparative form *länger* describes an activity which happens or is done after the usual or normal time:

- *Sie arbeitet heute **länger**.* – She is working **late** today.
- *Wir werden **lange** aufbleiben.* – We are going to stay up **late**.

'Late' as an adverb/adjective

(or translated as a reflexive verb or as a noun: spät sein, sich verspäten/ Verspätung haben)

To be late – *(zu) spät sein/sich verspäten*

You use *spät* when you arrive, come or get up after the time that was arranged or expected. The reflexive verb *sich verspäten* is a variant of *spät sein*.

- *Entschuldige, dass ich **zu spät bin**.* – I'm sorry for **being late**.
- *Entschuldigen Sie, ich habe **mich verspätet**.* – I apologize for **being late**.

- *Ich* ***kam*** 15 Minuten ***zu spät*** *zum Treffen.* – I **came** 15 minutes *late* for the meeting.
- *Wir sind heute* ***spät*** *dran.* – We're running **late** today.
- *Ich stand* ***später*** *auf als meine Frau.* – I got up **later** than my wife.

Late/to be late – *Verspätung haben*

Verspätung haben (the noun *die Verspätung* + auxiliary verb *haben*) are variants of *zu spät sein*; this expression is often used when a train, a bus or another form of public transport is late or delayed.

- *Wissen Sie, ob der Zug* ***Verspätung hat****?* – Do you know if the train **is late/delayed?**
- *Mein Zug* ***hatte Verspätung.*** – My train **arrived late**/My train *was delayed.*

'Late' as an adjective: *spät/verstorben*

Late – *spät*

Spät as an adjective is used to describe an activity which occurs or is done near the end of a particular stretch of time. In German you often merge nouns with adjectives, thus creating a new noun. In certain cases this is also possible with the adjective *spät*; e.g.: *der* ***späte*** *Nachmittag* (the **late** afternoon) becomes *der* ***Spät****nachmittag.*

- *Ich besuche dich am* ***späten*** *Nachmittag/am* ***Spät****nachmittag.* – I'll visit you in the **late** afternoon.
- *Seine Band war in den* ***späten*** *80ern sehr populär.* – His band was very popular in the **late** 1980s.
- *Diese Sonate gehört zu Bachs* ***Spät****werk.* – This sonata belongs to Bach's **late** work.
- *Sie ist eine* ***Spät****entwicklerin.* – She's a **late** developer.

late – *verstorben*

You use *verstorben* when you talk about someone who is dead, particularly someone who has died only recently.

- *Wir müssen mit Ihnen über Ihre* ***verstorbene*** *Ehefrau sprechen.* – We must talk with you about your **late** wife.
- *Morgen findet die Trauerfeier für den* ***verstorbenen*** *Präsidenten statt.* – Tomorrow is the funeral for the **late** President.

Exercise 10.7

Fill in the gaps using the appropriate adjective, adverb, reflexive verb or noun.

1. *Heute Morgen habe ich ___________ geschlafen.*
2. *Bitte kommen Sie nicht zu ___________ zum Unterricht.*
3. *Ich bin in den ________ 90ern für ein paar Jahre in Deutschland gewesen.*
4. *Entschuldigen Sie bitte, aber mein Zug hatte eine halbe Stunde _________.*
5. *Der _________ König wurde vor der Beerdigung in der Rotunde aufgebahrt.*
6. *Wenn Sie __________, sollten Sie sich bei Ihrem Vorgesetzten entschuldigen.*
7. *Mein Vater arbeitet heute – wie fast jeden Freitag – wieder __________.*
8. *Beeile dich doch, sonst kommen wir zu ___________!*
9. *Ihr ______________ Ehemann ist ein guter Freund von mir gewesen.*
10. *Wir sind wie immer ___________ dran.*

Exercise 10.8

Translate the following sentences into German.

1. Why are you always **late** for breakfast?
2. Mum, can we stay up **late** tonight?
3. I'm sorry, the train **was late/delayed**.
4. They honoured the **late** Chancellor.
5. The team scored two **late** goals.

Chapter 11: Choosing the Right Preposition

One-minute overview

In this chapter we shall take a closer look at prepositions. Prepositions are words that are used before a noun to indicate the relation of this noun to some other part of the sentence; as in: *Die Vase steht **auf** dem Tisch.* – The vase is standing **on** the table. In this case the preposition *auf* (**on**) shows the **position** (or **location**) – *auf dem Tisch* (on the table) – of an object, namely the vase. Besides position, prepositions indicate relations such as **time**, **manner** and **direction.** The noun following the preposition is declined, i.e. put in a case. Whereas in English prepositions are always followed by the same case, in German prepositions can be followed by the accusative, the dative, or the genitive case. Consequently, when learning prepositions in German, it is necessary to memorize which case each particular preposition requires. This chapter will show you:

- how to translate the most important English prepositions;
- the case which must be used after the various prepositions;
- useful words and sentences needed at an airport or railway station;
- helpful words and sentences used in a course or lesson at school or college;
- words and sentences needed when travelling;
- what to say if you want to pay by credit card;
- how to ask the way;
- how to book a flight.

The correct translation of the preposition 'at'

'At' indicates position, location (usually public places), direction, time and activity.

'At' indicating position

an*, *am (= *an* + *dem*) or ***bei*, *beim*** (= bei + dem) + dative.

- *Ich studiere **an** der Universität.* – I'm studying **at** university.

- *Ich treffe dich/Sie dann morgen* ***an/bei*** *der Mensa.* – I'll meet you tomorrow **at** the canteen then.
- *Der Student sitzt* ***am/beim*** *Fenster.* – The student is sitting **at** the window.
- *Wir treffen uns* ***bei*** *ihrer Freundin.* – We'll meet **at** her friend's.
- *Der Zug kommt immer pünktlich* ***am*** *Bahnhof an.* – The train always arrives **at** the station on time.

'At' indicating location (usually public places or institutions)
auf + dative or ***in*** + dative.

- *Hans wechselt sein Geld* ***auf*** *der Bank.* – Hans changes his money **at** the bank.
- *Andrea kauft gerade Briefmarken* ***auf*** *der Post.* – Andrea is buying stamps **at** the post-office.
- *Wir landeten* ***auf*** *einem kleinen Flughafen.* – We landed **at** a small airport.
- *Er wohnt* ***in*** *einem großen Hotel.* – He stays **at** a big hotel.
- *Anna ist Schülerin* ***auf*** *dem Albert-Schweitzer-Gymnasium.* – Anna is a pupil **at** the Albert Schweitzer Grammar School.

But: *Sie* ***geht auf/in*** *das Gymnasium.* – She **goes to** grammar school. Since **motion** is involved, the preposition *auf* takes the **accusative** instead of the **dative**, while in English the preposition 'at' is replaced by the preposition 'to'.

'At' indicating direction: *auf* + accusative.
Usually used after verbs that indicate a direction, such as *zeigen* (to point at), *zielen* (to aim at), *schießen* (to shoot at), *werfen* (to throw at), and also *ein Buch aufschlagen* (to open a book at a page).

- *In seiner Rede zielte er* ***auf*** *das Missmanagement der Firma ab.* – In his speech he was aiming **at** the company's mismanagement.
- *Er richtet die Kamera* ***auf*** *die Löwen.* – He's aiming the camera **at** the lions.
- *Der Jäger schoss* ***auf*** *den Hirsch.* – The hunter shot **at** the deer.
- *Der Lehrer zeigt* ***auf*** *die Tafel.* – The teacher's pointing **at** the board.
- *Schlagt euer Buch* ***auf*** *der zweiten Seite auf!* – Open your books **at** page two!

'At' indicating time, *um* + accusative or *bei/im* + dative
Um + accusative indicates a specific time of day – on the clock, whereas

bei/im + dative indicates a period of time during which something happens or the beginning or end of a period of time (*Bei Ende/bei Anfang der Show...*).

- ***Um*** *acht Uhr beginnt der Unterricht.* – The lesson starts **at** eight o'clock.
- *Der Zug fährt* ***um*** *zehn Uhr ab.* – The train leaves **at** ten o'clock.
- *Sie ging* ***um*** *zwölf Uhr/****um*** *Mitternacht nach Hause.* – She went home **at** midnight.
- ***Im/Beim*** *Morgengrauen verließ er die Stadt.* – He left the town **at** dawn.
- ***In der/Bei*** *Nacht sind alle Katzen grau.* (a saying) – All cats are grey **at** night.
- ***Bei*** *Beginn der Vorlesung fehlten noch einige Studenten.* – **At** the beginning of the lecture some students were still missing.

'At' indicating activity: *bei/beim* or *in/im* + dative

Bei/beim is followed by an activity someone is doing at the moment, *in/im* by an activity you are good **at** or bad **at.**

- *Sie sind gerade* ***bei der*** *Arbeit/****beim*** *Arbeiten.* – They are **at** work right now.
- *Thomas ist gerade* ***beim*** *Hausaufgabenmachen.* – Thomas is **at** his homework right now.
- *Die Kinder sind* ***beim*** *Spielen.* – The children are **at** play.
- ***Im*** *Vokabellernen ist sie sehr schwach.* – She's very weak **at** learning her vocabulary.
- *Er ist sehr schlecht* ***im*** *Schwimmen.* – He's very bad *at* swimming.

Exercises 11.1

Fill in the appropriate prepositions.

1. *Sie musste _______ der Ampel warten.*
2. *Kannst du mich ________ Flughafen abholen?*
3. *_______ Eintritt der Dämmerung erreichte er seinen Zielort.*
4. *Er setzt sich im Park ________ eine Bank.*
5. *Wir wollen uns ________ Stefan treffen.*
6. *Er ist gerade ________ einem wichtigen Treffen.*
7. *________ Beginn der Vorstellung waren noch einige Plätze frei.*
8. *Sie steht jeden Morgen ________ sechs Uhr auf.*
9. *Seine Tochter geht _____ das Gymnasium.*
10. *Wir kamen schließlich ______ einem Bahnhof an.*

Exercise 11.2

Translate the following sentences.

1. The bus leaves **at** seven o'clock.
2. Maria is waiting **at** the bus stop.
3. Do you want to meet **at** Susanne's place?
4. He woke up **at** dawn.
5. She stayed the night **at** her friend's place.
6. Mark always wins **at** cards.
7. We stopped reading **at** page 34.
8. **At** midnight he left the house.
9. She is staying **at** a youth hostel.
10. His remarks were aimed **at** her unfriendly behaviour.

The correct translation of the preposition 'by'

'By' indicating time: *bis* + accusative

Bis refers to a **future point in time**, when something will have to be finished or done, but not later than this point.

- *Der Aufsatz muss* ***bis*** *zum nächsten Montag fertig sein.* – The essay has to be finished **by** next Monday.
- *Sie müssen das Hotelzimmer* ***bis*** *Freitag gebucht haben.* – You have to book the hotel room **by** Friday.
- ***Bis*** *Ende April bin ich wieder in Berlin.* – I'll be in Berlin again **by** the end of April.
- *Wird mein Auto* ***bis*** *Donnerstag repariert sein?* – Will my car be repaired **by** Thursday?
- *Werden Sie es* ***bis*** *14.00 Uhr geschafft haben?* – Will you be able to make it **by** 2 p.m.?

Not translated:

- *Morgen werde ich in Frankreich sein.* – **By** tomorrow I'll be in France.

'By' indicating position

an, am (occasionally bei, neben) + dative or + accusative if **motion** is involved.

- *Sie saß den ganzen Nachmittag* ***am*** *Telefon.* – She sat **by** the phone all afternoon.
- *Wir werden unsere Ferien* ***an*** *der See verbringen.* – We're going to spend our holiday **by** the sea.

- *Warum setzen wir uns nicht* ***ans*** *Fenster?* – Why don't we (go and) sit **by** the window? *(motion)*
- *Sie saß* ***neben*** *mir.* – She sat **by** me.
- *Komm, setz dich* ***neben*** *mich!* – Come and sit **by** me! (**motion**)

Note: if a verb involves an action which takes place in a **fixed position,** the preposition (e.g. *an* or *neben*) following the verb takes the **dative case.**
If a verb involves motion, the preposition following the verb takes the accusative case. **Examples:** • Er stand ***an dem*** Schalter. – He was standing **by the** counter. (**fixed position**) • Er ging ***an den*** Schalter. – He went **to the** counter. (**motion**) • Sie sitzt gerade ***neben mir***. – Right now she's sitting **by me.** (**fixed position**) • Sie kommt und setzt sich ***neben mich***. – She comes and sits down **by me.** (**motion**)

'By' indicating manner or means: *mit* (+ dative)

- *Wir fahren* ***mit*** *dem Auto.* – We're going **by** car.
- *Sie fährt* ***mit*** *dem Bus zur Arbeit.* – She goes to work **by** bus.
- *Ich möchte gerne* ***mit*** *Kreditkarte bezahlen.* – I'd like to pay **by** credit card.
- *Wir werden* ***mit*** *dem Flugzeug reisen.* – We are going to travel **by** plane.

'By' indicating agent or cause

von (+ dative); ***durch/per*** (+ **accusative**)

The noun following the preposition ***per*** does not take an article.

- *Dieser Roman wurde* ***von*** *Thomas Mann geschrieben.* – This novel was written **by** Thomas Mann.
- *Dort sieht man ein Bild* ***von*** *Turner.* – There you can see a painting **by** Turner.
- *Das Paket wurde* ***durch*** *die Post/****per*** *Post versandt.* – The parcel was sent **by** mail.
- *Die Verben, welche* ***durch*** *ein/****mit*** *einem Sternchen versehen sind, gehören zu den unregelmäßige Verben.* – The verbs which are indicated **by** an asterisk belong to the irregular verbs.

'By' meaning 'according to'

nach/gemäß (+ dative); *laut* (+ genitive or dative); ***an*** (+ accusative).

- *Menschen werden oft **nach** ihrem Äußeren beurteilt.* – People are often judged **by** their appearances.
- ***Nach** meiner Uhr ist es halb zehn.* – **By** my watch it is half past nine.
- ***Gemäß/Laut** den Bestimmungen von Artikel I ist die Würde des Menschen unantastbar.* – **By** the terms of Article I human dignity is inviolable.
- *Es ist immer wichtig, sich **an** die Regeln zu halten.* – It is always important to go **by** the rules.

Exercise 11.3

Fill in the appropriate prepositions.

1. *„Wilhelm Tell" ist ein Theaterstück _______ Schiller.*
2. *________ Berichten der ARD ist die Arbeitslosigkeit zurückgegangen.*
3. *Komm, wir setzen uns _______ den Fluss.*
4. *Wir fahren immer _______ dem Zug in den Urlaub.*
5. *_______ ihrer Sprache zu urteilen ist sie nicht in Deutschland aufgewachsen.*
6. *_______ Artikel 21 des Grundgesetzes wurde die Partei verboten.*
7. *Sie müssen mir _________ Freitag Bescheid gegeben haben.*
8. *Ich schicke Ihnen das Paket ________ Schiff.*
9. *_______ wann können Sie fertig sein?*
10. *Ich sende Ihnen die Informationen _________ E-Mail.*

Exercise 11.4

Translate the following sentences into German, using the appropriate preposition.

1. Let's go **by** bus.
2. You often categorize people **by** the clothes they wear.
3. This poem was written **by** Friedrich Schiller.
4. We are crossing the Channel **by** hovercraft.
5. Thomas has sent us his regards **by** e-mail.
6. The paper has to be finished **by** the end of the week.
7. We sat **by** the fireplace.
8. We are thinking about spending our holiday **by** the sea.
9. I always go to work **by** bike.
10. We will be finished **by** Tuesday.

The correct translation of the preposition 'in'

'in' indicating place or position

in + **dative**, or + **accusative** if **motion** is involved

- *Er wohnt* ***in*** *einem großen Haus.* – He lives **in** a big house.
- *Sie sitzt gerade* ***im*** *Speisesaal.* – She's sitting **in** the dining-room.
- *Gehen Sie* ***in*** *diese Richtung!* – Go **in** that direction! (**motion**)
- *Er steckte seine Schlüssel* ***in*** *die Tasche.* – He put his keys **in** his pocket. (***motion***)

'in' indicating position

auf + dative

- ***Auf*** *diesem Foto sieht man seine Familie.* – **In** this photo you can see his family.
- *Die Kinder spielen* ***auf*** *der Straße.* – The children play **in** the street.
- *Der Flüchtige war* ***auf*** *dem Lastwagen.* – The fugitive was **in** the lorry.

'in' indicating time

With dates and in the sense of *during*: ***in/im*** + dative. 'in' referring to a time of day (e.g. in the evening, in the beginning): ***am***.

- *Ich wurde* ***im*** *Jahre 1974 geboren.* – I was born **in** 1974.
- ***In/Während*** *der Regierungszeit von Gerhard Schröder wurden die Steuern gesenkt.* – **In/During** the reign of Gerhard Schröder taxes were cut.
- ***Am*** *Morgen verlässt er Frankfurt.* – He leaves Frankfurt **in** the morning.
- *Die Kinder spielen immer* ***am*** *Nachmittag.* – The children always play **in** the afternoon.
- ***Am*** *Anfang gelang der Mannschaft ein Tor.* – **In** (**At**) the beginning the team scored a goal.

'in' ('within') indicating an interval of time

in + dative; *innerhalb* + genitive.

- ***In/Innerhalb*** *einer Woche muss er den Aufsatz geschrieben haben.* – **In** a week's time/**Within** a week he must have written the essay.
- ***In*** *kurzer Zeit kam ein Krankenwagen zur Unfallstelle.* – **In** a short time an ambulance arrived at the scene of the accident.

'in' indicating manner or condition

in/mit + dative.

- *Die Menschen dort leben* **im** *Luxus/***in** *Armut.* – The people there live **in** luxury/**in** poverty.
- *Der Bahnhof ist* **in** *gutem Zustand.* – The railway-station is **in** a good condition.
- *Stellen Sie sich bitte* **in** *einer Reihe auf!* – Please stand **in** a row.
- *Er spricht immer* **mit** *sehr leiser Stimme.* – He always speaks **in** a very soft voice.
- *Kann ich* **mit/in** *Euro bezahlen?* – Can I pay **in** euros?

Exercise 11.5

Fill in the appropriate preposition.

1. *Er kommt _______ Abend immer sehr spät von der Arbeit zurück.*
2. *Bitte sprechen Sie _______ lauter Stimme!*
3. *Wir fahren _______ Juni nach Deutschland.*
4. *Ich treffe ihn ________ Vormittag.*
5. *Sie können nicht _______ Dollar bezahlen.*
6. *Meine Frau ist _______ diesem Bild zu sehen.*
7. *________ eines Monats muss er die Arbeit geschrieben haben.*
8. *________ Jahre 2003 machte ich mein Examen.*
9. *Viele Menschen sind _______ den Straßen.*
10. *Herr Schmidt sitzt ______ Wartezimmer.*

Exercise 11.6

Translate the following sentences.

1. He put the machinery **in** the lorry.
2. He will arrive **in** Stuttgart **in** the morning.
3. She will finish her studies **in** August.
4. My uncle lives **in** a small flat.
5. **In** the summer it's always very hot here.
6. The children are playing **in** the garden.
7. They were **in** a state of shock.
8. Thomas learnt to drive **in** three months.
9. Many people **in** this district live **in** poverty.
10. He must have moved **in** a week's time.

The correct translation of the preposition 'on'

'On' indicating place or position

an/am/auf + dative, + accusative if **motion** is involved.

- *Wir sind gerade **am** (**an** + **dem**) Strand.* – We're **on** the beach at the moment.
- *Wir gehen **an den** Strand.* – We are going **to the** beach. (**motion**)

> Since **motion** is involved, the preposition ***auf*** takes the **accusative** instead of the **dative**, while in English the preposition **'at'** is replaced by the preposition **'to'**.

- *Wir sind gerade **auf** Seite 27.* – At the moment we're **on** page 27.
- *Die Vase steht **auf** dem Tisch.* – The vase is standing **on** the table.
- *Er stellte die Vase **auf** den Tisch.* – He put the vase **on** the table. (**motion**)

'On' indicating a vertical surface

(e.g. wall, board, etc.) or **parts of the body**: ***an/am*** **+ dative, + accusative** if **motion** is involved.

- *Die Informationen stehen **an** der Tafel.* – The pieces of information are **on** the board.
- *Er hat einen blauen Fleck **am** Kopf.* – He has got a bruise **on** his head.
- *Er hat einen Ring **am** Finger.* – He has got a ring **on** his finger.
- *Das Bild hängt **an der** Wand.* – The picture is hanging **on** the wall.
- *Er hängte das Bild **an die** Wand.* – He hung the picture **on** the wall. (**motion**)

'On' indicating means

von/mit + dative.

- *Er lebt **von** seinen Ersparnissen.* – He lives **on** his savings.
- *Sie ernähren sich **von** Reis.* – They live **on** rice.
- *Die Heizung wird **mit** Öl betrieben.* – The heating runs **on** oil.
- *Sie fuhren **mit** dem Zug.* – They went **on** the train.

'On' indicating time

an/am + dative.

- *Sie treffen sich immer **am** Samstag zum Fußballspielen.* – They always meet **on** Saturdays to play football.

- *Am ersten Juni fängt die Schule an.* – School begins **on** June the first.

'On' indicating an activity

in/im, an/am/auf + **dative, accusative** if **motion** is involved.

- *Sie ist gerade **im** Urlaub.* – She's **on** holiday at the moment.
- *Sie geht **in den** Urlaub.* – She's going **on** holiday. (**motion**)
- *Er ist samstags häufig **im** Dienst.* – He's often **on** duty **on** Saturdays.
- *Wir befinden uns **im** Streik.* – We are **on** strike.
- *Ich arbeite **an** einem neuen Projekt.* – I'm working **on** a new project.
- *Er ist **am** Telefonieren.* – He is **on** the phone.
- *Komm doch mit **auf** unsere Expedition!* – Join us **on** our expedition! ***(motion)***

'On' indicating at the time of

bei + **dative**.

- ***Bei*** seiner Ankunft in Deutschland war das Wetter schlecht. – **On** his arrival in Germany the weather was bad.

Exercise 11.7

Fill in the appropriate preposition.

1. *Sie hat eine Narbe _______ ihrem linken Arm.*
2. *Das Buch liegt _______ dem Tisch.*
3. *Er hängt das Gemälde ________ den Nagel.*
4. *Er hat _______ vierten Mai Geburtstag.*
5. *Sie legt das Buch _______ den Stuhl.*
6. *_______ meiner Abreise verabschiedeten mich viele Freunde.*
7. *Willst du mit ______ unseren Ausflug kommen?*
8. *Wir wollen morgen _______ den Urlaub fahren.*
9. *______ Sonntag wollen wir uns in der Stadt treffen.*
10. *Können Sie diese Aufgabe _______ die Tafel schreiben?*

Exercise 11.8

Translate the following sentences.

1. When do you go **on** holiday?
2. **On** examination the doctor didn't find anything.
3. The teacher wrote the words **on** the board.
4. He isn't able to join us, he's **on** duty.
5. **On** Tuesday we are going to visit our parents.
6. We were **on** page 34.

7. They live **on** eggs.
8. The heating runs **on** gas.
9. Write the answer to this exercise **on** a sheet of paper.
10. What project are you working **on**?

The correct translation of the preposition 'to'

'To' indicating direction

1. 'to' followed by a **person's name/shop/places** in town (e.g. streets, squares, etc.): ***zu/zur/zum*** + dative.

- *Du musst* ***zum*** *Arzt gehen.* – You have to go **to** the doctor's.
- *Wie komme ich* ***zum*** *Bahnhof/***zur** *Apotheke?* – How do I get *to* the station/***to*** the chemist's?
- *Können Sie mir den Weg* ***zum*** *Marktplatz/***zum** *Gericht/***zur** *Luisenstraße sagen?* – Can you tell me the way **to** the market square/ court/Luisenstraße.
- *Jeden Mittwoch gehe ich* ***zum*** *Metzger.* – Every Wednesday I go **to** the butcher.

2. 'To' followed by a **place/place to visit/institution/big stores/certain countries: *in/ins* + accusative.**

- *Wann gehst du* ***ins*** *Bett?* – When do you go **to** bed?
- *Heute Abend möchte ich* ***ins*** *Theater/***ins** *Museum/***in** *die Oper gehen.* – I would like to go **to** the theatre/museum/opera tonight.
- *Steffi geht noch* ***zur/in*** *die Schule.* – Steffi still goes **to** school.
- *Er geht jeden Sonntag* ***zur/in die*** *Kirche.* – He goes **to** church every Sunday.
- *Morgen werden wir mit dem Zug* ***in die*** *Schweiz/***in die** *Niederlande fahren.* – Tomorrow we are going to go by train **to** Switzerland/**to** the Netherlands.

3. **'To'** followed by a **place name** (villages, towns, cities, most countries, continents etc.) or **directions** (e.g. left/right/east/west): ***nach*** **+ dative.**

- *Wir wollen morgen* ***nach*** *Berlin fahren.* – We want to go **to** Berlin tomorrow.
- *Wir werden mit dem Zug* ***nach*** *Deutschland fahren.* – We are going to go by train **to** Germany.

- *Am Montag werden wir **nach** Amerika fliegen.* – On Monday we are going to fly **to** America.
- *Ich möchte einen Flug **nach** Frankfurt buchen.* – I would like to book a flight **to** Frankfurt.
- *Die Vögel fliegen **nach** Süden.* – The birds are flying **to** the south.

'To' meaning until/as far as

bis + **accusative.**

- *Du musst **bis** 10 zählen.* – You have to count up **to** 10.
- *Es sind 40 **bis** 50 Leute da.* – There are 40 **to** 50 people.
- ***Bis** München sind es 100 km.* – It's 100 km **to** Munich.

'To' not translated

In many cases the preposition **'to'** is not translated in German when an **indirect object** is used with the dative case.

- *Ich möchte **dir/Ihnen*** (= indirect objects, dative) *ein Geschenk überreichen.* – I would like to give a present **to you.**
- *Geben Sie **mir** das, bitte!* – Give it **to me**, please!
- ***Wem** hast du es gegeben?* – Who did you give it *to*?

Exercise 11.9

Put in the appropriate preposition.

1. *Wir wollen im Sommer ______ Skandinavien reisen.*
2. *Mein Sohn geht noch _______ den Kindergarten.*
3. *Können Sie mir den Weg ________ Stadion sagen?*
4. *Wie viele Kilometer sind es noch ______ Köln?*
5. *Ich muss dringend ______ Zahnarzt gehen.*
6. *Wir sollten wieder mal _______ Kino gehen.*
7. *Wie kommen wir am besten ______ Nürnberg?*
8. *Wir laufen im Moment ______ Westen.*
9. *Komm, wir gehen _______ diese Kneipe.*
10. *Kannst du auf Deutsch ________ 100 zahlen?*

Exercise 11.10

Translate the following sentences.

1. We have to go **to** the greengrocer's.
2. It's 50 kilometres **to** Frankfurt.
3. I want to go **to** bed now.

4. Can I give this ticket **to** you?
5. We are expecting 20 **to** 30 guests.
6. When do you go **to** Berlin?
7. Let's go **to** the museum tomorrow.
8. I said **to** him he should get up earlier.
9. He wants to travel **to** Canada next month.
10. Thomas goes **to** primary school.

Chapter 12: Choosing the Right Conjunction

One-minute overview

This chapter deals with conjunctions. A conjunction (e.g.: *und* – and, *aber* – but) connects words or clauses. We differentiate between **coordinating** and **subordinating conjunctions.** A coordinating conjunction links main clauses. Since main clauses are equal and parallel, coordinating conjunctions have no effect on the word order of the main clause they introduce. A subordinating conjunction connects a main clause and a subordinate clause. A subordinate clause is always dependent on the main clause it is connected to and therefore cannot stand on its own. In consequence the word order of the subordinate clause changes. Contrary to the English word order, in German the conjugated verb is put in final position. Example: *Ich weiß, dass er in dieser Stadt **wohnt**.* – I know that he *lives* in this town. This chapter will show you:

- some important coordinating and subordinating conjunctions and their usage;
- the word order in a subordinate clause introduced by a subordinating conjunction;
- how to get important information about trains (departure times, stops, dining-car, etc.);
- how to reserve seats on a train or aeroplane.

Coordinating conjunctions

But – *aber, doch*

The coordinating conjunctions *aber* and *doch*, which are used interchangeably, often connect two contrasting clauses. The clause introduced by *aber* or *doch* limits the preceding statement:

- *Er hat wenig Geld,* ***aber*** *seine Eltern sind reich.* – He hasn't got much money **but** his parents are rich.
- *Er hatte einen Verkehrsunfall, blieb unverletzt,* ***doch*** *das Auto war ein Totalschaden.* – He had a car accident, wasn't injured, **but** the car was a write-off.

Note: if the two clauses have the same subject and the same conjugated verb, subject and conjugated verb following the conjunction are usually omitted:

- *Der kleine Junge hat sich das Knie weh getan,* ***aber*** *(er hat) nicht geweint.* – The little boy hurt his knee **but** (he) didn't cry.
- *Die Lehrerin ist streng,* ***doch*** *(sie ist) gerecht.* – The teacher is strict **but** (she is) fair.

But – *sondern*

Sondern connects two clauses, in which the preceding clause consists of a statement made negative by *nicht* (not) or *nie* (never):

- *Sie hat das Zimmer nicht gebucht,* ***sondern*** *ihr Mann hat es getan.* – She didn't book the room **but** her husband did it.
- *Er zahlte nicht in bar,* ***sondern*** *überwies den Geldbetrag durch seine Bank.* – He didn't pay cash **but** transferred the amount of money through his bank.

Note: here again, if the two clauses have the same subject and the same conjugated verb, they are omitted in the clause introduced by *sondern*:

- *Er ist nicht nur ein guter Wissenschaftler,* ***sondern*** *(er ist) auch ein guter Lehrer.* – He is not only a good scientist **but** also a good teacher.
- *Das Wetter war nicht nur regnerisch,* ***sondern*** *auch kalt.* – The weather wasn't just rainy **but** also cold.
- *Wir fahren nicht nach Deutschland,* ***sondern*** *nach Frankreich.* – We're not going to Germany **but** to France.

Exercise 12.1

Connect the following sentences with the appropriate conjunction.

1. *Morgen könnt ihr sie nicht sehen, __________ erst übermorgen.*
2. *Sie haben zwar Recht, _________ wir müssen den Plan trotzdem ändern.*
3. *Beim Handballspiel steht es nicht 13:12, _________ es steht 14:12.*
4. *Sie ist nicht nur gut in Chemie, __________ auch in Physik.*
5. *Ich verdiene zwar viel Geld, _____ ich bin nicht zufrieden mit meinem Beruf*
6. *Er hat nicht nur schlechte Noten in Englisch, __________ auch in Deutsch und Kunst.*
7. *Die Schuhe sind schön, _________ leider zu klein.*
8. *Wir gehen heute Abend nicht in das Theater, __________ ins Kino.*

Exercise 12.2

Translate the following sentences into German.

1. *Her seminars are not only instructive* ***but*** *also funny.*
2. *He is not a very likeable person,* ***but*** *his teaching is instructive.*
3. *She is a rather unfriendly person* ***but*** *her husband is nice.*
4. *We're not taking the bus* ***but*** *a taxi.*

Subordinating conjunctions (I): *Wann, als, wenn*

Note that in German the conjugated verb used in the subordinate clause is put in final position.

'When' – *wann*

You use *wann* to introduce an indirect question in which you refer to a time at which something happens or happened. Here the interrogative or question word *wann* functions as a subordinate conjunction:

- *Sie wusste nicht,* ***wann*** *sie zurückkommen würde.* (Direct question: ***Wann*** *würde sie zurückkommen?*) – She didn't know **when** she was coming back.
- *Würden Sie mir bitte sagen,* ***wann*** *Sie abreisen?* – Would you please tell me **when** you will be leaving?
- *Können Sie mir sagen,* ***wann*** *der nächste Zug nach Berlin abfährt?* – Can you tell me **when** the next train to Berlin departs?
- *Der Termin,* ***wann*** *die Wahlen stattfinden, steht noch nicht fest.* – The day **when** the elections are held has not been fixed yet.

'When' – *als*

You use *als* to introduce a subordinate clause in which you mention the specific time or period at which a single action took place in the past:

- *Er verließ das College,* ***als*** *er 22 Jahre alt war.* – He left college **when** he was 22.
- *Die Mutter freute sich,* ***als*** *ihr Sohn das Examen machte.* – The mother was glad **when** her son passed the exam.

Note: when you put the subordinate clause in front position, the word order of the ensuing main clause changes. Subject and verb are inverted putting the conjugated verb (in bold type) in first position:

Als *der Student mit dem Lesen fertig war,* ***verließ*** *er die Bibliothek.* – **When** the student had finished reading, he went out of the library.

'When' – *wenn*

You use *wenn* in a conditional sentence that refers to a certain time in the present or in the future (i.e. could also be translated as 'if'):

- *Ich gehe joggen,* ***wenn*** *das Wetter schöner wird.* – I'll go jogging **when** the weather gets better.
- *Wir müssen ins Theater gehen,* ***wenn*** *du uns besuchen kommst.* – We must go to the theatre **when** you come and visit us.
- *Sie müssen rechts fahren,* ***wenn*** *Sie in Deutschland mit dem Auto unterwegs sind.* – You have to drive on the right-hand side **when** you're travelling by car in Germany.
- ***Wenn*** *ich etwas Freizeit habe, verbringe ich sie häufig beim Fischen.* – **When** I have some free time, I often spend it fishing.

It is possible to omit the subordinate conjunction; as a result of that the word order changes, inversion takes place and the conjugated verb (in bold type) is put in front position:

- ***Wird*** *das Wetter schön, gehe ich joggen.*
- ***Kommst*** *du uns besuchen,* ***müssen*** *wir ins Theater gehen.*
- ***Habe*** *ich etwas Freizeit,* ***verbringe*** *ich sie häufig beim Fischen.*

Exercise 12.3

Connect the following sentences with the appropriate conjunction.

1. *Manfred will dann in die Vereinigten Staaten fliegen, ______ er etwas mehr Geld hat.*
2. *Es flossen Tränen, _______ sich Ottmar von Anette verabschiedete.*
3. *Ich weiß nicht, _______ ich ihr das letzte Mal einen Brief geschrieben habe.*
4. *Ich müsste noch von Ihnen wissen, ________ Sie geboren wurden.*
5. *_____ ich mein Abitur bestanden habe, möchte ich Jura studieren.*
6. *_____ Wilfried und Ulrike am Bahnhof ankamen, wurden sie freundlich begrüßt.*
7. *Ich weiß noch nicht genau, ________ ich am Bahnhof ankommen werde.*
8. *________ ich 25 Jahre alt war, beendete ich mein Studium.*
9. *Wir werden nicht wandern gehen, ________ es regnen sollte.*
10. *______ Stefan die Tränen in ihren Augen sah, wusste er, dass sie ihn liebte.*

Exercise 12.4

Translate the following sentences.

1. Could you tell me **when** you will be back?
2. **When** the teacher entered the classroom, the pupils stopped talking.
3. I feel glad **when** I can spend some time with my wife.
4. **When** Thomas arrived at his friends' house, he received a friendly welcome.
5. We have to play this new game **when** you come and visit us in June.

Subordinating conjunctions (II): *ob, wenn, falls*

'If'/'whether' – *ob*

You use *ob* to introduce an indirect question where the answer is either yes or no. In English 'if' and 'whether' are interchangeable:

- *Wissen Sie,* ***ob*** *dieser Zug in Hamburg hält?* – Do you know **if/ whether** this train stops in Hamburg?
- *Können Sie mir sagen,* ***ob*** *es in diesem Zug einen Speisewagen gibt?* – Could you please tell me **if** there is a dining-car on this train?
- *Ich hätte gerne gewusst,* ***ob*** *ich noch zwei Plätze im ICE nach Berlin reservieren kann.* – I would like to know **if** it is possible to reserve two seats on the Intercity (train) to Berlin.

'If' – *wenn, falls*

You use *wenn* or *falls* in a conditional sentence. *Wenn* and *falls* are interchangeable.

- ***Wenn/Falls*** *ich es mir leisten kann, werde ich mir eine Villa kaufen.* – **If** I can afford it, I will buy a villa.
- ***Wenn*** *Sie es eilig haben, können Sie als Nächstes drankommen.* – **If** you are in a hurry, you can come next.
- *Wir wären pünktlich gewesen,* ***wenn*** *der Zug keine Verspätung gehabt hätte.* – We would have been on time, **if** the train hadn't been delayed.

Here the subordinate conjunction can be omitted. Remember that the conjugated verb (in bold type) is put in front position:

- ***Kann*** *ich es mir leisten, werde ich mir eine Villa kaufen.*

Exercise 12.3

Connect the following sentences with the appropriate conjunction.

1. *Ich würde dies nicht tun, ________ ich an deiner Stelle wäre.*
2. *Können Sie mir jetzt schon sagen, ________ Sie morgen zum Frühstück kommen?*
3. *Ich weiß nicht, ______ meine Freundin wirklich kommt.*
4. ________ *Sie sich noch anders entscheiden sollten, rufen Sie mich bitte an.*
5. ________ *er wirklich dazu in der Lage ist, kann ich zum jetzigen Zeitpunkt nicht sagen.*
6. ________ *du eine bessere Idee hast, gib mir bitte Bescheid.*
7. *Ich möchte gerne von dir wissen, _______ du mich wirklich liebst.*
8. *Der Arzt konnte mir nicht genau sagen, _______ ich ins Krankenhaus eingeliefert werden muss.*
9. ________ *du nichts anderes vorhast, kannst du ja bei uns vorbeikommen.*
10. ________ *du willst, kannst du mich in den Sommerferien besuchen kommen.*

Exercise 12.6

Translate the following sentences into German.

1. I'll phone you **if** I'm late.
2. Can you tell me **if** the weather will be fine tomorrow?
3. **If** you want to go to the cinema, just give me a ring.
4. Do you know **if** this bus stops at the town hall?
5. **If** you need some more help, just let me know and I'll take care of it.

Subordinating conjunctions (III): *als, da, wie, obwohl*

'As'/'when' – *als*

You use *als* to introduce a subordinate clause that describes an action that runs parallel to the one expressed in the main clause. In English 'as' has the same meaning as 'while' or 'when':

- *Als ich noch ein Kind war, bin ich oft bei meinen Großeltern gewesen.* – **When** I was still a child I often stayed at my grandparents'.
- *Als her älter wurde, ließ seine Sehkraft nach.* – **As** he grew older his eyesight deteriorated.
- *Als wir in das Kino gingen, trafen wir einen alten Freund.* – **As** we entered the cinema we met an old friend of ours.

'As'/'since' – *da*

You use *da* to introduce a subordinate clause in which you state a reason:

- ***Da*** *die Karten für die Oper sehr teuer sind, können es sich nur reiche Leute leisten dort hinzugehen.* – **As** the tickets for the opera are very expensive only rich people can afford to go there.
- *Ich möchte meinen Urlaub in Deutschland verbringen,* ***da*** *ich mich sehr für die Kultur dieses Landes interessiere.* – I would like to spend my holidays in Germany **as** I'm very interested in the culture of this country.
- ***Da*** *unser Auto kaputt war, mussten wir zu Fuß gehen.* – **As** our car was broken we had to go on foot.

'As'/'like' – *wie*

You use *wie* to introduce a clause that describes an action or a situation that is similar to the one expressed in the main clause:

- *Er stellte sich der Gruppe vor,* ***wie*** *das die Frau vor ihm getan hatte.* – He introduced himself to the group **as** the woman before him had done.
- ***Wie*** *ich bereits sagte, dieser Plan muss verändert werden.* – **As** I said before this plan has to be altered.
- *Im Jahr 2002 ging ich nach Deutschland um in einer Bank zu arbeiten,* ***wie*** *es mein Bruder im Jahr davor auch schon getan hat.* – In 2002 I went to Germany to work in a bank **as** did my brother in the year before.

'As'/'although' – *obwohl*

Obwohl is used when you mention something which you accept is true but which nevertheless does not affect the main thing you are saying:

- *Ich werde ihn nicht heiraten,* ***obwohl*** *er reich ist.* – Rich **as** he is (Although he's rich), I won't marry him.
- ***Obwohl*** *er noch sehr jung ist, spielt Mark bereits bei den Erwachsenen Fußball.* – Young **as** he is, Mark plays already football with the grown-ups.
- ***Obwohl*** *er sehr dumm sein mag, weiß er, wie man mit Tieren umgeht.* – Stupid **as** he may be, he knows how to treat animals.

Exercises 12.7

Connect the following sentences with the appropriate conjunction.

1. *Wir werden erst am Abend bei Ihnen eintreffen, ________ ich Ihnen bereits mitteilte.*
2. *Er ist ein sehr erfahrener und sachkundiger Lehrer, ________ er noch recht jung ist.*
3. *________ ich im Moment wenig Zeit habe, werde ich leider nicht mitkommen können.*
4. *Wir hörten ihm gespannt zu, ________ er uns eine spannende Geschichte aus seinem Leben erzählte.*
5. *________ ich ja bereits von Ihrer Frau erfahren haben, können Sie leider nicht an unserem Fest teilnehmen.*
6. *Seine Tochter kann schon sehr gut sprechen, ________ sie noch sehr klein ist.*
7. *________ bereits besprochen, können wir dem Entwurf vorbehaltlos zustimmen.*
8. *________ Max krank war, ging er zur Arbeit.*
9. *________ wir durch Deutschland reisten, besuchten wir viele schöne Städte.*
10. *________ wir noch viel lernen müssen, sollten wir jetzt den Unterricht fortsetzen.*

Exercise 12.8

Translate the following sentences into German.

1. **As** I told you yesterday, we will take the train to Frankfurt.
2. **As** we were watching television, the children were playing outside.
3. **As** we went by bike, we weren't able to take a lot of clothing with us.
4. Strong **as** he was, he wasn't able to win the fight.
5. **As** he was very good at playing football, he decided to become a professional.

Answers to exercises

Chapter 1

Exercise 1.1

2. *Eifersucht schafft Unfriede.*
3. *Fischer haben/besitzen Boote.*
4. *Lehrer unterrichten Schüler.*
5. *Häuser haben Dächer.*
6. *Polizisten jagen Verbrecher.*
7. *Computer ersetzen Menschen.*
8. *Schiffe transportieren Güter.*
9. *Nächstenliebe verbreitet Frieden.*
10. *Wolken schenken Regen.*
11. *Thomas liebt Kathrin./Kathrin liebt Thomas.*
12. *Herr Müller baut Brücken.*

Exercise 1.2.

2. *Der Student dankt dem Professor.*
3. *Der Junge gefällt dem Mädchen.*
4. *Die Schüler antworten dem Lehrer.*
5. *Das Haus hat eine Garage.*
6. *Der Polizist verfolgt einen Dieb.*
7. *Das Mädchen umarmt/besucht eine Freundin.*
8. *Das Spiel gefällt dem Kind.*
9. *Der Vogel frisst den Wurm.*
10. *Das Auto überholt den Radfahrer.*
11. *Die Familie besucht einen Zoo.*
12. *Die Tochter gehorcht der Mutter.*

Exercise 1.3

2. *Dem Professor dankt der Student.*
3. *Dem Mädchen gefällt der Junge.*
4. *Dem Lehrer antworten die Schüler.*
5. *Eine Garage hat das Haus.*
6. *Einen Dieb verfolgt der Polizist.*
7. *Eine Freundin umarmt das Mädchen.*
8. *Dem Kind gefällt das Spiel.*
9. *Den Wurm frisst der Vogel.*
10. *Den Radfahrer überholt das Auto.*
11. *Einen Zoo besucht die Familie.*
12. *Der Mutter gehorcht die Tochter.*

Exercise 1.4

2. *Der Lehrer gibt der Schülerin einen Rat.*
3. *Die Professorin macht der Studentin Mut.*
4. *Der Vater gibt dem Kind die Fahrkarte.*
5. *Andrea verkauft dem Arbeitskollegen das Auto.*
6. *Der Verkäufer macht dem Kunden ein Angebot.*
7. *Die Frau sendet der Tante eine Postkarte.*
8. *Der Junge gibt der Freundin ein Geschenk.*
9. *Der Lehrer macht dem Schüler ein Kompliment.*
10. *Die Direktorin überreicht dem Mitarbeiter eine Urkunde.*

Exercise 1.5

2. *Der Schülerin gibt der Lehrer einen Rat.*
3. *Der Studentin macht die Professorin Mut.*
4. *Dem Kind gibt der Vater die Fahrkarte.*
5. *Dem Arbeitskollegen verkauft Andrea das Auto.*
6. *Dem Kunden macht der Verkäufer ein Angebot.*
7. *Der Tante sendet die Frau eine Postkarte.*
8. *Der Freundin gibt der Junge ein Geschenk.*
9. *Dem Schüler macht der Lehrer ein Kompliment.*
10. *Dem Mitarbeiter überreicht die Direktorin eine Urkunde.*

Exercise 1.6

der alte Mann; dem alten Mann; den alten Mann
die junge Frau; der jungen Frau; die junge Frau
das treue Tier; dem treuen Tier; das treue Tier
der große Baum; dem großen Baum; den großen Baum
die gute Schülerin; der guten Schülerin; die gute Schülerin
das helle/harte/frische Brot; dem hellen Brot; das helle Brot

Exercise 1.7

3. *Die hilfsbereite Professorin macht der ängstlichen Studentin großen Mut.*
4. *Der fürsorgliche Vater gibt dem kleinen Kind die neue Fahrkarte.*
5. *Die kluge Andrea verkauft dem neuen Arbeitskollegen das alte Auto.*
6. *Der nette Verkäufer macht dem langjährigen Kunden ein gutes Angebot.*
7. *Die junge Frau sendet der lieben Tante eine wunderschöne Postkarte.*
8. *Der liebe Junge gibt der hübschen Freundin ein besonderes Geschenk.*
9. *Der angesehene Lehrer macht dem fleißigen Schüler ein nettes Kompliment.*
10. *Die beliebte Direktorin überreicht dem langjährigen Mitarbeiter eine schöne Urkunde.*

Exercise 1.8

2. *Er gibt ihr einen Rat.*
3. *Sie macht ihr Mut.*
4. *Er gibt ihm die Fahrkarte.*
5. *Sie verkauft ihm das Auto.*
6. *Er macht ihm ein Angebot.*
7. *Sie sendet ihr eine Postkarte.*
8. *Er gibt ihr ein Geschenk.*
9. *Er macht ihm ein Kompliment.*
10. *Sie überreicht ihm eine Urkunde.*

Exercise 1.9

3. *Die Professorin macht* ***ihrer*** *Studentin Mut.*
4. *Der Vater gibt* ***seinem*** *Kind die Fahrkarte.*
5. *Andrea verkauft* ***ihrem*** *Arbeitskollegen das Auto.*
6. *Der Verkäufer macht* ***seinem*** *Kunden ein Angebot.*
7. *Die Frau sendet* ***ihrer*** *Tante eine Postkarte.*
8. *Der Junge gibt* ***seiner*** *Freundin ein Geschenk.*
9. *Der Lehrer macht* ***seinem*** *Schüler ein Kompliment.*
10. *Die Direktorin überreicht* ***ihrem*** *Mitarbeiter eine Urkunde.*

Exercise 1.10

1. *Sie läuft zügig nach Hause.*
2. *Wir fahren häufig nach Berlin.*
3. *Sie spielt sehr gut Gitarre.*
4. *Er spricht sehr leise.*
5. *Herr Müller kommt häufig zu spät.*

Exercise 1.11

1. *Müde geht er ins Bett.*
2. *Schnell fährt der Zug.*
3. *Konzentriert macht sie ihre Arbeit.*
4. *Fröhlich geht er auf die Arbeit.*
5. *Manchmal gehe ich ins Kino.*

Exercise 1.12

2. *Er* ***stellt sich unter den Baum.***
3. *Der erfahrene Arzt* ***untersucht*** *das Kind* ***im Krankenhaus.***
4. *Der Professor* ***lobt*** *die Studentin* ***wegen ihrer guten Leistungen.***
5. *Der Lehrer* ***bittet*** *die lauten Schüler* ***um Ruhe.***
6. *Sie* ***stellt*** *das Fahrrad* ***gegen die Wand.***
7. *Die Urlauberin* ***verlässt*** *die Region* ***trotz des guten Wetters.***
8. *Ich* ***bewohne*** *dieses Haus* ***seit fünf Jahren.***
9. *Er* ***küsst*** *seine Freundin* ***auf den Mund.***
10. *Die junge Frau* ***wäscht*** *ihre langen Haare* ***mit einem teuren Shampoo.***

Exercise 1.13

1. ***Während*** *er nach Hause gehen konnte, musste ich leider bleiben.*
2. *Wir fahren mit dem Bus nach Hause,* ***weil*** *es in Strömen regnet.*
3. ***Wenn*** *du anrufst, fahre ich sofort los.*
4. *Sie ging in die Schule,* ***obwohl*** *sie krank war.*
5. *Mein Bruder ist Lehrer* ***und*** *meine Schwester studiert Jura.*
6. *Wir öffnen immer das Garagentor,* ***damit*** *Vater das Auto in die Garage fahren kann.*
7. *Wir wollten ins Kino gehen,* ***aber*** *wir bekamen keine Karten mehr.*
8. ***Als*** *das Glas umfiel, stand ich auf.*
9. *Es dauert noch etwas,* ***bis*** *der Zug abfährt.*
10. *Die Schauspieler verneigten sich,* ***bevor*** *sie die Bühne verließen.*

Chapter 2

Exercise 2.1

1. *Wann* ***beginnt*** *das Fußballspiel?*
2. *Der Mann* ***telefoniert*** *gerade.*
3. *Ich* ***studiere*** *in Köln.*
4. *Du* ***bleibst*** *zuhause.*
5. *Was* ***trinkt*** *ihr?*
6. *Das Baby* ***schreit*** *sehr laut.*
7. *Ich* ***glaube*** *an Gott.*
8. *Die Frau* ***liebt*** *ihren Mann.*
9. *Du* ***schreibst*** *gute Aufsätze.*

Exercise 2.2

1. *Ich* ***arbeite*** *in einem Supermarkt.*
2. *Seine Nase* ***blutet*** *sehr stark.*
3. *Wie* ***findest*** *du den Weg?*
4. *Wir* ***beobachten*** *gerade die Tiere.*
5. *Auf wen* ***wartet*** *ihr?*
6. *Ich* ***begegne*** *ihm regelmäßig.*
7. *Du* ***zeichnest*** *sehr schöne Portraits.*
8. *Das Mädchen* ***öffnet*** *das Buch.*
9. *Er* ***atmet*** *sehr schwer.*
10. *Die Mädchen* ***reden*** *sehr viel.*

Exercise 2.3

1. *Wie* ***heißt*** *du?*
2. *Warum* ***sitzt*** *du hier?*
3. *Warum* ***grüßt*** *du nicht diesen Mann?*
4. *Du* ***tanzt*** *gut.*
5. *Warum* ***hasst*** *du diese Frau?*

Exercise 2.4

1. _Ich **sammle** Briefmarken._
2. _Wir **klettern** in den Alpen._
3. _Das Kind **füttert** die Vögel._
4. _Die Touristen **bewundern** die alte Kirche._
5. _Ich **stehe** vor der Haustür und klingle._
6. _**Wandert** ihr am Sonntag?_
7. _Ich **behandl**e meine Patienten mit großer Fürsorge._
8. _Du **lächelst** ihn an._
9. _Ich **bewundere** seine Ausdauer._
10. _Wir **ändern** den Plan._

Exercise 2.5

1. _Sie **schlägt** den Hund._
2. _Wo **schläfst** du?_
3. _Was **isst** du?_
4. _Der Mann **trägt** einen Mantel._
5. _Welches Buch **empfiehlst** du mir?_
6. _Der Einbrecher **stiehlt** Juwelen._
7. _Was **liest** du?_
8. _Ein Wunder **geschieht** in dem Dorf._
9. _Wie weit **wirft** der Sportler?_
10. _Er **gibt** ihm etwas zu trinken._

Exercise 2.6

1. _Sie **ist/sind** nicht zuhause._
2. _Ich **habe** ein Auto._
3. _Du **wirst** ganz rot._
4. _Er **weiß** sehr viel._
5. _**Sind** Sie auch Lehrer?_
6. _Wir **sind** eine Familie._
7. _Die Kinder **haben** Durst._
8. _Ich **tue** nur meine Pflicht._
9. _Ihr **seid** gute Sportler._
10. _Du **hast** schöne Haare._
11. _Was **tut** ihr mir an?_
12. _Dem Kind **wird** kalt._
13. _Die Schüler **haben** Ferien._
14. _Ihr **werdet** wieder gesund._
15. _Woher **weißt** du das?_
16. _**Habt** ihr zwei Hunde?_

Exercise 2.7

1. _Er **spielte** gerne Fußball._
2. _Ich **bezahlte** mit Kreditkarte._

3. *Wir **brauchten** ein Auto.*
4. *Du **entdecktest** eine völlig neue Welt.*
5. *Ich **bestellte** ein Bier.*
6. *Ihr **besuchtet** eure Großmutter.*
7. *Sie **dankten** ihrer Gastfamilie.*
8. *Sie **hörte** gerne klassische Musik.*
9. *Er **lernte** Deutsch.*
10. *Ihr **wohntet** in Frankfurt.*

Exercise 2.8

1. *Der Junge **blutete** sehr stark.*
2. *Er **antwortete** auf ihre Frage.*
3. *Du **kanntest** das Mädchen.*
4. *Das Mädchen **zeichnete** gern.*
5. *Er **badete** im See.*
6. *Ich **öffnete** die Tür.*
7. *Er **wusste** es nicht.*
8. *Ihr **kanntet** diese Straße.*
9. *Ich **wusste** von nichts.*
10. *Die Häuser **brannten** lichterloh.*
11. *Du **nanntest** mich einen Lügner.*
12. *Sie **ordnete** die Akten.*
13. ***Dachtest** du an ihn?*
14. *Der Jäger **beobachtete** die Rehe.*
15. *Er **brachte** ihr das Essen.*
16. *Sie **wusste** über uns Bescheid.*

Exercise 2.9

1. *Wo **warst** du?*
2. ***Hattest** du Ferien?*
3. *Ich **wurde** krank.*
4. *Er **hatte** Hunger.*
5. *Sie **war** in der Schule.*
6. *Die Tiere **wurden** unruhig.*
7. *Er **war** Lehrer von Beruf.*
8. *Die Kinder **waren** in der Schule.*
9. *Ich **hatte** wenig Zeit.*
10. *Du **wurdest** müde.*
11. ***Wart** ihr böse auf uns?*
12. *Er **hatte** eine Schwester.*
13. *Die Frau **war** schwanger.*
14. *Sie **hatte** eine schwere Krankheit.*
15. *Ich **war** kaputt.*
16. *Du **wurdest** ganz blass.*

Exercise 2.10

1. *Er **hat** Medizin **studiert**.*
2. *Der Chor **hat** viele Lieder **gesungen**.*
3. *Ich **habe** den Kuchen **probiert**.*
4. *Der Student **hat** den Stoff **gelernt**.*
5. *Du **hast** die Wahrheit **gesagt**.*
6. *Ich **habe** ein Bier **bestellt**.*
7. *Die Frau **hat** diesen Mann **gekannt**.*
8. *Er **hat** eine Zigarette **geraucht**.*
9. *Ihr **habt** Blumen **geschenkt**.*
10. *Die Schüler **haben** den Test **bestanden**.*
11. *Der Film **hat** dem Mädchen **gefallen**.*
12. *Ich **habe** mein Auto **verkauft**.*
13. *Sie **hat** eine Geschichte **erzählt**.*
14. *Er **hat** Karten **gespielt**.*
15. *Du **hast** deinen Mann **geliebt**.*
16. *Ich **habe** den Brief **geöffnet**.*

Exercise 2.11

1. *Die Katze **ist** auf den Baum **geklettert**.*
2. *Wir **sind** gestern **gewandert**.*
3. *Die Läufer **sind** schnell **gerannt**.*
4. *Der Kanzler **ist** nach Italien **gereist**.*
5. *Ich **bin** in die Schule **gerannt**.*
6. *Ihr **seid** auf den Gipfel **geklettert**.*

Exercise 2.12

1. *Er **hat** den Apfel **gegessen**.*
2. *Wir **sind** nach Hause **gekommen**.*
3. *Ich **habe** die Königin **gesehen**.*
4. *Ihr **seid** sehr schnell **gelaufen**.*
5. *Er **hat** sein Kind **geschlagen**.*
6. *Ich **habe** mein Geld **vergessen**.*
7. *Die Polizisten **haben** ihn **gefangen**.*
8. *Das Kind **ist** in den Dreck **gefallen**.*
9. *Er **hat** ein Loch **gegraben**.*
10. *Ihr **habt** Plätzchen **gebacken**.*
11. *Die Frau **hat** ein Kleid **getragen**.*
12. *Du **bist** auf meinen Fuß **getreten**.*
13. *Das Mädchen **hat** das Buch **gelesen**.*
14. *Der Baum **ist** schnell **gewachsen**.*
15. *Sie **hat** die Hose **gewaschen**.*
16. *Ich **bin** nach Hamburg **gefahren**.*

Exercise 2.13

1. *Er* ***hat*** *mit ihm* ***gesprochen****.*
2. *Ich* ***habe*** *die Tür* ***geschlossen****.*
3. *Die Männer* ***haben*** *ein Lied* ***gesungen****.*
4. *Der Sträfling* ***ist geflohen****.*
5. *Der Hund* ***hat*** *einen Mann* ***gebissen****.*
6. *Wir* ***haben*** *das Spiel* ***verloren****.*
7. *Ihr* ***habt*** *meinen Freund* ***getroffen****.*
8. *Ich* ***habe*** *Ihnen ein Steak* ***empfohlen****.*
9. *Die Frauen* ***haben*** *Wein* ***getrunken****.*
10. *Du* ***hast*** *das Schnitzel* ***genommen****.*
11. *Er* ***hat*** *an einer Krankheit* ***gelitten****.*
12. *Ich* ***habe*** *eine Postkarte* ***geschrieben****.*
13. *Die Lehrerin* ***hat*** *dem Kind* ***geholfen****.*
14. *Wir* ***haben*** *das Hotel* ***gefunden****.*
15. *Meine Großmutter* ***ist gestorben****.*
16. *Du* ***hast*** *den Rekord* ***gebrochen****.*

Exercise 2.14.

1. *Ich* ***habe*** *Glück* ***gehabt****.*
2. *Du* ***bist*** *froh* ***gewesen****.*
3. *Das Kind* ***ist*** *hungrig* ***gewesen****.*
4. *Wir* ***sind*** *krank* ***geworden****.*
5. *Ihr* ***seid*** *hier* ***gewesen****.*
6. *Wir* ***haben*** *ein Haustier* ***gehabt****.*
7. *Du* ***bist*** *blass* ***geworden****.*
8. *Ich* ***habe*** *eine Erkältung* ***gehabt****.*
9. *Ihr* ***seid*** *immer dicker* ***geworden****.*
10. *Er* ***ist*** *alleine* ***gewesen****.*

Chapter 3

Exercise 3.1

1. *Er backte einen Kuchen.*
2. *Der Notarzt half dem Verletzten.*
3. *Die Schüler grüßen ihren Lehrer.*
4. *Er spielt Geige.*
5. *Sie befragte den Zeugen.*
6. *Der engagierte Lehrer unterrichtet fleißige Schüler.*

Exercise 3.2

1. *Einen Kuchen backte er.*
2. *Dem Verletzten half der Notarzt.*
3. *Ihren Lehrer grüßen die Schüler.*
4. *Geige spielt er.*

5. *Den Zeugen befragte sie.*
6. *Fleißige Schüler unterrichtet der engagierte Lehrer.*

Exercise 3.3

1. *Er hat eine Reise gebucht.*
2. *Sie hat eine Firma gegründet.*
3. *Er hat eine Wohnung gemietet.*
4. *Sie hat die meiste Arbeit gemacht.*
5. *Er hat seinen Chef angerufen.*
6. *Er ist zu schnell gefahren.*
7. *Sie hat den Artikel geschrieben.*
8. *Er wird die Rechnung bezahlen.*
9. *Wir müssen das Haus verkaufen.*
10. *Er hat gut gespielt.*

Exercise 3.4

1. *Den Herrn hat das Hotel angerufen.*
2. *Ihn hat man beraubt.*
3. *Das Haus werden sie kaufen.*
4. *Den FC Bayern hat Arsenal besiegt.*
5. *Das Bier hat er getrunken.*
6. *Eine Hose hat sie gekauft.*
7. *Das Bild hat das Kind gemalt.*
8. *Mich hat mein Chef entlassen.*
9. *Das Auto hat sie ausgeliehen.*
10. *Ein kleines Geschäft hat der Mann besessen.*

Exercise 3.5.

1. *Hinter dem Haus <u>steht ein großer Baum</u>.*
2. *In den Ferien <u>schläft er</u> gewöhnlich sehr lange.*
3. *Vor den Prüfungen <u>nimmt sie</u> immer eine Beruhigungstablette.*
4. *Morgen <u>werden wir</u> nach München <u>fahren.</u>*
5. *In der kommenden Woche <u>muss ich</u> meine Prüfungen <u>ablegen</u>.*
6. *Da <u>ich</u> keine Zeit <u>habe</u>, <u>kann ich</u> nicht in den Urlaub <u>fahren</u>.*
7. *Trotz ihrer Höhenangst <u>ist sie</u> auf den Turm <u>gestiegen</u>.*
8. *Aufgrund einer Erkältung <u>kann sie</u> nicht an der Wanderung <u>teilnehmen</u>.*
9. *Nach dem Mittagessen <u>macht er</u> seine Hausaufgaben.*
10. *Mit ihrem Mann <u>will sie</u> in die Schweiz <u>fahren</u>.*

Exercise 3.6

1. *Nächste Woche musst du wieder in die Schule gehen.*
2. *Mit diesem Zug werdet ihr pünktlich in Hamburg sein.*
3. *In zwei Stunden können wir den Berggipfel erreichen.*
4. *Um sich fit zu halten, geht er einmal täglich joggen.*

5. *Regelmäßig geht sie in die Mensa essen.*
6. *Nach ihrem Examen will sie in Amerika studieren.*
7. *Trotz des schlechten Wetters sind wir an die Küste gefahren.*
8. *Wegen seiner guten Qualifikation wurde er mit dieser Aufgabe betraut.*
9. *In Deutschland haben die Menschen schon immer gerne Fußball gespielt.*
10. *Über den Bergen sieht man einen wunderschönen Sonnenuntergang.*

Exercise 3.7

3. *Seinen Hund füttert der Junge mit viel Liebe.*
4. *Den Marathon sind sie trotz großer Hitze gelaufen.*
5. *Das Auto ist er nicht gefahren, weil er zu müde war.*
6. *Seine Arbeit konnte er unglücklicherweise nicht beenden.*
7. *Ihre Beine kann sie glücklicherweise noch fühlen und bewegen.*
8. *Seinen Arbeitsplatz hat er gewechselt um mehr Geld zu verdienen.*

Exercise 3.8

1. *Ich mache/machte das Fenster zu.*
2. *Sie kommt/kam immer spät heim.*
3. *Du bringst/brachtest etwas zu essen mit.*
4. *Wir gehen heute Abend aus.*
5. *Ich nehme/nahm meinen Bruder mit.*
6. *Du fährst/fuhrst das Auto weg.*
7. *Er sieht/sah sie an.*
8. *Wir kommen morgen früh an.*
9. *Ich ziehe/zog einen Mantel an.*
10. *Ihr ladet/ludet eure Freunde ein.*

Exercise 3.9

1. *Er fährt/fuhr gerne Auto.*
2. *Wir machen/machten an der Raststätte Halt.*
3. *Ihr lernt/lerntet euch in Deutschland kennen.*
4. *Sie gibt/gab mir Bescheid.*
5. *Du schreibst/schriebst dieses Wort getrennt.*
6. *Ich lasse/ließ meine Tasche hier liegen.*
7. *Ihr bekommt/bekamt ein Auto geschenkt.*
8. *Wir lassen/ließen ihn Auto fahren.*
9. *Er fährt/fuhr mit der Bahn.*
10. *Sie blieb letztes Jahr sitzen.*

Exercise 3.10

1. *Die Frau war sehr glücklich, als sie einen Blumenstrauß geschenkt bekam.*

2. *Peter legte sich gleich ins Bett, nachdem er übermüdet heimgekommen war.*
3. *Er hält sich auch im hohen Alter noch fit, indem er sehr viel Rad fährt.*
4. *Es wurde sehr kalt im Zimmer, nachdem sie das Fenster aufgemacht hatte.*
5. *Das Kind freute sich, weil ihm der Vater ein Geschenk mitgebracht hatte.*
6. *Seine Mutter informierte ihn, bevor ihm der Vater Bescheid geben konnte.*
7. *Die Wanderer waren so müde, dass sie am nächsten Rastplatz Halt machten.*
8. *Er kam zu spät, weil das Flugzeug nicht rechtzeitig abgeflogen war.*
9. *Sie war sehr erstaunt, als er sie mit ungläubigen Augen ansah.*
10. *Sie kam rechtzeitig an, weil sie statt Auto Bahn gefahren war.*

Exercise 3.11

1. *Bist du aus Deutschland?*
2. *Haben Sie noch ein Zimmer frei?*
3. *Studiert ihr in Berlin?*
4. *Lebst du in einer Kleinstadt?*
5. *Gehst du in die zehnte Klasse?*
6. *Kennen Sie diese Stadt?*
7. *Können Sie mich anrufen?*
8. *Fährt der Zug vom Bahnsteig 2 ab?*
9. *Ist er gestern nach Düsseldorf gefahren?*
10. *Schreibt man das Wort „spazieren gehen" getrennt?*
11. *Kommt der Zug heute Abend um 19.00 Uhr an?*
12. *Lernte er sie an der Universität kennen?*
13. *Hast du in München Betriebswirtschaft studiert?*
14. *Ziehen sie bald nach Berlin um?*
15. *Hat er in Frankfurt eine Wohnung gekauft?*
16. *Möchte sie in England Politik studieren?*

Exercise 3.12

1. *Wie alt sind Sie?/Wie alt bist du?*
2. *Wie viel kostet eine Fahrkarte?*
3. *Wie komme ich in das Stadtzentrum?*
4. *Was macht der Polizist da?*
5. *Wann besuchen Sie uns in England? Wann besuchst du uns in England?*

Exercise 3.13

1. *Wie lautet Ihre Telefonnummer?*
2. *Was können Sie empfehlen?*
3. *Wo ist das WC bitte?*

4. *Wie viel kostet die Hose?*
5. *Welcher Bus fährt in die Innenstadt?*
6. *Wo ist die nächste Bushaltestelle?*
7. *Wie komme ich am schnellsten zum Bahnhof?*
8. *Wie viele Kinder haben Sie?*
9. *Wessen Auto fährst du?*
10. *Wo findet die Konferenz statt?*

Exercise 3.14

1. *Warum studierten Sie in England?*
2. *Wie lernte dich dein Mann kennen?*
3. *Weshalb sagtest du das Treffen ab?*
4. *Wann kam dieser Beschluss zustande?*
5. *Wie ging deine Karriere an der Universität zu Ende?*

Exercise 3.15

1. *Warum bist du mit dem Zug gefahren?*
2. *Wann haben Sie in Frankfurt eine Wohnung gekauft?*
3. *Wie haben Sie die Aufgabe gelöst?*
4. *Wo findet die Tagung statt?*
5. *Wen triffst du heute Vormittag?*

Exercise 3.16

1. ***Sagt** mir Bescheid, wenn ihr kommen könnt!*
2. ***Lasst** mich bitte in Ruhe!*
3. ***Frag(e)** den Lehrer!*
4. ***Verkauf(e)** das Auto!*
5. ***Seid** euren Gästen ein guter Gastgeber!*
6. ***Sieh** dir das an!* (vowel change)
7. ***Hol(e)** mir bitte zwei Tüten Milch!*
8. ***Macht** nicht so viel Unfug im Urlaub!*
9. ***Gib** mir bitte etwas zu trinken!* (vowel change)
10. ***Sei** nicht immer so schlecht gelaunt!*

Exercise 3.17

1. *Fahren Sie mit der Straßenbahn!*
2. *Feiern Sie eine bestandene Prüfung!*
3. *Übersetzen Sie diesen Text!*
4. *Schreiben Sie einen Aufsatz!*
5. *Gehen Sie nach Deutschland!*
6. *Kaufen Sie am Schalter eine Fahrkarte!*
7. *Sprechen Sie mit meinem Chef!*
8. *Fragen Sie einen Polizisten!*
9. *Nehmen Sie die U-Bahn!*
10. *Lernen Sie für jeden Test!*

Chapter 4

Exercise 4.1

1. *Es bewegt* ***sich*** *dort etwas.*
2. *Ich habe* ***mich*** *am Bein verletzt.*
3. *Wir haben* ***uns*** *amüsiert.*
4. *Er rasiert* ***sich*** *jeden Morgen.*
5. *Ihr habt* ***euch*** *verändert.*
6. *Dann wende ich* ***mich*** *an die Polizei.*
7. *Die Studenten bereiten* ***sich*** *auf ihr Examen vor.*
8. *Du erinnerst* ***dich*** *doch auch an den Gast.*
9. *Bitte beklagen Sie* ***sich*** *beim Chef!*
10. *Bitte gebt* ***euch*** *doch Mühe beim Lernen!*

Exercise 4.2

1. *Männer rasieren sich.*
2. *Sie zieht/Sie ziehen sich gerade an.*
3. *Ich interessiere mich für Kunst.*
4. *Ich bereite mich auf den Vortrag vor.*
5. *Er nähert sich der Grenze.*
6. *Die Frau hat sich an den Vorfall erinnert.*
7. *Wir treffen uns im Konferenzzimmer.*
8. *Ich habe mich bei dem Unfall verletzt.*
9. *Du musst dich im Freien bewegen.*
10. *Ihr habt euch geschnitten.*
11. *Wie hat sich das Kind verletzt?*
12. *Wann hast du dich vorbereitet?*
13. *Wollen wir uns treffen?*
14. *Habt ihr euch gut erholt?*
15. *Kann ich mich auf dich verlassen?*
16. *Bereiten Sie sich auf die Prüfung vor!*
17. *Wascht euch mit Seife!*
18. *Versteck dich im Schrank!*
19. *Bitte legen Sie sich auf die Liege (hin)!*
20. *Freut euch auf den Urlaub!*

Exercise 4.3

1. *Wir holen* ***uns*** *ein Eis.*
2. *Ich bestelle* ***mir*** *ein Bier.*
3. *Wir machen es* ***uns*** *hier gemütlich.*
4. *Er hat* ***sich*** *die Haare gewaschen.*
5. *Ihr habt* ***euch*** *einen freien Tag gegönnt.*
6. *Du hast* ***dir*** *die Haare schneiden lassen.*
7. *Sie haben* ***sich*** *Urlaub genommen.*
8. *Ich schneide* ***mir*** *gerade die Fingernägel.*

9. *Bitte nehmen Sie **sich** ein Glas Wein.*
10. *Ihr habt **euch** ein Haus in Deutschland gekauft.*

Exercise 4.4

1. *Ich nehme mir ein Glas Wein.*
2. *Ihr macht euch das Frühstück.*
3. *Wir gönnen uns jeden Sommer einen Urlaub in Deutschland.*
4. *Er bestellt sich ein Schnitzel.*
5. *Ich verrenke mir den Hals.*

Exercise 4.5

1. *Was hast du dir bestellt?*
2. *Wie bereitet ihr euch auf die Prüfungen vor?*
3. *Wann haben Sie sich den Hals verrenkt?*
4. *Wie stellen Sie sich Ihre Arbeit vor?*
5. *Was hast du dir gekauft?*

Chapter 5

Exercise 5.1

1. *Nachdem er seinen entflohenen Kanarienvogel auf dem Baum gefunden hat, möchte er ihn nun **wieder**holen.*
2. *Diese Szene muss wieder**holt*** werden.
3. *Seine Frau und seine Kinder haben ihn durch**schaut**.*
4. *Könnten Sie mir bitte diese Broschüre zum **Durch**schauen geben?*
5. *Haben Sie das Buch über**setzt**?*
6. *In der Deutschprüfung musste er einen kurzen Text über**setzen**.*
7. *Wann wollen Sie mit der Fähre **über**setzen?*
8. *Wo können wir die Möbel während unserer Abwesenheit **unter**stellen?*
9. *Er hat mir unter**stellt**, eine falsche Aussage gemacht zu haben.*
10. *Kann ich mein Gepäck bei Ihnen **unter**stellen?*
11. *Sein Professor hat ihm deutlich gemacht, dass er die Seminararbeit **um**schreiben müsse.*
12. *Ich habe diesen Ausdruck nicht verstanden. Könnten Sie ihn bitte mit anderen Worten um**schreiben**?*
13. *Der Bankangestellte muss jede Woche den Zugangscode **um**stellen.*
14. *Die Soldaten haben das Gebäude komplett um**stellt**.*
15. *Er hat die 800 m in weniger als zwei Minuten durch**laufen**.*
16. *Der Kaffee ist gerade am **Durch**laufen.*

Exercise 5.2

1. *Sie hat dieses mathematische Problem **durchschaut**.*
2. *Hast du mir meinen Ball **wiedergeholt**?*
3. *Ich habe gerade schon **durchgeschaut**.*

4. *Er hat das Schuljahr* ***wiederholt****.*
5. *Der Dolmetscher hat für die ausländischen Gäste* ***übersetzt****.*
6. *Die Autorin hat die Kurzgeschichte* ***umgeschrieben****.*
7. *Sein bester Freund hat seine Absichten* ***durchschaut****.*
8. *Wir sind mit der Fähre nach Fehmarn* ***übergesetzt****.*
9. *Mein Chef hat mir diese Aufgabe* ***unterstellt****.*
10. *Ich habe meine Fahrweise* ***umgestellt****.*

Exercise 5.3

1. *Sie* ***durchschaute*** *dieses mathematische Problem.*
2. ***Holtest*** *du mir meinen Ball* ***wieder****?* (used rather rarely)
3. *Ich* ***schaute gerade*** *schon* ***durch****.*
4. *Er* ***wiederholte*** *das Schuljahr.*
5. *Der Dolmetscher* ***übersetzte*** *für die ausländischen Gäste.*
6. *Die Autorin* ***schrieb*** *die Kurzgeschichte* ***um****.*
7. *Sein bester Freund* ***durchschaute*** *seine Absichten.*
8. *Wir* ***setzten*** *mit der Fähre nach Fehmarn* ***über****.*
9. *Mein Chef* ***unterstellte*** *mir diese Aufgabe.*
10. *Ich* ***stellte*** *meine Fahrweise* ***um****.*

Chapter 6

Exercise 6.1

1. *Wer ist in der Firma für* ***die Einnahmen und Ausgaben*** *zuständig?*
2. *Bitte schreiben Sie* ***einen Bericht*** *über Ihre Erfahrungen in Deutschland!*
3. *Ich habe* ***ein Konto*** *bei der Commerzbank.*

Exercise 6.2

1. *Dieser Professor hatte* ***eine Affäre*** *mit einer Studentin.*
2. *Sie haben mit* ***dieser Sache*** *nichts zu tun. Das ist* ***meine Angelegenheit****.*
3. *Ich komme in* ***einer*** *dienstlichen* ***Angelegenheit*** *zu Ihnen.*

Exercise 6.3

1. *Der Professor hat* ***die Berufung*** *an die Universität in München abgelehnt.*
2. *Er hat sich um* ***die Stelle*** *als Botschafter beworben.*
3. *Um vier Uhr habe ich* ***eine*** *geschäftliche* ***Verabredung****.*
4. *Ich muss die Sitzung auf* ***einen*** *späteren* ***Termin*** *verschieben.*

Exercise 6.4

1. *Und in* ***welcher Branche*** *sind Sie tätig?*
2. *Er besitzt* ***ein*** *rentables* ***Geschäft*** *in der Innenstadt.*
3. *Ich habe mit* ***der*** *ganzen* ***Sache*** *nichts zu tun.*
4. *Ich halte mich in Deutschland auf um* ***Geschäfte*** *zu tätigen.*

Exercise 6.5

1. *Sie hat keine guten* ***Aussichten/Chancen*** *ein Stipendium zu bekommen.*
2. *Wenn ich an deiner Stelle wäre, würde ich kein* ***Risiko*** *eingehen.*
3. *Werde ich noch einmal* ***die Chance/die Gelegenheit*** *bekommen nach Berlin zu fahren?*
4. *Es war purer* ***Zufall****, dass wir uns in Hamburg begegnet sind.*

Exercise 6.6

1. *Ich benötige etwas* ***Kleingeld*** *für den Zigarettenautomaten.*
2. *Das Leben in diesem Ort bietet* ***keine Abwechslung****.*
3. *Ich habe Ihnen noch nicht* ***Ihr Wechselgeld*** *gegeben.*
4. *Im Sommer kommt es zu* ***einem Wechsel*** *an der Spitze des Unternehmens.*
5. *Wir sehen zur Zeit eine drastische* ***Veränderung*** *in der Arbeitsmoral.*

Exercise 6.7

1. ***Eine Schauspieltruppe*** *aus Deutschland führt morgen ein Theaterstück auf.*
2. *Er arbeitet an der Spitze* ***eines*** *großen deutschen* ***Konzerns****.*
3. *Wir können dir heute Abend etwas* ***Gesellschaft*** *leisten.*
4. *Wie wiele Soldaten haben Sie in* ***Ihrer Kompanie****?*
5. *Hast du gerade* ***Besuch****?*

Exercise 6.8

1. *Die großen* ***Konzerne*** *bauen zur Zeit viele Arbeitsplätze ab.*
2. ***Seine*** *größte* ***Sorge/Besorgnis*** *war, dass sein Arbeitsplatz in Gefahr ist.*
3. *Das ist nicht* ***meine Angelegenheit****.*
4. *Die Energieversorgung ist eine Angelegenheit von immenser* ***Bedeutung****.*

Exercise 6.9

1. *Sie macht Ihrer Heimatstadt alle* ***Ehre****.*
2. *Wie viele* ***Scheine*** *bis zum Examen musst du noch machen?*
3. *Die Namen aller Mitwirkenden wurden* ***im Nachspann*** *des Films genannt.*
4. *Es tut mir Leid, aber ich kann dieser Sache nur wenig* ***Glauben*** *schenken.*
5. *Sie hat ein beachtliches* ***Guthaben*** *auf der Bank.*
6. *Die Bank hat mir leider keinen* ***Kredit*** *gewährt.*

Exercise 6.10

1. ***Die Forderung*** *nach besseren Arbeitsbedingungen bestimmte die Diskussion.*
2. ***Die Nachfrage*** *nach Fernsehgeräten geht zurück.*

Exercise 6.11

1. *Viele unserer Kunden befürworten längere* ***Geschäftszeiten/ Öffnungszeiten****.*
2. *In den* ***Stunden*** *der Einsamkeit wird sie sehr schnell melancholisch.*

Exercise 6.12

1. *Wir müssen noch* ***einen*** *größeren* ***Posten*** *Kochtöpfe bestellen.*
2. ***Dieser Bericht*** *über die Anhebung der Steuern erschien in der Stuttgarter Zeitung.*
3. *Die Partei muss die einzelnen* ***Punkte*** *ihres Wahlprogramms überarbeiten.*

Exercise 6.13

1. *Ich muss Ihnen leider* ***eine Kündigung*** *erteilen.*
2. *Sie werden bald von Ihrer Krankenkasse* ***einen Bescheid*** *erhalten.*
3. *Er ist bei einer Zeitung angestellt und schreibt vor allem* ***Kritiken/ Rezensionen****.*
4. *Könnten Sie bitte* ***diese Notiz/Mitteilung*** *am schwarzen Brett aufhängen?*

Exercise 6.14

1. *Diese Entscheidung ist gegen alle Regeln* ***der Vernunft****.*
2. *Können Sie triftige* ***Gründe*** *für Ihre Kündigung vorlegen?*
3. *Mein Verstand sagt mir, dass ich* ***diesen Beschluss*** *nicht mittragen kann.*

Chapter 7

Exercise 7.1

1. *Meiner Meinung nach fehlt diesem Hollywood-Streifen* ***die Action****.*
2. *Wir müssen jetzt endlich diesen Plan in* ***die Tat*** *umsetzen.*
3. ***Die Handlung*** *des Romans spielt in Alsfeld, einer Kleinstadt in Oberhessen.*

Exercise 7.2

1. *Er stammt* ***aus kleinen Verhältnissen*** *und hat sich hochgearbeitet.*
2. *Wir müssen* ***die Zusammenhänge/Hintergründe*** *dieser Tat bis ins Detail aufdecken.*
3. *Die Handlung des Theaterstücks hat* ***einen*** *geschichtlichen* ***Hintergrund****.*

Exercise 7.3

1. *Die Schüler müssen bis* ***zu einem*** *gewissen* ***Maß/Grad*** *belastbar sein.*
2. *Um bei uns arbeiten zu können, brauchen Sie* ***einen Hochschulabschluss****.*
3. *Das Thermometer steigt im Laufe des Tages auf 30* ***Grad****.*

Exercise 7.4

1. *Nach meinem Abitur möchte ich gerne* ***Erziehungswissenschaft/ Pädagogik*** *studieren.*
2. *Sie befindet sich noch* ***in der Ausbildung****.*
3. *Er ist sehr belesen und verfügt über eine umfassende* ***Bildung****.*
4. *In seiner Kindheit wurden Fehler* ***in der Erziehung*** *gemacht.*

Exercise 7.5

1. *Morgen muss ich* ***wegen einer Untersuchung*** *zum Arzt gehen.*
2. *Sie müssen sich während der Verhandlung* ***einem Verhör*** *unterziehen.*
3. *Eine gründliche* ***Prüfung*** *Ihres Autos dauert bis zu drei Stunden.*
4. *Ihre mündliche* ***Prüfung*** *ist am Freitag um 14.00 Uhr.*

Exercise 7.6

1. *Das Nichterreichen des Viertelfinals muss als* ***Misserfolg*** *gewertet werden.*
2. *Nach der nichtbestandenen Prüfung fühlte er sich als* ***Versager****.*
3. *Durch* ***den Ausfall****/Wegen* ***des Ausfalls*** *der Heizung bekamen die Kinder schulfrei.*

Exercise 7.7

1. ***Der Glaube*** *kann Berge versetzen.*
2. *Welchem* ***Glauben/Bekenntnis*** *gehören Sie an?*
3. ***Der*** *jüdische und* ***der*** *christliche* ***Glaube*** *haben gemeinsame Wurzeln.*
4. *Nach diesem Vorfall hat sie* ***ihr Vertrauen*** *in ihn verloren.*

Exercise 7.8

1. *Er ist ein Mann von kleiner und untersetzter* ***Figur****.*
2. *Es handelt sich bei diesem Herrn um* ***eine*** *hochgestellte* ***Persönlichkeit****.*
3. *Im dichten Nebel konnte ich* ***diese Gestalt*** *nur sehr schwer erkennen.*
4. *Haben Sie die* ***Zahlen*** *von diesem Jahr mit denen vom letzten Jahr verglichen?*

Exercise 7.9

1. *Er hat* ***eine*** *schlechte* ***Note*** *im Fach Deutsch.*
2. *Er hat* ***eine*** *blutige* ***Schramme*** *in seinem Gesicht.*
3. *Auf der Tischdecke ist* ***ein*** *dicker* ***Fleck****.*
4. *Als* ***ein Zeichen*** *der Freundschaft überreichte er ihm das Geschenk.*
5. *Nach dem Umzug hatten die Möbel mehrere* ***Kratzer/Schrammen****.*

Exercise 7.10

1. *Im Musikunterricht müssen wir* ***Noten*** *lernen.*
2. ***Der Ton*** *in ihrer Stimme verriet mir, dass sie Angst hatte.*
3. *Machen Sie sich während der Vorlesung* ***Notizen****.*

4. *An ihre Freundin schrieb sie noch* ***ein paar Zeilen*** *auf ein Blatt, welches sie an ihrer Zimmertür befestigte.*
5. *Sie müssen* ***die Fußnoten*** *an das Ende des Buches platzieren.*

Exercise 7.11

1. *Der Lehrer rief die Schüler* ***zur Ordnung/Disziplin****.*
2. *Ich kann Ihnen dieses Produkt nur auf* ***Bestellung*** *liefern.*
3. *Der Kapitän gab* ***den Befehl*** *die Segel zu setzen.*
4. *Die Spieler müssen sich* ***in der Reihenfolge*** *ihrer Platzierung aufstellen.*
5. *Sie müssen diese Angelegenheit* ***in Ordnung*** *bringen.*
6. *Der Präsident betonte, dass* ***die*** *politische* ***Ordnung*** *in Europa bewahrt werden soll.*

Exercise 7.12

1. *Er ist völlig* ***aus der Übung/aus dem Training****.*
2. *Die theoretische Ausbildung stimmt oft nicht* ***mit der Praxis*** *überein.*
3. *Wenn er mit der Facharztausbildung fertig ist, möchte er* ***eine Praxis*** *aufmachen.*
4. *Wir haben bei uns im Betrieb eine andere* ***Praktik/Verfahrensweise****.*
5. *Ein warmes Abendessen ist bei uns (so)* ***Sitte/Brauch****.*
6. *Sie hat* ***die Gewohnheit*** *nach dem Essen zu schlafen.*

Chapter 8

Exercise 8.1

1. *Könnten Sie bitte* ***Ihre Adresse*** *auf einem Zettel notieren?*
2. *Er hält heute Abend* ***eine Ansprache*** *vor dem Kongress.*

Exercise 8.2

1. *Der Schüler rechnete die Aufgabe* ***an der Tafel****.*
2. *Auf der letzten Mitgliederversammlung wurde* ***ein*** *neuer* ***Vorstand*** *gewählt.*
3. *Was hattest du in deinem Urlaub für Unterkunft und* ***Verpflegung*** *ausgegeben?*
4. *Um auf dem Gerüst arbeiten zu können, brauchen die Handwerker noch längere* ***Bretter****.*

Exercise 8.3

1. *Substantive werden im Deutschen am Anfang* ***mit einem Großbuchstaben*** *geschrieben.*
2. *Wir müssen* ***unser*** *gesamtes* ***Kapital*** *in das Geschäft stecken.*
3. ***Sein*** *ganzes* ***Kapital*** *waren seine schnellen Beine.*
4. ***Die Hauptstadt*** *des Bundeslands Hessen ist Wiesbaden.*

Exercise 8.4

1. *Wie möchten Sie damit **durch den Zoll** kommen?*
2. *Während meines Aufenthaltes in Deutschland habe ich viele fremde **Sitten** und Gebräuche kennen gelernt.*
3. *Der Geschäftsinhaber hat **seine Kundschaft** verärgert. Nun bleibt sie weg.*
4. *Sie hat **die Angewohnheit** während des Essens fernzusehen.*

Exercise 8.5

1. *Ich möchte noch ein paar **Geschenke** für meine Eltern und Freunde kaufen.*
2. *Sie ist eine junge Frau mit vielen **Gaben**.*

Exercise 8.6.

1. *Um darüber Bescheid zu wissen, sollten Sie sich **ein Handbuch** zur Gartenkunde kaufen.*
2. *Wir haben uns mit mehreren Touristen **einem Führer** angeschlossen.*
3. *Bevor wir mit dem Stadtrundgang beginnen, will ich mir noch schnell **einen Stadtführer** kaufen.*

Exercise 8.7

1. *Das ist **meine Vorstellung** von einem schönen Urlaub.*
2. *Sie hat **keine Ahnung**, wie das passieren konnte.*
3. *Manche Deutsche haben etwas schräge **Ansichten** über die Engländer.*
4. *Hast du **eine Idee**, was wir morgen Abend machen wollen?*

Exercise 8.8

1. *Wenn Sie ins Ausland reisen, vergessen Sie nicht **Ihre Ausweispapiere mitzunehmen.***
2. *Junge Menschen sind auf der Suche nach **Identifikation**.*
3. *Wir brauchen Sie **zur Identifizierung** des Toten.*

Exercise 8.9

1. *Ich hätte gerne **die** heutige **Ausgabe** des „Daily Telegraph".*
2. ***Diese Frage** wird uns auch noch in 100 Jahren beschäftigen.*

Exercise 8.10

1. ***Diese Linie** führt direkt nach Frankfurt.*
2. *Sie haben gerade **eine Zeile** übersprungen.*
3. *Wenn Sie **die Grenze** passiert haben, dürfen Sie nicht schneller als 130 km/h fahren.*
4. *Auf allen innerdeutschen **Linien** werden die modernsten Flugzeuge eingesetzt.*
5. *Unsere **Gesellschaft/Linie** bietet unseren Passagieren den besten Komfort.*
6. *Wie heißt die erste Ortschaft **hinter der Grenze**?*

7. *Stellen Sie sich bitte* ***in einer Reihe*** *auf!*
8. *Er ist nicht in der Lage,* ***eine*** *gerade* ***Linie*** *zu zeichnen.*

Exercise 8.11

1. *Nach seinem Schulabschluss möchte er gerne* ***Medizin*** *studieren.*
2. *Ich muss jeden Abend* ***meine Arznei/Medizin*** *schlucken.*

Exercise 8.12

1. ***Die*** *ländliche* ***Bevölkerung*** *im Raum Nordhessen geht immer mehr zurück.*
2. *Der neue Präsident hat* ***das Volk*** *auf seiner Seite.*
3. *Wir wollen versuchen, die einfachen* ***Menschen/Leute*** *auf der Straße zu erreichen.*
4. *Die Deutschen sind* ***das Volk*** *der Dichter und Denker.*

Exercise 8.13

1. *Gibt es in diesem Restaurant denn* ***keine Bedienung****?*
2. ***Der Gottesdienst*** *in unserer Kirchengemeinde ist immer gut besucht.*
3. ***Meinen Militärdienst*** *leistete ich bei der Luftwaffe ab.*
4. *Dieser Fahrkartenautomat ist zur Zeit leider nicht in* ***Betrieb****.*
5. *Er ist* ***im Dienst*** *der Weltgesundheitsorganisation unterwegs.*
6. *Aufgrund der geringen Zahl von Reisenden wurde* ***der Busverkehr/die Busverbindung*** *an die Küste eingestellt.*
7. *Als eine der führenden Banken bieten wir Ihnen* ***Dienstleistungen*** *aller Art an.*

Exercise 8.14

1. *Wir können Ihnen in unserer Pension noch ein* ***freies Zimmer*** *anbieten.*
2. *In unserer Firma haben wir zur Zeit einige* ***freie Stellen****.*

Chapter 9

Exercise 9.1

1. *Er hat ein Geschenk für* ***mich*** *gekauft.*
2. *Die Katze legte sich auf* ***mich****.*
3. *Sie hat* ***mir*** *das Auto gewaschen.*
4. *Nicola fährt in dem Auto vor* ***mir****.*
5. *Wilfried hat* ***mich*** *beim Schach geschlagen.*
6. *Die Polizei hat im Wald nach* ***mir*** *gesucht.*
7. *Bitte denkt an* ***mich****, wenn ich morgen in meine Prüfung gehe.*
8. *Komm, wir gehen einfach zu* ***mir****.*
9. *Meine Freundin Riki hat* ***mir*** *zum Abschied einen Kuss gegeben.*
10. *Kannst du* ***mir*** *bitte die Butter reichen?*

Exercise 9.2

1. *Mein Sohn liebt* ***mich****.*
2. *Meine Freunde warteten auf* ***mich****.*
3. *Gib es* ***mir****, bitte!*
4. *Sie gab* ***mir*** *ein Geschenk.*
5. *Dies ist ein Buch über* ***mich****.*

Exercise 9.3

1. *Ich möchte* ***mich*** *gerne vorstellen.*
2. *Ich habe* ***mich*** *in eine sehr nette Frau verliebt.*
3. *Ich schneide* ***mir*** *regelmäßig beim Kartoffelschälen in den Finger.*
4. *Nach der Arbeit auf der Baustelle habe ich* ***mich*** *erst mal gewaschen.*
5. *Ich erinnere* ***mich*** *an diesen Schüler.*
6. *Gestern habe ich* ***mir*** *ein Auto gekauft.*
7. *Ich habe* ***mich*** *für das Foul bei meinem Gegenspieler entschuldigt.*
8. *Ich fühle* ***mich*** *gut.*
9. *Gestern habe ich* ***mich*** *beim Fußballspielen verletzt.*
10. *Meine Mahlzeiten mache ich* ***mir*** *immer selbst.*

Exercise 9.4

1. *Ich möchte* ***mir*** *einen Stadtführer von Frankfurt kaufen.*
2. *Ich sagte* ***zu mir*** *selbst, die Zeit zum Handeln ist gekommen.*
3. *Um noch den Zug rechtzeitig zu erreichen, musste ich* ***mich*** *beeilen.*
4. *Schau, ich habe* ***mir*** *einen schönen Rock gefertigt.*
5. *Gestern habe ich* ***mich*** *geschnitten.*

Exercise 9.5

1. *Uli hat* ***dir*** *ein köstliches Essen zubereitet.*
2. *Dein Lehrer hat sich über* ***dich*** *beschwert.*
3. *Max hat* ***dich*** *fotografiert.*
4. *Er steht direkt vor* ***dir*** *in der Schlange.*
5. *Ich habe* ***dir*** *einen Hut aus Deutschland mitgebracht.*
6. *Wir verlassen uns auf* ***dich****.*
7. *Ich bin nach* ***dir*** *an der Reihe.*
8. *Zu deinem Geburtstag möchten wir* ***dir*** *herzlich gratulieren.*
9. *Sie hat mir einiges über* ***dich*** *erzählt.*
10. *Ich habe* ***dich*** *vermisst.*

Exercise 9.6

1. *Sie hasst* ***dich****.*
2. *Der Hund folgt* ***dir****, wo auch immer du hingehst.*
3. *Ich möchte* ***dich*** *gerne im Mai besuchen.*
4. *Er hat* ***dir*** *einen Brief geschrieben.*
5. *Ich kaufe* ***dir*** *ein Geschenk.*

Exercise 9.7

1. *Herr Müller, kann ich* ***Sie*** *etwas fragen?*
2. *Kann ich* ***Ihnen*** *helfen?/Kann ich* ***Ihnen*** *behilflich sein?*
3. *Was kann ich für* ***Sie*** *tun?*
4. *Sie möchte* ***Ihnen*** *Deutsch beibringen.*
5. *Ich habe ein großartiges Angebot für* ***Sie****.*

Exercise 9.8

1. *Sie müssen* ***sich*** *selbst entscheiden.*
2. *Würdest du* ***dich*** *als Marxisten bezeichnen?*
3. *Wann kaufst du* ***dir*** *ein Auto?*
4. *Sie dürfen* ***sich*** *auf keinen Fall überanstrengen.*
5. *Bleib ruhig! Du regst* ***dich*** *zu sehr auf.*
6. *Machen Sie* ***sich*** *nicht so viele Gedanken!*
7. *Du kannst* ***dich*** *hier im Badezimmer waschen.*
8. *Du musst* ***dir*** *Zeit lassen.*
9. *Wie hast du* ***dich*** *verletzt?*
10. *Du hast* ***dich*** *gestern aber dumm verhalten.*

Exercise 9.9

1. *Benimm* ***dich****!/Benehmen Sie* ***sich****!*
2. *Du musst* ***dich*** *beeilen./Sie müssen* ***sich*** *beeilen.*
3. *Du musst* ***dich*** *deutlich ausdrücken./Sie müssen* ***sich*** *deutlich ausdrücken.*
4. *Möchtest du* ***dich*** *selbst vorstellen?/Möchten Sie* ***sich*** *selbst vorstellen?*
5. *Du kannst* ***dir*** *eine Tasse Tee machen./Sie können* ***sich*** *eine Tasse Tee machen.*

Exercise 9.10

1. *Sie können* ***ihn*** *anrufen.*
2. *Könnten Sie* ***ihm*** *einen Gruß ausrichten?*
3. *Die Straße wurde nach* ***ihm*** *benannt.*
4. *Ich werde* ***ihm*** *eine Email schicken.*
5. *Ich habe von* ***ihm*** *ein Fax erhalten.*
6. *Wir haben auf* ***ihn*** *gesetzt.*
7. *Du musst* ***ihm*** *die Wahrheit sagen.*
8. *Wir sind* ***ihm*** *gefolgt.*
9. *Wann werden Sie* ***ihn*** *sehen?*
10. *Die Leute werden über* ***ihn*** *reden.*

Exercise 9.11

1. *Ich schicke* ***ihm*** *eine Postkarte.*
2. *Gehe einfach zu* ***ihm*** *und frage* ***ihn****!*
3. *Wer gibt* ***ihm*** *das Geschenk?*

4. *Versuche **ihn** zu stoppen/**ihn** aufzuhalten.*
5. *Ich habe **ihn** einmal unterrichtet.*

Exercise 9.12

1. *Ich werde mich an **sie** wenden.*
2. *Wir schenken **ihr** eine Reise nach Italien.*
3. *Du musst **ihr** jetzt helfen.*
4. *Wir wollen **sie** freundlich begrüßen.*
5. *Ich werde **sie** vermissen.*
6. *Fährst du zu **ihr** nach Hamburg?*
7. *Können Sie **ihr** die Bestellung zufaxen?*
8. *Du musst dich auf **sie** einstellen.*
9. *Bitte richte **ihr** einen Gruß von mir aus.*
10. *Hast du diesen Brief von **ihr** erhalten?*

Exercise 9.13

1. *Wann kann ich **sie** wiedersehen?*
2. *Bitte, sag **ihr**/sagen Sie **ihr**, sie soll mich im Büro anrufen.*
3. *Was kann ich für **sie** tun?*
4. *Wo kann ich **sie** finden?*
5. *Könntest du/Könnten Sie **ihr** etwas Geld leihen?*

Exercise 9.14

1. You are late.
2. Mr Clemens, you can wash yourself here.
3. He was ashamed of himself.
4. Hurry up, please!
5. The bird has hurt itself.
6. She made herself comfortable.
7. He wants to buy himself a tent.
8. Dear colleagues, bring yourselves up to date!
9. She feels good.
10. She introduced herself briefly to the audience.

Chapter 10

Exercise 10.1

1. *Dies ist heute der **einzige** Bus nach München.*
2. *Sie müssen **nur/bloß** die Straße hinuntergehen, bis Sie zum Postamt kommen.*
3. *Dieses Auto kostet **nur/bloß** €5000; Sie würden ein gutes Geschäft machen.*
4. *Wir sind doch **erst** vor einer Viertelstunde hier angekommen.*
5. ***Nur** in Mathematik hatte Ulrike eine schlechte Note.*
6. *Sie müssen mir **nur** Ihre Bankverbindung geben.*

7. *John ist der **einzige** Engländer in dieser Touristengruppe.*
8. *Das Flugzeug ist **erst** vor fünf Minuten gelandet.*
9. *Du musst dich **nur** etwas mehr anstrengen; dann klappt es auch.*
10. *Ich bin der **einzige** Schüler, der eine Eins in Deutsch bekommen hat.*

Exercise 10.2

1. *Ich bin der **einzige** Sohn.*
2. *Es gibt **nur** einen Professor, der deutsche Linguistik lehrt.*
3. *Wir sind **erst** seit zwei Monaten hier.*
4. *Sie ist das **einzige** Mädchen in diesem Kurs.*
5. *Du musst **nur**/Sie müssen **nur** auf den Knopf drücken.*

Exercise 10.3

1. *Wir fuhren an Darmstadt vorbei; und **dann** erreichten wir endlich Frankfurt.*
2. *Und **dann/außerdem** musst du dich fragen, warum du diesen Weg gegangen bist.*
3. *Ich war **damals** gerade mal sechs Jahre alt, als dies passiert ist.*
4. *Der **damalige** Bürgermeister ließ eine neue Stadthalle bauen.*
5. *Und **dann/außerdem** ist da noch das Problem der hohen Jugendkriminalität.*
6. *Zuerst war er voller Zuversicht; **dann** verließ ihn aber der Mut.*
7. *Die **damaligen** Klassenkameraden ließen ihn im Stich.*
8. *Ich war **damals** Student in Hamburg, als ich meine Frau kennen lernte.*
9. *Und **dann/außerdem** müssen wir uns noch über das bevorstehende Treffen unterhalten.*
10. ***Damals** glaubte ich noch, er würde mich lieben.*

Exercise 10.4

1. *Der **damalige** Außenminister war/hieß James Baker.*
2. *Zuerst werden wir München besuchen und **dann** haben wir vor nach Köln zu fliegen.*
3. *Und **dann/außerdem** muss man auch an die hohe Arbeitslosenquote denken.*
4. *Ich war **damals** in Deutschland, zusammen mit meiner Familie.*
5. *Und falls sie auch keine freien Zimmer haben, wo werden wir **dann** schlafen?*

Exercise 10.5

1. *Sie haben diese Aufgabe sehr **gut** gelöst.*
2. *Dieser Mann dort nahm **auch** an der Konferenz teil.*
3. *Schau dir seine Gesichtsfarbe an; ich finde, er sieht nicht sehr **gesund** aus.*
4. *Die Mannschaft hat sehr **gut** Fußball gespielt.*

5. *Es kann* ***ohne weiteres/gut*** *möglich sein, dass Sie in zwei Wochen wieder laufen können.*
6. *Die deutschen Fußballer wurden von dem starken Gegner aus England* ***gründlich*** *in ihre Schranken verwiesen.*
7. *Sie möchte* ***auch*** *mit nach Süddeutschland fahren.*
8. *Es könnte* ***ohne weiteres/gut*** *sein, dass es bald anfängt zu schneien.*
9. *Das letzte Mal, als ich ihn traf, sah er recht* ***gesund*** *aus.*
10. *Ich werde mich auf das anstehende Examen* ***gründlich/gut*** *vorbereiten.*

Exercise 10.6

1. *Es kann* ***ohne weiteres*** *sein, dass der Konflikt bis zum Ende des Jahres vorbei sein wird.*
2. *Ihrem Großvater geht es nicht* ***gut***.
3. *Du hast* ***leicht/gut*** *reden; du kannst im Bett liegen bleiben.*
4. *Sie will* ***auch*** *ein Auto kaufen.*
5. *Meine Schwester spielt sehr* ***gut*** *Violine.*

Exercise 10.7

1. *Heute Morgen habe ich* ***lange*** *geschlafen.*
2. *Bitte kommen Sie nicht zu* ***spät*** *zum Unterricht.*
3. *Ich bin in den* ***späten*** *90ern für ein paar Jahre in Deutschland gewesen.*
4. *Entschuldigen Sie bitte, aber mein Zug hatte eine halbe Stunde* ***Verspätung***.
5. *Der* ***verstorbene*** *König wurde vor der Beerdigung in der Rotunde aufgebahrt.*
6. *Wenn Sie* ***sich verspäten****, sollten Sie sich bei Ihrem Vorgesetzten entschuldigen.*
7. *Mein Vater arbeitet heute – wie fast jeden Freitag – wieder* ***länger***.
8. *Beeile dich doch, sonst kommen wir zu* ***spät****!*
9. *Ihr* ***verstorbener*** *Ehemann ist ein guter Freund von mir gewesen.*
10. *Wir sind immer* ***spät*** *dran.*

Exercise 10.8

1. *Warum kommst du immer* ***zu spät*** *zum Frühstück?*
2. *Mama, können wir heute Abend* ***lange*** *aufbleiben?*
3. *Es tut mir Leid, der Zug* ***hatte Verspätung***.
4. *Sie ehrten den* ***verstorbenen*** *Kanzler.*
5. *Die Mannschaft schoss zwei* ***späte*** *Tore.*

Chapter 11

Exercise 11.1

1. *Sie musste* ***an*** *der Ampel warten.*

2. *Kannst du mich* ***am*** *Flughafen abholen?*
3. ***Vor*** *Eintritt der Dämmerung erreichte er seinen Zielort.*
4. *Er setzt sich im Park* ***auf*** *eine Bank.*
5. *Wir wollen uns* ***bei*** *Stefan treffen.*
6. *Er ist gerade* ***bei*** *einem wichtigen Treffen.*
7. ***Bei*** *Beginn der Vorstellung waren noch einige Plätze frei.*
8. *Sie steht jeden Morgen* ***um*** *sechs Uhr auf.*
9. *Seine Tochter geht* ***auf*** *das Gymnasium.*
10. *Wir kamen schließlich* ***an*** *einem Bahnhof an.*

Exercise 11.2

1. *Der Bus fährt* ***um*** *sieben Uhr ab.*
2. *Maria wartet* ***an*** *der Bushaltestelle.*
3. *Wollt ihr euch* ***bei*** *Susanne treffen?*
4. *Er wachte* ***im/beim*** *Morgengrauen auf.*
5. *Sie verbrachte die Nacht* ***bei*** *ihrem(ihrer) Freund(in).*
6. *Mark gewinnt immer* ***beim*** *Kartenspielen.*
7. ***Auf*** *Seite 34 hörten wir* ***auf*** *zu lesen.*
8. ***Um*** *Mitternacht verließ er das Haus.*
9. *Sie ist* ***in*** *einer Jugendherberge untergebracht.*
10. *Seine Bemerkungen zielten* ***auf*** *ihr unfreundliches Verhalten.*

Exercise 11.3

1. *„Wilhelm Tell" ist ein Theaterstück* ***von*** *Schiller.*
2. ***Laut*** *Berichten der ARD ist die Arbeitslosigkeit zurückgegangen.*
3. *Komm, wir setzen uns* ***an*** *den Fluss.*
4. *Wir fahren immer* ***mit*** *dem Zug in den Urlaub.*
5. ***Nach*** *ihrer Sprache zu urteilen ist sie nicht in Deutschland aufgewachsen.*
6. ***Gemäß/Nach*** *Artikel 21 des Grundgesetzes wurde die Partei verboten.*
7. *Sie müssen mir* ***bis*** *Freitag Bescheid gegeben haben.*
8. *Ich schicke Ihnen das Paket* ***per*** *Schiff.*
9. ***Bis*** *wann können Sie fertig sein?*
10. *Ich sende Ihnen die Informationen* ***per*** *E-mail.*

Exercise 11.4

1. *Komm, wir fahren* ***mit*** *dem Bus.*
2. *Häufig kategorisiert man Menschen* ***nach*** *ihrer Kleidung.*
3. *Dieses Gedicht wurde* ***von*** *Friedrich Schiller geschrieben.*
4. *Wir überqueren den Kanal* ***mit*** *dem Luftkissenboot.*
5. *Thomas hat uns* ***per*** *Email Grüße gesandt.*
6. *Das Paper muss* ***bis*** *zum Ende der Woche fertig sein.*
7. *Wir saßen* ***am*** *Kamin.*
8. *Wir denken darüber nach, unseren Urlaub* ***an*** *der See zu verbringen.*

9. *Ich fahre immer* ***mit*** *dem Fahrrad zur Arbeit.*
10. ***Bis*** *Dienstag werden wir fertig sein.*

Exercise 11.5

1. *Er kommt* ***am*** *Abend immer sehr spät von der Arbeit zurück.*
2. *Bitte sprechen Sie* ***mit*** *lauter Stimme!*
3. *Wir fahren im Juni* ***nach*** *Deutschland.*
4. *Ich treffe ihn* ***am*** *Vormittag.*
5. *Sie können nicht* ***in*** *Dollar bezahlen.*
6. *Meine Frau ist* ***auf*** *diesem Bild zu sehen.*
7. ***Innerhalb*** *eines Monats muss er die Arbeit geschrieben haben.*
8. ***Im*** *Jahre 2003 machte ich mein Examen.*
9. *Viele Menschen sind* ***auf*** *den Straßen.*
10. *Herr Schmidt sitzt* ***im*** *Wartezimmer.*

Exercise 11.6

1. *Er legte die Maschinen* ***auf/in*** *den Lastwagen.*
2. *Er wird* ***am*** *Morgen* ***in*** *Stuttgart ankommen.*
3. *Sie wird ihr Studium* ***im*** *August beenden.*
4. *Mein Onkel lebt* ***in*** *einer kleinen Wohnung.*
5. ***Im*** *Sommer ist es hier immer sehr heiß.*
6. *Die Kinder spielen* ***im*** *Garten.*
7. *Sie waren* ***in*** *einem Schockzustand.*
8. ***In*** *drei Monaten/****Innerhalb*** *von drei Monaten lernte Thomas das Autofahren.*
9. *Viele Menschen* ***in*** *diesem Distrikt leben* ***in*** *Armut.*
10. ***Innerhalb*** *einer Woche muss er umgezogen sein.*

Exercise 11.7

1. *Sie hat eine Narbe* ***an*** *ihrem linken Arm.*
2. *Das Buch liegt* ***auf*** *dem Tisch.*
3. *Er hängt das Gemälde* ***an*** *den Nagel.*
4. *Er hat* ***am*** *vierten Mai Geburtstag.*
5. *Sie legt das Buch* ***auf*** *den Stuhl.*
6. ***Bei*** *meiner Abreise verabschiedeten mich viele Freunde.*
7. *Willst du mit* ***auf*** *unseren Ausflug kommen?*
8. *Wir wollen morgen* ***in*** *den Urlaub fahren.*
9. ***Am*** *Sonntag wollen wir uns in der Stadt treffen.*
10. *Können Sie diese Aufgabe* ***an*** *die Tafel schreiben?*

Exercise 11.8

1. *Wann fährst du* ***in*** *den Urlaub?/Wann fahren Sie* ***in*** *den Urlaub?*
2. ***Bei*** *der Untersuchung hat der Arzt nichts gefunden.*
3. *Der Lehrer schrieb die Wörter* ***an*** *die Tafel.*
4. *Er kann nicht mit uns kommen, er ist* ***im*** *Dienst.*

5. ***Am*** *Dienstag werden wir unsere Eltern besuchen.*
6. *Wir waren* ***auf*** *Seite 34.*
7. *Sie ernähren sich* ***von*** *Eiern.*
8. *Die Heizung läuft* ***mit*** *Gas.*
9. *Schreibe die Antworten zu dieser Übung* ***auf*** *ein Blatt Papier!*
10. ***An*** *welchem Projekt arbeitest du?*

Exercise 11.9

1. *Wir wollen im Sommer* ***nach*** *Skandinavien reisen.*
2. *Mein Sohn geht noch* ***in*** *den Kindergarten.*
3. *Können Sie mir den Weg* ***zum*** *Stadion sagen?*
4. *Wie viele Kilometer sind es noch* ***bis*** *Köln?*
5. *Ich muss dringend* ***zum*** *Zahnarzt gehen.*
6. *Wir sollten wieder mal* ***ins*** *Kino gehen.*
7. *Wie kommen wir am besten* ***nach*** *Nürnberg?*
8. *Wir laufen im Moment* ***nach*** *Westen.*
9. *Komm, wir gehen* ***in*** *diese Kneipe.*
10. *Kannst du auf Deutsch* ***bis*** *100 zählen?*

Exercise 11.10

1. *Wir müssen noch* ***zum*** *Gemüsehändler (gehen).*
2. ***Bis*** *Frankfurt sind es 50 Kilometer.*
3. *Ich möchte jetzt* ***ins*** *Bett gehen.*
4. *Kann ich dir diese Fahrkarte geben?/Kann ich Ihnen diese Fahrkarte geben?* (not translated)
5. *Wir erwarten 20* ***bis*** *30 Gäste.*
6. *Wann fährst du* ***nach*** *Berlin?*
7. *Komm, wir gehen morgen* ***ins*** *Museum.*
8. *Ich sagte ihm, er sollte früher aufstehen.* (not translated)
9. *Er möchte nächsten Monat* ***nach*** *Kanada verreisen.*
10. *Thomas geht* ***in/auf*** *die Grundschule.*

Chapter 12

Exercise 12.1

1. *Morgen könnt ihr sie nicht sehen,* ***sondern*** *erst übermorgen.*
2. *Sie haben zwar Recht,* ***aber/doch*** *wir müssen den Plan trotzdem ändern.*
3. *Beim Handballspiel steht es nicht 13:12,* ***sondern*** *es steht 14:12.*
4. *Sie ist nicht nur gut in Chemie,* ***sondern*** *auch in Physik.*
5. *Ich verdiene zwar viel Geld,* ***aber/doch*** *ich bin nicht zufrieden mit meinem Beruf.*
6. *Er hat nicht nur schlechte Noten in Englisch,* ***sondern*** *auch in Deutsch und Kunst.*
7. *Die Schuhe sind schön,* ***aber/doch*** *leider zu klein.*

8. *Wir gehen heute Abend nicht in das Theater,* ***sondern*** *ins Kino.*

Exercise 12.2

1. *Ihre Seminare sind nicht nur lehrreich,* ***sondern*** *auch lustig.*
2. *Er ist keine sehr sympathische Person,* ***aber/doch*** *sein Unterricht ist lehrreich.*
3. *Sie ist eine ziemlich unfreundliche Person,* ***aber/doch*** *ihr Ehemann ist nett.*
4. *Wir nehmen nicht den Bus,* ***sondern*** *das Taxi.*

Exercise 12.3

1. *Manfred will dann in die Vereinigten Staaten fliegen,* ***wenn*** *er etwas mehr Geld hat.*
2. *Es flossen Tränen,* ***als*** *sich Ottmar von Anette verabschiedete.*
3. *Ich weiß nicht,* ***wann*** *ich ihr das letzte Mal einen Brief geschrieben habe.*
4. *Ich müsste noch von Ihnen wissen,* ***wann*** *Sie geboren wurden.*
5. ***Wenn*** *ich mein Abitur bestanden habe, möchte ich Jura studieren.*
6. ***Als*** *Wilfried und Ulrike am Bahnhof ankamen, wurden sie freundlich begrüßt.*
7. *Ich weiß noch nicht genau,* ***wann*** *ich am Bahnhof ankommen werde.*
8. ***Als*** *ich 25 Jahre alt war, beendete ich mein Studium.*
9. *Wir werden nicht wandern gehen,* ***wenn*** *es regnen sollte.*
10. ***Als*** *Stefan Tränen in ihren Augen sah, wusste er, dass sie ihn liebte.*

Exercise 12.4.

1. *Kannst du mir sagen,* ***wann*** *du zurück sein wirst?*
2. ***Als*** *der Lehrer den Klassenraum betrat, hörten die Schüler auf zu reden.*
3. *Ich fühle mich froh,* ***wenn*** *ich etwas Zeit mit meiner Frau verbringen kann.*
4. ***Als*** *Thomas am Haus seiner Freunde eintraf, wurde er freundlich empfangen.*
5. *Wir müssen dieses neue Spiel spielen,* ***wenn*** *du uns im Juni besuchen kommst.*

Exercise 12.5

1. *Ich würde dies tun,* ***wenn*** *ich an deiner Stelle wäre.*
2. *Können Sie mir jetzt schon sagen,* ***ob*** *Sie morgen zum Frühstück kommen?*
3. *Ich weiß nicht,* ***ob*** *meine Freundin wirklich kommt.*
4. ***Falls/Wenn*** *Sie sich noch anders entscheiden sollten, rufen Sie mich bitte an.*
5. ***Ob*** *er wirklich dazu in der Lage ist, kann ich zum jetzigen Zeitpunkt nicht sagen.*

6. ***Wenn** du eine bessere Idee hast, gib mir bitte Bescheid.*
7. *Ich möchte gerne von dir wissen, **ob** du mich wirklich liebst.*
8. *Der Arzt konnte mir nicht genau sagen, **ob** ich ins Krankenhaus eingeliefert werden muss.*
9. ***Wenn** du nichts anderes vorhast, kannst du ja bei uns vorbeikommen.*
10. ***Wenn** du willst, kannst du mich in den Sommerferien besuchen kommen.*

Exercise 12.6

1. *Ich rufe dich an, **wenn/falls** ich zu spät bin.*
2. *Können Sie mir sagen, **ob** das Wetter morgen schön wird?*
3. ***Wenn/Falls** du ins Kino gehen willst, ruf mich an.*
4. *Wissen Sie, **ob** dieser Bus an der Stadthalle hält?*
5. ***Wenn/Falls** du etwas mehr Hilfe brauchst, lass es mich wissen und ich werde mich darum kümmern.*

Exercise 12.7

1. *Wir werden erst am Abend bei Ihnen eintreffen, **wie** ich Ihnen bereits mitteilte.*
2. *Er ist ein sehr erfahrener und sachkundiger Lehrer, **obwohl** er noch sehr jung ist.*
3. ***Da** ich im Moment wenig Zeit habe, werde ich leider nicht mitkommen können.*
4. *Wir hörten ihm gespannt zu, **als** er uns eine spannende Geschichte aus seinem Leben erzählte.*
5. ***Wie** ich ja bereits von Ihrer Frau erfahren habe, können Sie leider nicht an unserem Fest teilnehmen.*
6. *Seine Tochter kann schon sehr gut sprechen, **obwohl** sie noch sehr klein ist.*
7. ***Wie** bereits besprochen, können wir dem Entwurf vorbehaltlos zustimmen.*
8. ***Als** Max krank war, ging er zur Arbeit.*
9. ***Als** wir durch Deutschland reisten, besuchten wir viele schöne Städte.*
10. ***Da** wir noch viel lernen müssen, sollten wir den Unterricht fortsetsen.*

Exercise 12.8

1. ***Wie** ich dir/Ihnen bereits gestern gesagt habe, wir werden den Zug nach Frankfurt nehmen.*
2. ***Als** wir fernsahen, spielten draußen die Kinder.*
3. ***Da** wir mit den Rädern unterwegs waren, konnten wir nicht viel Kleidung mitnehmen.*
4. ***Obwohl** er sehr stark war, konnte er den Kampf nicht gewinnen.*
5. ***Da** er sehr gut Tischtennis spielte, entschied er sich ein Profi zu werden.*

Websites for Students of German

Websites for travellers

German for travellers
www.germanfortravellers.com/
This is a website in English and therefore ideal for speakers of English who want to visit Germany. Besides offering online courses on German grammar, vocabulary and sounds, it provides useful information on German culture (food and drink, music, principal holidays, etc.). There is also a travel toolbox with destination guides and travel tips.

How to Germany
www.howtogermany.com/
The homepage of *How To Germany* magazine. It tells you everything you need to know about living and working in Germany.

For students

Forum Deutsch als Fremdsprache
www.deutsch-als-fremdsprache.de/
This website offers a wide range of study material for students of German as a foreign language: tests, web-projects, practice exercises, useful information about jobs and exchange programmes.

Stufen International by Klett Publishers
www.stufen.de/
The online forum of a leading German publisher of teaching material provides information about books on German as a foreign language as well as teaching projects and discussions. It also offers an e-mail exchange-service.

Institut für internationale Kommunikation
www.iik-duesseldorf.de/
This homepage of the Institute for International Communication in Düsseldorf provides information about courses of German as a foreign language, summer school programmes, scholarships and documentaries, as well as free-time activities and cultural events for international students.

Institut für internationale Kommunikation in Bayern, Berlin und Thüringen
www.iik.com/
This homepage of the Institute for International Communication in Bavaria, Berlin and Thuringia offers a wide range of information about the study and teaching of German as a foreign language. Here you can find practice exercises and language games, as well as information about courses and examinations. It also lists important publications.

Das Internetportal für Deutsch als Fremdsprache
www.daf-portal.de/
This website gives you a lot of study and teaching material for German as a foreign language. You can find plenty of information about jobs, seminars, courses as well as tests, lesson plans and exercises. There is also a calendar listing important events for students and teachers of German as a foreign language.

Klett Edition – Deutsch lehren und lernen
www.edition-deutsch.de/
On this website Klett publishers presents its publications on German as a foreign language. It also offers downloads of teaching and study material such as worksheets and articles.

Forum Wirtschaftsdeutsch im Internet
www.wirtschaftsdeutsch.de/
On this website the Institute for International Communication in Düsseldorf offers a wide range of information on business German. Here you can find teaching and study material as well as useful pieces of information on courses, scholarships and jobs.

Lernforum Deutsch, Bonn – Deutsch als Fremdsprache
www.lernforum.uni-bonn.de/
This website designed for international students in Germany offers practice material as well as book reviews about and fictional texts for the study of German as a foreign language. You can also find reports by international students about their experiences in learning German.

GFL – Journal homepage
www.gfl-journal.de/
The homepage of the *GFL-Journal*, an internet journal designed for professors, teachers and students of German as a foreign language. It

features numerous articles on approaches and methods in language learning and teaching.

Portal – Fremdsprache Deutsch
www.deutsch-online.com/
This website offers a wide range of study material and a lot of information for students of German as a foreign language. You can find numerous practice exercises on sounds, grammar, spelling and vocabulary. It also provides downloads and offers useful study and travel tips.

Interdeutsch.de – Deutsch lernen via Internet
www.interdeutsch.de
The homepage of a company that offers online courses on German for one's everyday life and work.

Reinhard Donath: Deutsch als Fremdsprache & das Internet
www.englisch.schule.de/DaF.htm
The homepage by Reinhard Donath, a teacher of English and German and an expert on teaching German as a foreign language. On this website you can find e-mail and internet projects as well as publications and literature for students of German as a foreign language.

Goethe-Verlag
www.goethe-verlag.com/
This website of the Goethe-Verlag in Munich offers free language tests and vocabulary exercises as well as free downloads of language puzzles.

Websites about Germany

World Wide Websites for German
www.mtholyoke.edu/acad/germ/workshops/urls/index.html/
This is a very useful compilation of websites about all kinds of aspects of German life and language (politics, culture, media, literature, education, history, etc.).

Goethe-Institut
www.goethe.de/
The homepage of the very prestigious Goethe-Institute which has academies and institutes in over 70 countries of this world fostering German language and culture. Besides offering online study material this website provides a lot of information about German culture and society.

Das Deutschland-Portal
www.deutschland.de/
The official homepage of the Federal Republic of Germany where you can find a lot of information about the country and its people (education, health, sports, the state, tourism, economy, science, etc.).

German Life – Culture, History, Travel
www.germanlife.com/
The homepage of an American magazine written for all who are interested in German culture.

Deutschland aus der Luft
www.ausderluft.de/
This website shows numerous photos of German cities from a bird's-eye view.

Medien im Internet
www.burks.de/medien.html/
A compilation of websites listing the homepages of international as well as German newspapers, magazines, radio and television channels.

Die Zeit
www.zeit.de/
The homepage of the famous German weekly.

Frankfurter Allgemeine Zeitung
www.faz.net/s/homepage.html/
The homepage of the famous German daily newspaper.

Die Welt
www.welt.de/
The homepage of one of the most important German daily newspapers.

Die Süddeutsche Zeitung
www.sueddeutsche.de/
The homepage of one of the most important German daily newspapers.

Der Spiegel
www.spiegel.de/
The homepage of the famous weekly news magazine.

Focus
www.focus.msn.de/
The homepage of the weekly news magazine.

ARD
www.ard.de/
The homepage of one of the most important television channels in Germany.

ZDF
www.zdf.de/
The homepage of one of the most important television channels in Germany.

Useful addresses and websites for travellers

Deutsche Zentrale für Tourismus (DZT)
(German Centre for Tourism)
Beethovenstr. 69
D-60325 Frankfurt am Main
0049 (0)69 97 46 40
www.deutschland-tourismus.de

Deutscher Tourismusverband (DTV)
(German Association of Tourism)
Bertha-von-Suttner-Platz 13
D-53111 Bonn
0049 (0)228 98 52 20
www.deutschertourismusverband.de

Deutscher Heilbäderverband
(German Association of Spas)
Schumannstr. 111
D-53113 Bonn
0049 (0)228 20 12 00
www.deutscher-heilbaederverband.de

Tourismus-Verband Baden-Württemberg
(Tourism Association of Baden-Württemberg)
Tourismus Marketing GmbH
Esslinger Str. 8
D-70182 Stuttgart
0049 (0)711 23 85 80
www.tourismus-baden-wuerttemberg.de

Bayern Tourismus Marketing GmbH
(Bavaria Tourism Marketing)
Leopoldstr. 146
D-80804 München (Munich)
0049 (0)89 2 12 39 70
www.btl.de

Berlin Tourismus Marketing GmbH
Am Karlsbad 11
D-10785 Berlin
0049 (0)190 75 40 40
www.berlin.de

Tourismus-Marketing Brandenburg GmbH
Am Neuen Markt 1
D-14467 Potsdam
0049 (0)331 2 00 47 47
www.tmb-brandenburg.de

Bremer Touristik Zentrale
(Bremen Tourism Centre)
Findorffstr. 105
D-28215 Bremen
0049 (0)1805 10 10 30
www.bremen-tourism.de

Tourismus-Zentrale Hamburg GmbH
(Hamburg Tourism Centre)
Steinstr. 7
D-20095 Hamburg
0049 (0)40 30 05 13 00
www.hamburg-tourism.de

Hessen Touristik Service e.V.
(Hesse Tourism Service)
Abraham-Lincoln-Str. 38-42
D-65189 Wiesbaden
0049 (0)611 77 88 00
www.hessen-tourismus.de

Tourismusverband Mecklenburg-Vorpommern
(Mecklenburg and Western Pomerania)
Platz der Freundschaft 1
D-18059 Rostock
0049 (0)381 5 00 02 23
www.tmv.de

Tourismusverband Niedersachsen e.V.
(Lower Saxony)
Vahrenwalder Str. 7
D-30165 Hannover
0049 (0)511 9 35 72 50
www.tourismus.niedersachsen.de

Tourismusverband Nordrhein-Westfalen e.V. (North Rhine-Westphalia)
Emil-Hoffmann-Str. 1a
D-50996 Köln (Cologne)
0049 (0)2226 96 72 55
www.nrw-tourismus.de

Fremdenverkehrs- und Heilbäderverband Rheinland-Pfalz
(Association of Tourism and Spas in Rhineland-Palatinate)
Postfach (PO box number) 20 04 63
D-56005 Koblenz
0049 (0)261 91 52 00
www.rlp-info.de

Tourismus Zentrale Saarland GmbH
Franz-Josef-Röder-Str. 9
D-66119 Saarbrücken
0049 (0)681 92 70 20
www.tourismus.saarland.de

Tourismus Marketing Gesellschaft Sachsen mbH (Saxony)
Bautzener Straße 45/47
D-01099 Dresden
0049 (0)351 49 17 00
www.sachsen-tour.de

Landesmarketing Sachsen-Anhalt
(Saxony-Anhalt)
Am Alten Theater 6
D-39104 Magdeburg
0049 (0)391 5 67 70 80
www.lmg-sachsen-anhalt.de

Tourismusverband Schleswig-Holstein
Niemannsweg 31
D-24105 Kiel
0049 (0)431 5 60 01 00
www.sht.de

Thüringer Tourismus GmbH
(Thuringia)
Weimarische Straße 45
D-99099 Erfurt
0049 (0)361 3742-0
www.thueringen-tourismus.de

Deutsches Jugendherbergswerk (DJH)
(German Youth-Hostel Association)
Postfach (PO box number): 1455
D-32704 Detmold
0049 (0)5231 7 40 10
www.djh.de

British Embassy Berlin
Wilhelmstr. 70-71
D-10117 Berlin
0049 (0)30 2 04 57-0
www.britischebotschaft.de

British Consulate General in Düsseldorf
Yorckstr. 19
D-40476 Düsseldorf
0049 (0)211 9 44 80

British Consulate General in Frankfurt
Bockenheimer Landstraße 42
D-60323 Frankfurt am Main
0049 (0)69 1 70 00 20

British Consulate General in München (Munich)
Bürkleinstr. 10
D-80538 München
0049 (0)89 21 10 90

British Consulate General in Stuttgart
Breite Straße 2
D-70173 Stuttgart
0049 (0)711 16 26 90

British Consulate General in Hamburg
Harvestehuder Weg 8a
D-20148 Hamburg
0049 (0) 4 48 03 20

British Consulate Honorary in
Bremen
Herrlichkeit 6
Postfach (P.O. box number): 10 38 60
D-28199 Bremen
0049 (0)421 59 07 08

British Consulate Honorary in Nürnberg (Nuremberg)
Hadermühle 9-15
D-90402 Nürnberg
0049 (0)911 2 40 43 03

British Consulate Honorary in Kiel
Maklerstraße 11-14
D-24159 Kiel
0049 (0)431 33 19 71

British Consulate Honorary in Hannover (Hanover)
Karl-Wiechert-Allee 50
D-30625 Hannover
0049 (0)511 3 88 38 08

Index of Grammatical Terms

Index of German Words

Useful Sentences and Phrases for Travellers, Students, and Businessmen

Words and expressions a tourist or businessman needs in Germany

- booking a flight: p. 150
- booking/making a reservation for seats on a train: p. 156
- buying tickets (at the railway station, at the airport): p. 121
- asking whether it is possible to pay in euros: p. 146
- enquiring about ferry and train departure times: pp. 66, 154
- asking whether a train is late: p. 137
- talking about matters of identification (e.g. passport): p. 110
- enquiring about board and lodging/vacancies: pp. 105, 116
- enquiring about railway and bus lines: pp. 112, 116
- asking for a city guide: p. 108, 109
- asking the way: pp. 119, 149
- complaining about hotel facilities (room, bed, etc.): pp. 54, 156
- ordering a meal in a restaurant: pp. 58, 59
- paying by credit-card: p. 143
- asking for someone's e-mail address: p. 104
- opening a bank account: p. 77
- asking how much credit is on one's account, p. 84
- transferring a booking from one account to another: p. 69
- enquiring about business hours: p. 86
- asking someone to give you change for your large money: p. 81
- placing an order with a business partner: p. 101
- asking someone to leave a message: p. 125
- apologizing: p. 121
- apologizing when being late: p. 136

Classroom language – what a teacher/professor/student might say

- a teacher's advice to be prepared for tests and exams: p. 55
- a teacher stating that a student has grasped the given problem: p. 64
- a teacher saying that the student has to rewrite an essay: p. 69
- saying that you have understood the grammar: p. 64
- asking the teacher if he could repeat a question: p. 73

At the doctor's – what to say in case of injuries and illnesses